FROMMER'S TOURING GUIDE TO AUSTRALIA

Author
Pierre Grundmann

Translation
Angus Cameron

Adaptation
Mary Hyman

With special thanks to:
HE Mr P. Curtis, Australian Ambassador to France.
Barbara Whiteman, First Press Secretary, Australian Embassy, Paris.
Hanspeter Rohrer, European Director of the Australian Tourist Commission and of Australian Tourist Commission Services in Frankfurt London and Melbourne.
The Australian Information Service
The tourist offices of the states, territories and cities of Australia, and their representatives in Europe.
Jean-Paul Delamotte, President of the French-Australian Cultural Association.
Rita Rakus, Bronte Douglass, Sam Parsons

Photo credits: Pierre Brouwers: pp. 21, 64 and 166. - Robert Solway pp. 45, 48, 61, 73, 77, 89, 123, 131, 135, 139, 183 and 195. - Australian Tourist Commission: pp. 12, 37, 53, 114, 146, 151, 155 and 175. - Northern Territory Tourist Commission: pp. 32, 191 and 198.

This edition published in the United States in 1988 by Prentice Hall Press
A division of Simon & Schuster, Inc.
Gulf + Western Building
One Gulf + Western Plaza
New York, New York 10023
PRENTICE HALL PRESS is a trademark of Simon & Schuster, Inc.

Library of Congress Cataloging-in-Publication Data
Grundmann, Pierre.
  [En Australie. English]
  Frommer's touring guide to Australia / author, Pierre Grundmann
translation, Angus Cameron ; adaptation, Mary Hyman.
      p. ·   cm.
  Translation of : En Australie.
  Bibliography : p. 199.
  Includes index.
  ISBN 0-13-331174-0 : $9.95
  1. Australia — Description and travel — 1981 — Guide-books.
I. Title.
DU95.G7813 1988
919.4'0463- -dc19   87-35965
Printed in France by Aubin-Imprimeur, Poitiers   CIP

FROMMER'S TOURING GUIDE TO AUSTRALIA

PRENTICE HALL PRESS

NEW YORK

HOW TO USE YOUR GUIDE

● Before you leave home, read **Planning Your Trip**, p. 10 and **Practical Information**, p. 18. **Geography**, p. 29, **Australia's Past**, p. 34, **Australia Today**, p. 43 and **Who are the Australians**, p. 49, will also be of interest before you leave.

● The rest of the guide is divided into sections treating either the large cities (Sydney, Melbourne) or areas of Australia such as Brisbane and Northern Queensland or Adelaide and South Australia. There are also two driving itineraries, one going from Sydney to Brisbane, the other from Sydney to Melbourne, which give you a chance to see parts of the country most profitably visited by car.

Each of these sections contains **practical information** specific to the area being discussed (access, accommodation, restaurants, useful addresses etc.), followed by what to see: sights, monuments etc.

● Each chapter includes a **general map** of the area being discussed. Those on Sydney and Melbourne contain a map of the city and corresponding **grid references** [(B5), (C1), etc.] are included after each address located on the map. Note also that most cities are divided into neighbourhoods (described under the heading 'Getting to Know...'). The city centre or downtown area is referred to as the 'City'; other neighbourhoods have specific names, such as Kings Cross or Fitzroy. These areas are also indicated on the city map and included as part of addresses.

● At the back of the guide there is a list of specifically **Australian words or phrases**, a short **bibliography** and an **index**.

SYMBOLS USED

Places of interest, monuments, museums, works of art

★★★ not to be missed

★★ very interesting

★ worth a look

Hotel classification

For details see pp. 18-19.

▲▲▲▲ International-standard

▲▲▲ First-class

▲▲ Moderately priced

▲ Inexpensive

MAPS

■ CONTENTS

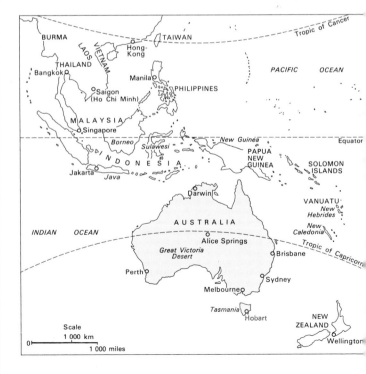

INTRODUCING AUSTRALIA

'New worlds must be experienced before they can be explained.' The author of these words, Alejo Carpentier, was referring to his own country of Cuba but they sum up perfectly the approach taken to Australia in this guide. The size of the United States, over 30 times larger than Britain and 28 times larger than New Zealand, with 16 million inhabitants (nine million of them in the five major cities), 40,000 years of prehistory and 200 years of white settlement, Australia does not strive to explain itself, nor does it lend itself to conventional tourism. Australia is simply Australia.

Australia can be found in the rhythm of the drover's horse, as he drives his herd through the dust of bush and desert; or aboard a yacht on Sydney Harbour, surrounded by one of the most beautiful cities on earth; or on the bleachers of the Olympic Stadium in Melbourne, shoulder-to-shoulder with 120,000 'footy' (Australian football) fans. Australia can be found in the footsteps of the Gold Rush 'diggers'; in the clear, warm waters of the Great Barrier Reef 1250 mi/2000 km long; beneath the deep blue of the sky; in the heart of magnificent yet harsh deserts, where Acacia bushes, legendary kangaroos and Aborigines cling obstinately to life. Australia can be found beneath the tiled 'sails' of the Sydney Opera House; at a rock concert on the manicured lawns of a park in Brisbane; in front of a Rembrandt at the National Gallery in Melbourne, or an ageless rock painting deep in the desert. Australia can be found on a straight highway, 70 mi/112 km long, where road signs warn motorists to watch out for kangaroos; or in the quiet streets of a suburb, where the Victorian architecture of the houses is characterized by delicate wrought-iron lacework; in a pub, with an ice-cold beer in hand; on a beach, enjoying a summer that never seems to end...

Whether you are visiting Australia for several days on a business trip, for several weeks to explore the continent, or permanently, in search of a new life, this guide will help you draw up an itinerary, one which will concentrate on simple and authentic encounters with the country—and which will let you experience the real Australia.

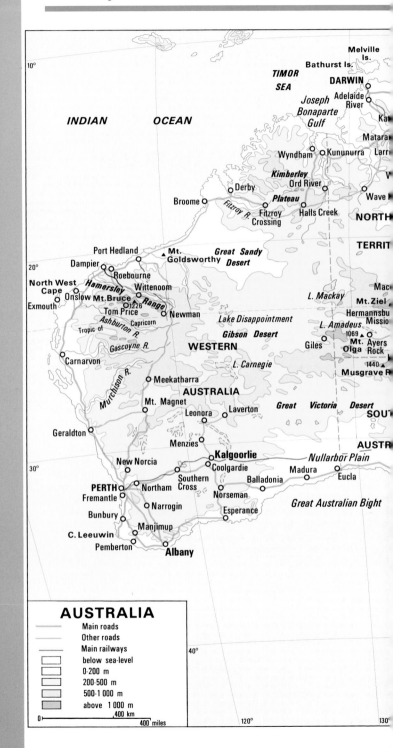

AUSTRALIA

- Main roads
- Other roads
- Main railways
- below sea-level
- 0-200 m
- 200-500 m
- 500-1 000 m
- above 1 000 m

0   400 km
400 miles

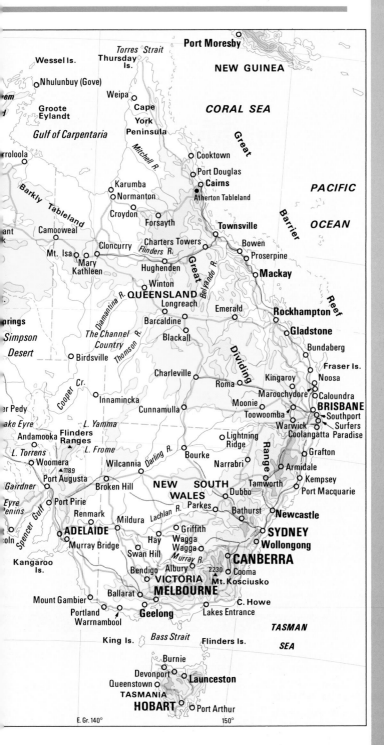

PLANNING YOUR TRIP

This chapter will give you all the information you need before setting out: how to get there, customs formalities, currency, climate and lots of tips and useful contacts.

▬▬ HOW TO GET THERE

Plane

There are flights from Europe and the west coast of North America to the east and west coasts of Australia every day of the year. Contact your travel agent, tour operator or airline company (see specific airline addresses below) for purchase and reservation of plane tickets and other tourist services.

When you arrive at the airport in Australia, don't let first impressions turn you off. After your aircraft lands, two officials from the Ministry of Agriculture will come aboard and spray the aircraft cabin with an insecticide designed to kill any insects and microbes which might endanger local crops. Officers from the Department of Immigration will then use their computers to check your papers from every angle before releasing you into the hands of a customs officer skilled in the art of locating foodstuffs and other prohibited imports. If any are found, they will be destroyed. But take heart—travel within the country is unrestricted. The only official piece of paper you are likely to be asked for is your driver's license, and then only if you're actually at the wheel.

Flights from North America

Regularly scheduled flights to Australia from North America are operated exclusively with Jumbo 747 and DC-10 aircraft by **Qantas Airways** (the Australian national carrier), **United, Continental, Air New Zealand,** and **CP Air.** The flight from Los Angeles to Sydney takes about 13 or 14 hours.

Other flights leave North America for Australia from San Francisco and Vancouver. Since most flights to Australia depart from the west coast in the evening, there is no problem with connecting flights from the east, south and midwest. The same applies on the way back, with most flights to North America leaving Australia in the afternoon and arriving on the west coast at approximately the same time they departed, on the same day (you gain a day crossing the International Dateline in the Pacific). Flights from North America arrive in Australia at Sydney, Melbourne, Brisbane and Cairns.

For each airline below, the address and telephone number of the main office is given, followed by other numbers that can be called for information and reservations ('800' numbers are toll-free).

Qantas (QF), 360 Post St., San Francisco, CA 94108, USA. Tel. (415) 761 8000.

Other numbers
Eastern and Midwestern USA, Puerto Rico, Virgin Islands. Tel. (800) 227 4500.

California. Tel: (800) 622 0850.
Alaska, Hawaii. Tel: (800) 227 3000.
Bermuda. Tel: (217) 764 0200.
Canadian East Coast, Quebec. Tel: (800) 663 3423.
Eastern Ontario. Tel: (800) 663 3493.
Manitoba, Saskatchewan, Western Ontario. Tel: (800) 663 3797.
Alberta, British Columbia. Tel: (800) 633 3411.
Vancouver. Tel: (604) 684 8231.

Air New Zealand (TE), 9841 Airport Blvd., Suite 1020, Los Angeles, CA 90045, USA. Tel: (213) 642 0196.

Other numbers:
Continental USA. Tel: (800) 262 1234.
Alaska, Hawaii. Tel: (800) 521 4059.
Quebec (French). Tel: (800) 268 8000.
Quebec (English). Tel: (800) 268 9021.
Canadian East Coast. Tel: (800) 268 9110.
Canada 519, 613, 705. Tel: (800) 268 9011.
Ontario 416. Tel: (800) 268 9038.
Toronto. Tel: (416) 928 0550.
Western Canada. Tel: (800) 663 9811.
Vancouver. Tel: (604) 689 3331.

Continental (CO), 2929 Alban Pkwy., Houston, TX 77210-4607, USA. Tel: (713) 821 8150.

Other numbers:
USA. Tel: (800) 231 0856 or (800) 525 0280.
Toronto. Tel: (416) 968 7139.
Vancouver. Tel: (604) 734 4534.

Canadian Pacific Airlines (CP), 1 Grant McConachie Way, Vancouver International Airport, BC Canada V7B 1V1. Tel: (604) 641 2000.

Other numbers:
USA. Tel: (800) 426 7000.
For other numbers in Canada, see local telephone directory.

United (UA), PO Box 66100, Chicago IL 60666. Tel: (312) 952 4000.

Other numbers:
USA and Canada. Tel: (800) 631 1500.
A great many more numbers are listed in telephone directories.

Flights from Europe

It is possible to fly to Australia from most European capitals. Flights are plentiful and take from 16 to 26 hours depending on the city of departure and the number of stop-overs. The following airlines offer direct flights from Europe: **Qantas, British Airways, KLM, Lufthansa, Alitalia, Olympic,** and **JAT.** Other carriers, with stop-overs in Asia, include **Singapore Airlines, Thai International Airlines,** and **Air India.**

Great Britain

British Airways, PO Box 10, Heathrow Airport, Hounslow, Middlesex, TW6 2JA. Tel: (01) 897 4000.

Singapore Airlines, 143 Regent St., London W1. Tel: (01) 439 8111.

Qantas Airlines, 182 The Strand, London WC2. Tel: (01) 836 3013.
Other numbers can be found in telephone directories.

Boat

Cruise packages allow travelers to fly from North America to a port in Australia or elsewhere in the Pacific, joining a cruise ship there. On completion of the cruise, travelers fly home to North America. Alternatively, travelers to Australia may wish to start their voyage from Britain or avail themselves of the 'jet/ship' option (see below).

Several world cruises and circle Pacific cruises include Australian ports in the itinerary. The world cruises and the circle Pacific cruises leave North America and sail to Australia via the South Pacific. It is possible to purchase the North America to Australia segment only.

Cruise information:

USA and Canada
Cunard Line/NAC, 555 Fifth Ave., New York, NY 10017. Tel: (212) 661 7777 or 880 7500.
Other numbers.
USA. Tel: (800) 221 4770.
Canada. Tel: (800) 268 3705.
Royal Viking Line, 750 Battery St., San Francisco, CA 94111.
Phone numbers.
USA. Tel: (800) 422 8000.
Canada. Tel: (800) 233 8000.

Great Britain
CTC Lines (Soviet ships), 1 Regent St., London SW1 Y4NN. Tel: (01) 930 5833.
P&O, 77 New Oxford St., London WC1A 1PP. Tel: (01) 831 1331.

Jet/ship:
Far-East Travel Centre, 35 Piccadilly, London W1V 9PD. Tel: (01) 734 9318. Flights from London to Singapore, then by boat from Singapore to Fremantle (Western Australia).

ENTRY FORMALITIES

Upon entering Australia you must produce your passport and visa, a completed incoming passenger card (issued on the aircraft or ship), a round-trip or continuing passage ticket and must pay a A$5 entrance fee. Clearance is straightforward if your documents are in order.

Passport

A passport is required, and must be valid for longer than the period of your stay in Australia. Two (unused) facing pages are needed for the Australian visa and entry stamps. Although not a requirement, it is advisable to have your passport valid for a period of three months after your departure from Australia.

Visa

All visitors must obtain a visa prior to their arrival in Australia with the exception of New Zealanders, who need only a valid passport. A Visitor's Visa is easily obtained for genuine short-term visits (max. three months) for the purposes of tourism, business discussions or negotiations, special pre-arranged medical treatment or visiting relatives. A visa may be obtained from the Australian Embassy or Consulate nearest you (see 'Before you leave: some useful addresses' pp. 16-17). Visas may take several days to process and are issued free of charge. If you intend visiting Australia more than once, you should ask for a multiple-entry visa.

Customs

Visitors may bring their personal effects into Australia without paying duty, and those over 18 years of age may include 200 cigarettes or 8.75 oz/250 g of cigars or tobacco, and 1 litre/1.057 qts of alcohol. Dutiable goods up to the value of A$200 (200 Australian dollars) included in personal baggage are exempt from duty. A duty of 20 percent applies to the next A$160 in value.

Strict regulations apply to all drugs, narcotics and controlled substances. Penalties for drug offences are severe.

Australia's cultural heritage—an Aboriginal rock painting.

Because Australia is free from many exotic insect pests and diseases, the importation of fresh or packaged food, fruit, vegetables, seeds, bacteria cultures, animals and plants, or animal or plant products, is strictly controlled. Prohibited imports include furs, skins, ivory and other items from animals and birds declared as endangered species. If you have any doubts when you arrive, ask the uniformed quarantine staff in the Customs Hall. More detailed information may also be obtained from the Australian Tourist Commission or any of the regional tourist commissions before you leave home (see 'Before you leave: some useful addresses' pp. 16-17)

■■■ MONEY

Australian currency is decimal, the basic unit being the Australian dollar (A$) divided into 100 cents. The 2, 5, 10, 20, 50 and 100 dollar notes feature historical or cultural scenes. The 1, 2, 5, 10, 20 and 50 cent coins as well as the 1 and 2 dollar coins have a portrait of Queen Elizabeth II on one side.

There is no limit on the importation of currency into Australia but only A$5000 may be exported without permission from the Reserve Bank of Australia. Currency and travelers' checks can be exchanged at all major hotels, airports and banks throughout the country (banks are generally open from 9.30am to 4.30pm, Mon.-Thurs. and from 9.30am to 5.00pm on Fri.) Travelers' checks in Australian dollars can be very convenient because they are considered as cash by the Australians and offer security without the constraints of foreign currency.

Credit cards

The most commonly accepted credit cards are American Express, Bankcard, Carte Blanche, Diners Club, MasterCard, Visa and their affiliates. Usage in smaller towns and country areas may be restricted.

Your budget

The most important item by far in your budget will be travel expenses. First there's the cost of the flight to Australia, followed by all your internal trips which, because of the enormous distances involved, will make heavy demands on your wallet. However, many fare concessions are available for travelers to Australia and travel agents can advise on these. Except for travel costs, you'll be pleasantly surprised at Australian prices.

Thanks to the recent devaluation of the Australian dollar, hotels are reasonably priced and home or farm stays virtual giveaways (see p. 19). Safari excursions are not expensive and food is cheap. Broadly speaking, and no matter how you travel, Australian prices compare very favourably with those in the United States and Great Britain (air fares excepted).

■■■ WHEN TO GO?

Any season is a good one to visit Australia. Why not spend Christmas at the beach? If you want to skip the hottest times, the rain and the local vacation crowds, September to November and March to May are especially good choices. Don't forget that Australia is situated entirely in the southern hemisphere, and the seasons are the opposite of those in Europe or North America. Winter lasts from June to August, spring from September to November, summer from December to February and autumn from March to May. Christmas, accompanied traditionally by Santa Claus, Christmas trees and sleighs, even in Australia, is occasionally spent in 38 °C/100 °F heat around a barbecue.

Because of its size, Australia has several distinct climatic zones. A Mediterranean climate prevails along the coast, whether near Sydney or Perth, with hot summers and pleasantly cool winters. The north of the continent is tropical, with heavy rain from January until March (the 'wet' season) and very warm winters during the 'dry' season. The rest of the country experiences a desert climate: very hot and dry except in winter, when the nights are cool and rains can be torrential.

Lastly, the island of Tasmania enjoys a temperate climate, with warm summers but humid, windy and cold winters. The temperature drops below 0 °C/32 °F only in the mountains, where it snows.

Note: Australians, like everyone else, take their vacations in summer. Airline, hotel and tour reservations can be hard to come by then, so it is best to make reservations well in advance.

Average temperatures

	Jan min	Jan max	Mar min	Mar max	May min	May max	Jul min	Jul max	Sep min	Sep max	Nov min	Nov max
SYDNEY °F	64	79	63	77	52	66	46	61	52	68	59	75
°C	18	26	17	25	11	19	8	16	11	20	15	24
BRISBANE °F	81	84	66	82	55	73	48	68	65	75	64	82
°C	27	29	19	28	13	23	9	20	13	24	18	28
CAIRNS °F	75	90	72	86	68	81	63	77	56	82	72	88
°C	24	32	22	30	20	27	17	25	19	28	22	31
CANBERRA °F	55	82	50	70	37	59	32	52	37	61	48	73
°C	13	28	10	24	3	15	0	11	3	16	9	23
MELBOURNE °F	57	79	55	75	48	63	43	55	46	63	52	72
°C	14	26	13	24	9	17	6	13	8	17	11	22
HOBART °F	54	72	52	68	45	57	39	52	43	59	48	66
°C	12	22	11	20	7	14	4	11	6	15	9	19
ADELAIDE °F	61	86	59	81	50	66	45	59	48	66	55	77
°C	16	30	15	27	10	19	7	15	9	19	13	25
PERTH °F	64	86	63	82	54	70	48	63	50	66	57	77
°C	18	30	17	28	12	21	9	17	10	19	14	25
DARWIN °F	77	90	77	90	72	90	68	86	73	91	77	93
°C	25	32	25	32	22	32	20	30	23	33	25	34
ALICE SPRINGS °F	72	99	64	91	48	73	39	66	50	79	64	93
°C	22	37	18	33	9	23	4	19	10	26	18	34

WHAT TO PACK

Australians dress like Americans or, rather, like Americans in summer and possibly even more casually. In the southern cities, from October to April, Australians wear clothing suited to the heat: shorts, shirts, blouses and light dresses, T-shirts, jeans, sandals or bare feet. Refinement does shine through on some occasions—a tie, though not necessarily a jacket, is required in up-market restaurants and clubs. Civil servants often wear 'dress' shorts, long socks up to the knee, white shirt and tie to the office. In most instances, a pullover or cardigan over shirt or blouse is sufficient for evening wear. Except for employees of government ministries, stock-broking firms and banks, the three-piece suit is something of a curiosity.

The outback requires desert-style clothing: stout walking shoes, sun-hat, a soft travel bag, jeans or similarly rugged trousers if you're planning to ride a horse, motorbike or camel. Don't forget your sunglasses and swimsuit. Suntan lotion is a must (quality lotions can be found just about everywhere in Australia). For winter in the mountains you'll need woolen garments and a raincoat. If you're thinking of indulging in your favourite sport in Australia, don't load yourself down with equipment: surfboards, tennis rackets or fishing rods may be rented or bought when you get there. You'll need a sleeping bag if you're going on a safari tour—check with your travel agency to see whether the tour operator supplies sleeping bags or not.

TIPS FOR PHOTOGRAPHERS

Australia is relatively easy to photograph. The natural light is very beautiful and the deep violet-blue of the sky provides a great backdrop to the scenery. Eucalyptus trees make fine photographs and the cities are full of contrasts and well lit. If you want a more restrained photograph of the desert, use a polarizing filter. Kangaroos move very quickly and require speed, accuracy and a good zoom lens. There's no problem photographing most people—just ask and they will cooperate. Aborigines are the most difficult to photograph, firstly because they are very shy of the camera, and secondly because their dark brown skin and sunken eyes call for strong lighting on the face. Protect your equipment from dust and sand, and keep your films safe from the humid heat of the tropics in a sealable bag. You can buy film and have it developed in Australia. Kodachrome 64 is a good colour film. Finally, if you intend taking photos on the Great Barrier Reef, don't forget to bring along your underwater equipment (see p. 104).

BEFORE YOU LEAVE: SOME USEFUL ADDRESSES

Britain

Australian High Commission
London: Australia House, The Strand, WC2B 4LA. Tel: (01) 438 8000.

Consulates
Edinburgh: Hobart House, 80 Hanover St., EH2 2DL. Tel: (031) 226 6271.
Manchester: Chatsworth House, Lever St., M1 2DL. Tel: (061) 228 1344.

Agent-General for New South Wales
London: 66 The Strand, WC2. Tel: (01) 839 6651.

Agent-General for Queensland
London: 392 The Strand, WC2. Tel: (01) 836 3224.

Agent-General for South Australia
London: 50 The Strand, W2. Tel: (01) 930 7471.

Agent-General for Victoria
London: Melbourne Place, W2. Tel: (01) 836 2656.

Agent-General for Western Australia
London: 115 The Strand, W2. Tel. (01) 240 2881.

Australian International Travel Centre
London: 31 Melbourne Place, WC2. Tel: (01) 240 2000.

Northern Territory Tourist Commission
London: Heathcoat House, 20 Savile Row, W1. Tel: (01) 439 2727.

Canada

Australian High Commission
Ottawa: National Bldg., 13th Floor, 130 Slater St., ONT K1P 5H6. Tel: (613) 236 0841.

Consulates
Toronto: Suite 2324, Commerce Court West, corner King and Bay Sts., ONT M5L 1B9. Tel: (416) 367 0783.

Vancouver: 1066 West Hastings St., BC V6E 3X1. Tel: (604) 684 1177.

Australian Tourist Commission

Toronto: 3080 Yonge St., Suite 5052, ONT M4N 3N1. Tel: (416) 487 2126.

Queensland Tourist and Travel Corporation

Vancouver: 890 West Pender St., Suite 600, BC V6C 1J9. Tel: (604) 687 7975.

Victorian Tourism Commission

Toronto: 120 Eglington Ave. East, Suite 220, ONT M4P 1E2. Tel: (416) 487 1151.

United States

Embassy

Washington: 1601 Massachusetts Ave. NW, DC 20036. Tel: (202) 797 3000.

Consulates

Chicago: 321 North Clark St., Suite 2930, IL 60610. Tel: (312) 645 9440.

Honolulu: 1000 Bishop St., HI 96813. Tel: (808) 524 5050.

Houston: 1990 South Post Oak Blvd., Suite 800, TX 77056-9998. Tel: (713) 629 9131.

Los Angeles: 611 North Larchment Blvd., CA 90004. Tel: (213) 380 0980.

New York: 636 Fifth Ave., NY 10111. Tel: (212) 245 4000.

San Francisco: Qantas Bldg., 360 Post St., CA 94108. Tel: (415) 362 6160.

Australian Tourist Commission

Los Angeles: 3550 Wilshire Blvd., Suite 1740, CA 90010. Tel: (213) 380 6060.

New York: 489 Fifth Ave., 31st Floor, NY 10017. Tel: (212) 687 6300.

New South Wales Tourist Commission

Los Angeles: 2049 Century Park East, Suite 2250, CA 90067. Tel: (213) 552 9566.

Northern Territory Tourist Commission

Los Angeles: 3550 Wilshire Blvd., Suite 1610, CA 90010. Tel: (213) 383 7092 or (800) OUTBACK.

Queensland Tourist and Travel Corporation

Los Angeles: 3550 Wilshire Blvd., Suite 1738, CA 90010. Tel: (213) 687 6300.

New York: 489 Fifth Ave., 31st Floor, NY 10017. Tel: (212) 687 6300.

South Australian Department of Tourism

Los Angeles: 3550 Wilshire Blvd., Suite 1740, CA 90010. Tel: (213) 380 5422.

Tasmanian Department of Tourism

Los Angeles: 3550 Wilshire Blvd., Suite 1740, CA 90010. Tel: (213) 380 6060.

Victorian Tourism Commission

Los Angeles: 3550 Wilshire Blvd., Suite 1736, CA 90010. Tel: (213) 387 3111.

Western Australian Tourism Commission

Los Angeles: 3550 Wilshire Blvd., Suite 1610, CA 90010. Tel: (213) 383 7122.

New York: 489 Fifth Ave., NY 10017. Tel: (212) 687 1442.

PRACTICAL INFORMATION

The information in this chapter will be useful to you upon arrival in Australia. Advice on accommodation, food and drink, organizing your time, transportation etc. appears in alphabetical order. For specific page references, see the contents page at the beginning of the guide.

▬▬ *ACCOMMODATION*

Hotels, motels, pubs etc.

With its long nomadic tradition, Australia has many kinds of accommodation, from the most luxurious establishments to youth hostels. The recent tourist boom throughout the country has seen the growth of first-class tourist resorts. We divide hotels into the following categories:

▲▲▲▲ **International-standard** hotels (*premier* hotels in Australia) are modern, luxurious, comfortable, fully equipped, well located and fairly expensive (A$100-120 for a single room, A$130-150 for a double). They all offer rooms and suites with private bath, colour television, and air conditioning; other amenities include first-rate service, swimming pool, one or more restaurants, parking and conference facilities. Major cities and important tourist centres offer an excellent choice of hotels in this category, at significantly lower prices in some areas, especially on Barrier Reef islands (A$100 per person for full board in a double room on Dunk Island, one of the most comfortable and best-equipped locations on the Great Barrier Reef).

▲▲▲ **First-class** hotels (also *premier* hotels in Australia) offer service and comfortable rooms similar to those of the international-standard hotels but generally do not include conference facilities and may or may not have a pool or restaurant. Consequently they are less expensive: A$50-70 for a single room, A$80-100 for a double.

▲▲ **Moderately priced** (*moderate*) accommodation includes fully equipped private hotels, motels or pubs (rooms with private bath, television, etc.), comfortable but not luxurious: A$30-50 for a single, A$40-60 for a double.

The term *private* hotel is used to distinguish the ordinary hotel from the pub, short for *public* hotel. Pubs, mostly built in the latter half of the 19th century with splendid wrought-iron verandahs, are more than hotels in that they are licensed to sell alcohol, which private hotels are not. At the bar you can meet the entire town or suburb. In the bush, you'll encounter everyone from several hundred miles around and in summer it is not uncommon to simply 'doss down' on the verandah after an evening of emptying cans of beer with the locals (bars close at 10 or 11pm during the week and at various times during the weekend, depending on the state). You can get a good, inexpensive meal in a pub. Not all pubs, however, take guests. Those which do display the sign 'accommodation'.

▲ **Inexpensive** (*budget*) accommodation includes small private hotels, motels, pubs, guest houses and hostels: prices range from A$15-20 for a single room to A$25-30 for a double, except for the youth hostels which belong to the International Federation of Youth Hostels or are of the American YMCA-YWCA variety; they charge about A$5-7 per night. There are about 110 youth hostels in Australia, in the bush as well as the city. Don't forget your membership card. Address in Australia: **Australian Youth Hostels,** 60 Mary St., Surry Hills, NSW 2010. Tel: (02) 212 1151.

In the bush, the choice is generally between the old, 'atmospheric' pub and the modern, air-conditioned motel. Motels, which tend to be better equipped, are unfortunately replacing the pubs which have much more character.

Private hotels, hostels and guest houses, with their pleasant family atmosphere and meals, are often very inexpensive but are quite rare outside tourist centres.

Camping and caravan parks

To be recommended if you're traveling by car or campervan. In caravan (trailer) parks in the bush, you'll meet Australia's nomadic population: contract labourers and their families moving from job to job or from farm to farm. Camping grounds are numerous and well-equipped. If you like the wide-open spaces, ask property owners for permission to camp on their land. Be careful with fires and remember the phrase 'don't rubbish Australia'. Don't leave trash lying about. Guides to camping grounds are available from tourist offices in Australia. Camping cost: about A$3.50 per person.

Home stays

If you can understand the local accent, you might enjoy the simple, warm Australian hospitality to be found through a specialized organization or just by making friends. Prices range from A$25 to A$40 per person for a room and breakfast.

Information and reservations
Bed & Breakfast Australia, 396 Kent St., Sydney, NSW 2025. Tel: (02) 264 3155.

Australian Home Accommodation, 209 Toorak Rd., South Yarra, Melbourne. Tel: (03) 241 3694.

Farm stays

Above all, don't miss the unique and fabulous Australian experience of a stay on a farm or ranch in the outback. There, you'll be treated like one of the family and can take part in all farm activities: riding, motor-biking, working cattle, drives in a Land Rover and bush walks on properties which can be as large as several thousand square miles. This 'Wild West' adventure costs about A$60 to A$80 per day per adult (special rates for children), food and activities included. The oldest and finest properties are located in Victoria, NSW, southern Queensland and Tasmania, whereas the biggest and most isolated stations are found throughout the outback. The Australian Tourist Commission publishes a very comprehensive guide to farm holidays (see 'Before you leave: some useful addresses' pp. 16-17).

Information and reservations
Farm Holidays, 98 Fletcher St., Woollahra, NSW 2025. Tel: (02) 387 6681.

Farmhost Border Promotions, PO Box 65, Culcairn. NSW 2660. Tel: (060) 29 6521.

Homestay of WA, Lot 40, Union Rd., Carmel, WA. Tel: (09) 293 5347.

Quirindi Host Farms, PO Box 293, Quirindi, NSW 2343. Tel: (067) 46 1545.

▬ BUSINESS HOURS

Shops are usually open from 8.30 or 9am to 5 or 5.30pm from Mon.-Fri., from 9am to noon on Sat., and are closed on Sun. Small shops, especially those operated by 'new Australians', tend to have more flexible hours.

EMERGENCIES

Dial 000 for emergency help from the police, fire or ambulance services.

FOOD AND DRINK

Food

Australian food is good food. The basic ingredients, especially meat and a great variety of seafoods, are excellent and the contributions of immigrants to the country have greatly changed Australians' eating habits. In the bush, food may be merely functional but, in the cities, the choice is endless. The influence of the Europeans who manage most of the city markets can now be detected in Australian homes, where people have learned to vary the menu and to eat well.

In the countryside, the main purpose of eating is to regain one's strength after a long working day. The hearty food is based mostly on meat, although it may be a little heavy when it's 100 °F/38 °C in the shade.

As in all Anglo-Saxon countries, the main meals are breakfast, lunch and dinner. Breakfast, especially in the bush, is formidable: porridge or cornflakes, steak and eggs, sausages or lamb chops accompanied by French fries, toast, coffee or strong tea with milk—in a word, fortifying.

The noon meal, lunch, is usually little more than a formality: some kind of sandwich on white or whole-grain bread, or a meat pie, one of the classics of the Australian cuisine, consumed quickly at the beach or in a park. There is also the counter lunch, a larger repast often eaten standing at a pub bar and washed down with copious quantities of beer.

The evening meal is more elaborate: soup or starters, a meat dish (roast leg of lamb accompanied by fresh vegetables is another classic dish), salad, cheese and dessert. Dinner is served fairly early, about 6pm. This enables people to go out and take advantage of the few cool hours before nightfall or enjoy an evening at the pub which, by law, must close at 10 or 11pm, depending on the state.

Australians rarely invite people to dinner, preferring instead to go out or, if it's a weekend, to organize a traditional barbecue in the garden, in the sunshine, with steak, chops, sausages and beer in abundance.

Drink

Australians are proud of the fact that, after the Germans and the Czechs, they are the greatest beer drinkers in the world. Australian beer is really first-class. It is drunk cold from the can at home or on tap (draught) in the pub; at a picnic kept cold in a polystyrene container (an *Esky*). There are different names for the glasses of beer served at the bar: you'll hear schooner, middy, glass, and pot (see 'A guide to Australian English' pp. 200-201).

Each state has its own beer brands. Tastes vary, but many prefer Melbourne beers such as Foster's Lager or Carlton Draught from Carlton-United Breweries. Connoisseurs also favour Cooper's beer from Adelaide, Hannan's (named after the founder of Kalgoorlie in Western Australia) and Swan Lager from Perth. There are also beers from Queensland and New South Wales.

Drinking a beer with your 'mates' is a ritual that takes place in the evening between dinner and closing time. For some, it involves consuming as many glasses of the amber fluid as possible, while ensuring that their companions do the same.

Metropolitan mounted police.

In the last 20 years, as an alternative pleasure, Australians have grown very fond of the wines produced in their own vineyards. They are proud of them, and rightly so: some vineyards, such as those in the Barossa Valley of South Australia, produce high quality vintages, especially in white wines.

A lot of tea is also drunk in Australia (unions have won two tea breaks per day from employers in numerous branches of industry), as well as coffee, delicious cold milk-shakes, American-style soft drinks such as Coke and lemonade, and superb fruit juices.

Restaurants and pubs

The major cities are justifiably proud of their restaurants which are more and more becoming part of the cultural heritage and which bear witness to the diversity of the Australian population. You will find any number of different cuisines: Italian, Greek, Chinese, French, Indian, Lebanese, Indonesian, American (plenty of McDonalds), and British (fish and chips unlike any you'll find in Britain). Many pubs also offer counter lunches at noon. These are quick, inexpensive and often very good, eaten either at a table or at the bar.

The very strict licensing laws on the sale of alcohol have produced three kinds of restaurant:

— Conventional restaurants which have a liquor license.

— Cafés, sandwich bars and fast-food outlets which do not have liquor licenses (this is changing—some Pizza Huts have been licensed). The consumption of alcohol is forbidden in these establishments but you can take your food outside and wash it down with a beer bought at the pub.

— BYO (Bring Your Own) establishments invite you to bring your own 'hard liquor'. This is a way for the restaurant owner to circumvent having a liquor license which is difficult to procure and expensive. Such restaurants are often the most interesting, inexpensive, fashionable and friendly.

■■■ LANGUAGE: DO YOU SPEAK 'STRINE'?

The Australian accent is broad, not quite English or American. There are no regional accents in Australia but socio-cultural differences, which date back to colonial times, do have an effect on the way people speak. On the one hand, you have the 'educated', English-sounding accent which may be an affectation or merely the result of a person's education and friends. On the other, there is 'strine' (rhymes with 'wine' and means 'Australian'), the accent of the majority of Australians who do not seek to conceal their working-class Irish or Cockney origins. In 'strine', vowels are strongly nasalized, especially the 'a' and 'ay' sounds (approximate pronunciation = 'eye'). Long words are typically shortened to two syllables ending with an 'i' or 'o': *Aussie* (pron. 'ozi') = an Australian; *vegies* = vegetables; *sunnies* = sun glasses; *Uie* (youi) = U-turn; *mozzie* = mosquito; *garbo* = garbage collector; *smoko* = tea break, etc.

'Strine' is also characterized by what North Americans and British travelers will undoubtedly find to be an excessive use of slang and swear words—rest assured, no offense is meant. The most frequently encountered slang expressions include: *G'day mate* (hi, hullo); *no worries* or *she's right* (that's OK); a *beaut shiela* (an attractive girl); *pom* or *pommy* (an Englishman/woman); *yank* (an American); *dinkum, fair dinkum* or *dinkie die Aussie* (a real Australian); *my shout* (my round of drinks). See also 'A guide to Australian English' pp. 200-201.

METRIC SYSTEM AND ELECTRICITY

In 1966, Australia converted to the metric system with few problems and after an excellent public education program, although some people—mainly older people educated in the Imperial System—still refer to feet, miles, gallons and Fahrenheit. It may be helpful to know the following conversions: 10°C/50°F, 20°C/68°F, 30°C/86°F, and 40°C/104°F; 80 km/50 miles; and 1 litre/approx. 1 US quart or 1.8 British pints.

Electricity in Australia is supplied at 240 volts AC (260 volts AC in Western Australia). An adapter is needed if you wish to use any British 3-pin or any round-pin plugs in Australian sockets. Major hotels and motels have 110 volt outlets into which US appliances can be plugged directly but, otherwise, a transformer will have to be used to convert 240-260 sockets to 110 volts.

ORGANIZING YOUR TIME

Australia is as large as the United States, so it requires careful budgeting of time. Just the length of the journey to Australia and the time changes involved mean that you've lost two days before you start. You should also consider the time required for internal travel, even by plane, but especially by train or bus (three days from Sydney to Perth), and by car (few roads are suitable for high-speed driving). For these reasons, even if you're on a long vacation of at least two weeks, you should plan your itinerary bearing in mind that you cannot 'do' Australia in one go. You can, however, see the country adequately in two or three months. Concentrate on the centres of interest, the 'musts'. They are easy to define, despite the distances involved: the major cities of the south (especially Sydney); the bush (Ayers Rock); and the Great Barrier Reef.

Another factor to be considered is your port of entry. Sydney is the usual choice but you could equally well select Melbourne, Darwin, Perth, Adelaide or several cities in Queensland. This is an excellent means of cutting down on traveling time.

The following are some basic itineraries, with variations governed by the time available to you and your finances. All travel is by air except where otherwise mentioned.

Two weeks (arrival and departure from Sydney)
— In and around Sydney: 3-4 days.
— Townsville or Cairns and the Great Barrier Reef (stay on an island): 3-4 days.
— Alice Springs-Ayers Rock: 3 days.
— Transfers and air travel: approx. 2 days.

Two and a half weeks
(arrival and departure from Sydney)
The same itinerary as above, plus a two-day visit to Melbourne, returning from Melbourne with a stop in Canberra.

Two and a half weeks
(arrival in Sydney, departure from Perth)
— Sydney and the Great Barrier Reef: 7-8 days.
— Alice Springs-Ayers Rock: 2 days.
— In and around Perth (Kalgoorlie): 2-3 days.
— Transfers and air travel: approx. 2 days.

Two and a half weeks
(arrival in Sydney, departure from Darwin)
— Sydney and the Great Barrier Reef: 8 days.
— Darwin and Kakadu National Park: 6 days.
— Transfers and travel: approx. 2 days.

Three weeks
The same basic itinerary, plus a stay of several days on a station (ranch) and an extra road journey.

Four weeks
— The grand tour: arrival in Melbourne, then Sydney, Brisbane, the Great Barrier Reef, Darwin, Alice Springs, Adelaide and departure from Perth with a three-day stay in each place.
— One of the basic itineraries above, allowing the maximum time in each place, plus one or other of the following 3 or 4-day modules: ranch stay; Barrier Reef cruise; visit to Tasmania (from Melbourne); trip on the Murray River (from Adelaide); bush safari (from Darwin or Alice Springs in the Northern Territory, Cairns in Queensland, Broome or Derby in Western Australia); transcontinental train journey (Sydney-Perth or Sydney-Adelaide-Alice Springs); walking in a national park; the gold route (around Kalgoorlie in Western Australia); the opal route (Coober Pedy in central Australia); the North Coast (of New South Wales, to Brisbane via the Gold Coast); the Great Ocean Road (from Melbourne to Adelaide):
— Another possibility if you have four weeks at your disposal is to rent a campervan and follow one of the basic itineraries above, with the added benefit of being able to leave the van in a city other than the one you started from.

Longer stays (six weeks or more)
The same basic itineraries, but exclusively by land i.e. bus, train or car. Here, the best solution is to buy a second-hand car in Australia and sell it again before you leave. This guide contains several suggestions in the chapters devoted to various regions for trips 'off the beaten track', but there are many others. Inquire at travel offices when you arrive and, more importantly, ask the locals.

Business trips (two-three days)
This guide contains a selection of short excursions (from one-half to two days) from the main cities. They can be taken individually or through a local tour operator.

▬ *POST OFFICE AND TELECOMMUNICATIONS*

Telephone
The telephone system is efficient and cheap: local calls cost only 30 cents for an unlimited amount of time. Most areas are connected directly on STD, the Standard Trunk Dialing system. International dialing can be automatic or via the operator, and collect calls are also possible from the grey-green STD public phones. For calls to North America or Britain, ask the operator for prices; there are special low rates at night and on Sundays. Telegrams can be sent via the telephone or from a post office.
The Yellow Pages are a mine of information, listing hotels, car rentals and the like. The ordinary, alphabetical phone book contains information on how to phone, prices, and the area codes for all the cities in Australia. However, Australia is updating its telephone system and numbers are subject to change. In the bush, communication often takes place via the Flying Doctor network (see p. 196) or on the ultra-high frequencies used by truck-drivers and prospectors.

Post office
Poste restante (general delivery) offices are found in post offices at all major centres. The post can be slow and deliveries leisurely and infrequent. Some years ago, postal workers decided unilaterally to abandon Saturday deliveries. If you can, post airmail letters from large towns and cities. In the bush, despite the extraordinary helpfulness of local post office personnel, mail moves almost at walking pace.

▬ *PUBLIC HOLIDAYS, FESTIVALS AND LEISURE ACTIVITIES*

Public holidays
Australia as a whole has eight public holidays per year. They include New Year's Day, Christmas, Easter, Anzac Day, Australia Day and Labor Day. Although Anzac Day is celebrated on April 25 throughout Australia, holidays like Australia Day and Labor Day are celebrated on different days in every state.

Anzac Day commemorates the defeat of Australian and New Zealand forces at Gallipoli during World War I and is considered a solemn event by many Australians. All cities and towns have very moving processions by former service personnel. Labor Day sees good-natured processions. States also have their individual public holidays, the most famous of which is Victoria's Melbourne Cup Day, celebrated the first Tuesday in November, when the state shuts down for a horse race. Important local festivals and celebrations are indicated in the appropriate chapter.

Other events

Religious holidays, Christmas and Easter, are observed nationally but do not involve any public rejoicing, except in Latin communities. Other important events are the Royal Shows (regional agricultural exhibitions); cultural festivals such as the Adelaide Festival of Arts; popular festivals such as *Moomba* in Melbourne; rodeos and bush horse races; and major sporting competitions. Australians also love getting together at regional or town level. Saturday markets are a favourite rendez-vous for the local population which gathers just as people have done for ages to exchange baskets of puppies, organically grown vegetables and gossip. Auctions, of produce or cattle, are an excuse for celebrating at the pub and parties or barbecue gatherings are almost daily events.

Australian bicentennial: 1988

The year 1988 marks the 200th anniversary of Australia's founding. Bicentennial celebrations and festivities of all kinds are held throughout the country between January 1 and December 31, 1988. For complete information and lists of these events, ask your travel agent or the Australian Tourist Commission representative nearest you (see pp. 16-17).

SHOPPING

When you come to consider souvenirs and presents, you will be especially attracted to two kinds of items: opals and Aboriginal artifacts. About 95 percent of the world's opals come from Australia, mainly from the mines of Coober Pedy and Lightning Ridge. Black opals are the most precious and they, together with the multi-coloured varieties, are sold polished, mounted or rough. Aboriginal arts and crafts such as 'x-ray' design bark paintings and carved wooden objects (boomerangs, animals, dishes) are extremely beautiful. They can be purchased at specialized galleries, whether in the cities or in the bush. You can also take home toy kangaroos and koalas, sheep-skin garments, sporting outfits and accessories, and works of art.

TIME

Australia has three time zones, more or less separated by state borders. Queensland, New South Wales, Victoria and Tasmania operate on GMT (Greenwich Mean Time) + 10 hours. South Australia and the Northern Territory are on GMT + 9.5 hours and Western Australia on GMT + 8 hours. In other words, if it is 12 noon GMT in Britain, it will be 10pm in Sydney, Melbourne, Canberra, Brisbane and Hobart; 9:30pm in Adelaide and Darwin; and 8pm in Perth (it will also be 6am in New York and Montreal, 3am in Los Angeles and Vancouver).

Daylight-saving time confuses things a bit, however; during the North American and European summer months, one hour must be subtracted from the above figures because clocks are set ahead one hour in the Northern hemisphere. Australia, with the exception of Western Australia and Queensland, goes on daylight-saving time during the North American and European winter, so one hour must be added to the above figures during those months.

▬▬ *TIPPING*

Tipping is not as widespread or expected in Australia as in the United States and Europe, and service charges are not added to accounts at hotels and restaurants. Porters at airports and hairdressers do not expect to be tipped. Porters at railway terminals have set charges; those at hotels do not but you may tip for service. In restaurants, food and drink waiters may be tipped from 10 to 15 percent of the bill for special service. Tipping in taxis is not compulsory, though taxi drivers will not refuse a small tip. Generally speaking, tipping is up to you, in appreciation of some extra service received.

▬▬ *TOURIST INFORMATION*

Every city and tourist centre in Australia has excellent tourist offices. They are usually most efficient and friendly. Don't hesitate to get in touch with them for help in locating a hotel, transport or general tourist information. One other feature of these offices is that you can make your bookings there (transport, hotel, tours etc.).

▬▬ *TRANSPORTATION*

Before choosing any means of transport, bear in mind the size of the country. It takes almost three days to travel by road from Sydney to Perth, and almost a day by plane. The drive from Sydney to Melbourne takes a minimum of 10 hours. Your choice will depend on the time at your disposal and the amount of money you want to spend. If you have lots of time, rent a car or buy a second-hand car when you arrive. If you don't have much time, it might be better to fly. If you don't like flying and don't want to drive, you might find the train or bus more appealing.

Driving

If you'll be staying for a long time and want to see the country, the best solution is to buy a second-hand car. Older Holdens (General Motors) or Falcons (Ford) can be located quite easily. The prices may seem high by comparison with what you'd pay at home, but you will also be able to demand a good resale price when you leave.

Car rental

Renting a vehicle is no problem in the cities and tourist centres. Prices vary in accordance with size and type of car (from a small Datsun to a Rolls Royce) and the rental period (per day, per week, per month, etc.). The main rental companies are Avis, Budget, Hertz and Thrifty. A glance through the Yellow Pages of the phone book will also provide the addresses of local rental firms. Some of these offer attractive discounts and some most original vehicles: Mini Mokes, off-road vehicles, motorbikes and camper-vans (motorhomes). A fully equipped campervan can carry five people and is a good idea if you want to travel with children and go when and where you like. Various tour operators offer attractive fly-drive packages and your car can be waiting for you when you arrive or at each stopover.

Highway driving

Before you take to the highway, you should know the following: Australians drive on the left, the speed limit varies between 62-70 mi/100-110 km per hour outside the cities and the wearing of seat-belts is compulsory. The road network is extensive but not always in very good condition. Expressways are rare and usually fairly short. Tarred roads are not very wide (two lanes is the norm) and extreme caution should be exercised on the busy routes, such as the Princes Highway linking Sydney to Melbourne and Brisbane. If you stray from the main roads in the bush, you will find the often untarred minor roads dusty in summer and muddy in winter (to make up for this, Australia is a paradise for off-road vehicles and Land Rovers).

In general, watch out for sudden turns after long straight stretches as well as cattle, kangaroos, potholes, ditches and 'road trains'. The latter are giant trucks with up to four trailers. Traveling at speeds above 60 mi/100 km per hour, they resemble super-tankers and take just about as long to stop. You should also avoid the combination of sun and alcohol.

Desert driving

If you intend to drive in the desert, there are a number of precautions to take even if it doesn't look like the Sahara. You'll need to carry water, extra fuel, food and spare wheels, and your vehicle will need to be in A-1 condition. One last piece of advice: if you're driving in the bush, even along main roads, you'll constantly come across gates intended to keep the cattle in. The rule is to leave the gate in the position you found it—open if it was open and closed if you had to open it to drive through.

Motor vehicle insurance

Your own insurance policy will not be valid in Australia. At the very least you will have to take out insurance to cover third-party damage. If you buy a registered second-hand vehicle, this insurance is included in the price. It is also included in car rental prices but extra insurance (partial or comprehensive) is recommended.

Plane

Flying in Australia, especially in the bush, is as common as taking the train elsewhere in the world. There are three major domestic airlines: **Ansett** (privately owned), **Australian Airlines** (government-owned) and **East-West Airlines** (privately owned). They are among the safest airlines in the world, fly regular schedules and are quite expensive. However, all airlines offer special discount fares for overseas visitors. Other packages offered are comprehensive tours and fly/drive vacations. Information can be obtained from any of the above airlines or your travel agent.

Regional connections can be arranged with East-West Airlines (which has ambitions to be the third national airline), subsidiaries of Ansett (**Air New South Wales, Ansett Northern Territory, Ansett Western Australia**) and **Air Queensland.** Other companies, such as **East Coast Airlines, Kendell** or **Skywest** operate at the local level. Air Queensland, East-West Airlines and several other local companies offer discount fares on certain routes. Farmers and prospectors in the outback usually have their own aircraft and it is often a cowboy pilot who will personally take you to his farm for a stay in an isolated ranch. The ultimate tourist experience in Australia is to rent a plane, with or without pilot, or to join several other adventurers for an air safari or air tour in a small business jet (Air New South Wales, **Jolly Swagman Tours, Tasair,** etc.).

Train

Aside from the two transcontinental lines that serve Perth and Alice Springs, the entire Australian rail network is concentrated within a triangle formed by Cairns, Sydney and Adelaide. Each state is responsible for its own rail system and for a long time travelers were obliged to change trains at state borders because the tracks were of different gauges in each state. Thanks to efforts by the federal government, the quality of travel on the major lines has now been standardized. If you like train travel, these comfortable, scenic journeys will make you feel that you are aboard a kind of tropical Trans-Siberian Express. The *Indian-Pacific* links Sydney and Perth via Melbourne, Adelaide and the Nullarbor Plain (three times a week, 65-hour journey); other lines connect Sydney to Brisbane (daily, 16-hour journey) and Brisbane to Cairns (six times a week, 34 to 37-hour journey) and there is the *Ghan,* which runs from Adelaide to Alice Springs (once a week normally, twice a week between May and October, 24-hour journey). Over longer distances, such as Sydney-Perth, the train is considerably more expensive than the bus (about three times as much for a 2nd-class ticket). However, the train ticket includes sleeping facilities and all meals. Over shorter distances, such as Sydney-Melbourne or Sydney-Brisbane, the bus is about 30 percent cheaper than the train. Before you leave home, you can buy an Austrailpass through your travel agent. This gives you a reduced, unlimited-mileage ticket that can be used on all rail lines, including suburban networks. Tickets are valid for periods from two weeks to three months and are not too expensive.

Tip: reserve your seats before you leave home through your travel agent. That way you can also benefit from a 30 percent reduction on certain routes provided you make your reservation at least seven days in advance. Some discount fares are also available on the spot for individual state networks.

Bus

As elsewhere in the world, buses or coaches provide truly economical means of transportation, much cheaper than the train on transcontinental routes and 30 percent cheaper over short distances. Above all, buses go where trains do not and connect the rest of the country with those small bush townships not served by regular airlines. Long-distance buses are air conditioned and have lavatories, an indispensable comfort given the heat and the distances involved (more than 60 hours from Sydney to Perth and 75 hours from Sydney to Darwin). Australia has two national bus companies: Greyhound, linked in name only with its American counterpart, and Ansett-Pioneer. There are also numerous local companies, such as Deluxe and Centralian. Greyhound and Ansett-Pioneer both offer unlimited mileage discount fares to foreign travelers (from 14 to 60 days) on their routes. These fares are not transferable between companies and must be bought outside Australia from a travel agent before you leave home.

Bus tours are very popular with Australians themselves. Whether they involve major tourist excursions lasting several weeks or a few days, visits to a city or safari-camping trips in the outback, all are well-proven and inexpensive.

Boat

Tasmania is connected to Melbourne three times a week by the ferry Abel Tasman (14-hour crossing) and certain Barrier Reef islands are served by launch. River journeys are available along the Murray River.

Hitch-hiking

Hitch-hiking is still quite safe in Australia and is an efficient means of getting about on major routes. It is, nevertheless, best to hitch in pairs rather than alone and to use common sense in accepting or not accepting rides.

In cities

Public transport is more or less adequate in all major cities and towns. There are no extensive underground train systems but buses are frequent. Melbourne has its famous trams and Sydney its ferries. Taxis are common, efficient and inexpensive and it's considered good form to sit in front, next to the driver.

Excursions and organized tours

Tour-operators and excursion organizers offering the most interesting trips will be indicated for each geographical region among the useful addresses in the 'Practical Information' section of the appropriate chapter.

GEOGRAPHY

Australia is a huge country—2,967,906 sq mi/7,686,884 sq km—as big as the United States and as large as Europe from Ireland to the Caspian Sea. Sydney, in the east, is 2569 mi/4135 km from Perth, in the west, or 5 hours 20 minutes by plane and 60 hours by bus. Darwin in the north, is 2545 mi/4095 km away, or 6 hours 30 minutes by plane and 75 hours by bus, not counting transfer time.

THE FORMATION OF AUSTRALIA

Australia is perhaps the most ancient, the most isolated, the flattest and the driest of the continents. Its harsh, monotonous and barren landscape, crowned by a violet-blue sky, is a boundless domain of red earth, grey-green scrub and shimmering heat haze. Its solemn, stark naturalness cannot fail to impress.

In geological terms, Australia is over 3 billion years old. One hundred and fifty million years ago, *Gondwanaland,* a supercontinent comprising Australia, Africa, South America, India and Antarctica, gradually separated (Europe and Asia were still submerged). Australia slowly drifted to its present position just south of the Equator. Bordered to the west by the Indian Ocean, to the east by the Pacific and to the south by the Southern Ocean, Australia has only New Guinea, Timor, New Zealand and New Caledonia for near neighbours.

THE FLAT AUSTRALIAN LANDMASS

The 23,000 mi/37,000 km of coastline surround a country which is fairly even and flat, except for some dips to below sea-level in central Australia. The coast traces the shape of a very ancient continent; it has neither volcanic activity nor chains of high mountains. Even during the glacial eras, there was no significant glaciation. Australia grew old where it stood, wrinkling, cracking, slowly changing, unknown for millions of years to the rest of the world. The result is a huge, flat continent, with sweeping plains and low plateaux, their monotony relieved occasionally by low, rounded hills. Only a few sections of the Great Dividing Range, which runs along the coast from Cape York in the far north of Queensland to Tasmania, exceed 4900 ft/1500 m. The highest point in the Australian Alps is Mount Kosciusko, at 7310 ft/2228 m. Only these mountainous regions are snow-covered in winter.

To the east of the Australian Alps is an area of low alluvial plains, where Australia's only important river, the Murray, winds its languid course. With its companion river, the Darling, the Murray forms a system over 3000 mi/4800 km long, before emptying into the Great Australian Bight, over a drainage basin of 386,000 sq mi/1,000,000 sq km.

To the west there is desert. Sand, rock and red earth are interspersed with several spectacular monoliths (Ayers Rock among them) and a few large salt lakes, such as Lake Eyre. All of Western Australia and much of the central region forms an ancient, low plateau scarcely touched by erosion. The Nullarbor Plain, which terminates abruptly in the south at an uninterrupted cliff-face, has been there since the beginning of time. In the north-west, the ancient plateaux of the Kimberley and Arnhem Land rise above huge basins and swampy coastal plains. Finally, there is the Great Barrier Reef, stretching for 1250 mi/2014 km along the Queensland coast.

THE DRIEST CONTINENT ON EARTH

Australia is the world's least-watered landmass, with an average 18.5 in/470 mm of rainfall per year as compared to 26.1 in/720 mm for the rest of the world. A desert or semi-desert climate prevails in more than half of the continent, and in those areas drought is continuous. In contrast, the coast from Cape York to Adelaide, the 'mountains' and Tasmania are quite well watered as is the area around Perth. The north of the continent experiences a tropical climate, including cyclones which can be extremely violent, like *Tracy* which, on Christmas morning 1974, virtually wiped Darwin off the face of the earth.

The Australian landscape spreads from the centre, in more or less concentric rings. Red-earth desert and sand dunes are bordered by grassy savanna, shimmering amid a scattering of acacias where the vast cattle ranches are. Then come the low hills, where forests of eucalypts give way to pastures, followed by low plateaux suited to wheat and other cereal crops. Denser forests signal the higher hills of the coastal strip, followed by orchards and vegetable gardens close to the population centres. The tropical north is the domain of rain forest and sugar cane. Tasmania is covered in a dense, moist forest (part of it unexplored) and apple trees. Remember, as soon as you leave the cities, you're in the bush, or the outback.

FLORA AND FAUNA

The poverty of the soil, the dryness and the isolation of the continent are reflected in Australia's flora and fauna. Most species of plant and animal are endemic and have adapted well to the harshness of their environment.

Flora

The best-known Australian plant species is the *eucalyptus*. A native tree, it boasts more than 500 varieties, suited to all kinds of conditions, from wintry snow-covered mountains to the humid tropics, from plains to dry hillsides. The largest eucalypts thrust their silvery-white trunks almost 330 ft/100 m skyward. Their grey-green, upward-facing leaves offer minimal shade but filter a golden light through to the undergrowth below. The eucalypt has a very pleasant smell but its wood is often of no value because of its sap content—hence its alternative name of *gum tree*. Some varieties, however, such as the *jarrah,* are among the hardest of hardwoods.

The other well-known species of Australian plant is the *acacia.* It is not endemic and is found in all dry regions of the world. Australia has 700 varieties, known as *mulga* or *wattle.* A few species of indigenous pine-tree occur in the moist forests to the north, and in Tasmania. The *black boy,* with its black scaly trunk and dry grass 'afro hairstyle' is a typical feature of the Western Australian savanna, as are *baobabs* or *bottle trees* in the central and northern deserts. Australia is also famous for the wild flowers which carpet its undergrowth and plains in spring. The coastal *waratah,* with its blood-red flowers, is the floral emblem of New South Wales. *Kangaroo paws* are among the 2000 known plant species in Western Australia. Watch out, too, for the *Christmas bush* which opens its striking orange flowers in the southern spring, the very impressive *fern trees* and the magnificent *orchids* which thrive in the humid undergrowth in Victoria.

Bush animals

Australia's fauna are remarkable, as much for the number of species unique to the continent as for the absence of species common to other parts of the world. Virtually untroubled by predators and the usual herbivores, Australia's marsupials have had the country to themselves, quite unlike the normal distribution of mammals elsewhere. Australia's mammals include grass-eaters, leaf-eaters, insect-eaters and flesh-eaters. Nearly one-half of the 230 species of mammal found in Australia are marsupials, that is, they have a ventral pouch in which their young develop after birth.

The king of Australian animals is the *kangaroo* (or 'roo'). There are scores of varieties, from the red or giant grey kangaroo, taller than a man and weighing up to 200 lbs/90 kg, to the kangaroo-rat which only attains a height of 12 in/30 cm. *Wallabies* and *wallaroos* are medium-sized kangaroos. Kangaroos can be found all over the country, except in those areas where they compete for food with sheep. Regarded as a pest by pastoralists, their numbers are culled by licensed hunters who keep the population down. Nonetheless, you can see them easily outside the big cities, and the sight of kangaroos bounding along a track or through the bush at 25 mi/40 km per hour is certainly one of nature's finest offerings.

Koalas are also stars of the marsupial kingdom, although they are almost impossible to spot in their natural habitat. Most live on the east coast of southern Queensland, one of the few regions where the variety of eucalypts they feed on grows. All Australian zoos house a number of these lovable-looking, but short-tempered, lethargic bears. Other tree-living marsupials include the *cuscus,* which resembles a lemur, and the *sugar gliders* of northern Queensland, which fly from tree to tree. Another marsupial which is very common and very much loved in Australia is the *wombat,* a

A jabiru, one of Australia's 700 bird species.

creature looking something like an enormous, slothful rat. Finally there are the carnivorous marsupials, ranging from a mouse which feeds on insects, to the legendary Tasmanian Tiger, a kind of striped dog, which some naturalists would have us believe still inhabits the unexplored forests of Tasmania.

The *monotremes* are an especially strange variety of mammal, like living fossils which have retained a number of features from their reptilian past. The *platypus,* for example, is a small furry animal about 23 in/60 cm long, with a duck's beak and webbed feet, and an egg pouch. It is rarely seen and lives in streams in the southeast of the country. The *echidna,* about 18 in/45 cm long, feeds exclusively on ants and has a body covered in spines, just like a porcupine.

The best-known, non-marsupial Australian mammal is the *dingo,* a wild dog which accompanied the ancestors of the Aborigines to Australia. The dingo is shunned by dog breeders (it sometimes attacks sheep), and remains the domesticated traveling companion of the Aborigine.

All Australia's indigenous mammals are threatened to varying degrees by the successful introduction of foreign animals such as cats, dogs, rabbits, camels and donkeys, which have been released into the desert, and especially sheep, which tolerate no rivals.

Australia's wildlife includes 700 species of bird, 530 of which are endemic. Among the most famous are the *emu,* the Australian cousin of the ostrich; the *cassowary,* another running bird; the *black swan;* the *kookaburra* with its mocking laugh to enliven suburban barbecues; the *lyre-bird,* a sort of peacock ventriloquist; and scores of species of *parrot* and *budgerigar,* all brightly coloured and as common throughout the bush as the sparrow on the American and European continents.

Reptile species are also well represented: 360 kinds of lizard, 140 kinds of snake, as well as crocodiles, and terrestrial and marine tortoises. The freshwater crocodiles in the rivers and estuaries of the tropical Northern Territory and Queensland can grow to lengths of 23 ft/7 m and more. Watch out also for the 20 or so species of venomous snake if traveling in some of the remoter areas. Their bite can be fatal. The *Tiger Snake, Brown Snake, Copperhead, Death Adder* and the *Taipan* are the most dangerous. Thankfully, deaths from snake bites are extremely rare.

Potentially even more dangerous are the bites of two spiders, the *Red Back* and the *Funnel Web,* which have the unfortunate habit of setting up house in lavatories, especially outdoor ones. One seldom hears of people being bitten by these spiders but it is best to exercise caution outside the city limits. Mosquitoes can be numerous in warm, wet weather, but carry neither malaria nor yellow fever.

The oceans around Australia contain large numbers of huge and ferocious sharks but it is safe to swim at the beaches near big cities which are well protected by a system of nets, by boat patrols and spotter planes. Sea snakes can be a problem in the north, as can the *sea wasp,* a kind of jellyfish with long stinging tendrils. The sting from a sea wasp can easily be fatal and swimming should be strictly avoided along the far northern coastline around Darwin from November to April. Offshore islands do not seem to be affected by the problem and the beaches of the Northern Territory are very pleasant and popular during the rest of the year. For more detailed information contact the Northern Territory Government Tourist Office, either before you leave (see pp. 16-17) or in Australia (see p. 188).

AUSTRALIA'S PAST

Recent archaeological discoveries continue to push back the approximate date of arrival of mankind on the Australian continent. Carbon-14 dating of a cremated female skeleton found on the banks of Lake Mungo in western New South Wales suggest 26,000 years of occupation. Archaeologists who have studied stone tools recovered from the same site would add another 10,000 year. Researchers investigating stone artifacts found near the Murchison River in Western Australia opt for a figure of 100,000 years. The most common of current estimates is 40,000 years.

40,000 YEARS OF ABORIGINAL PREHISTORY

Little is known of the history of Australia's first inhabitants, the Aborigines. These people, whose civilization has been austere rather than primitive, have made do without writing, metals of permanent dwellings, preferring to turn their minds to the development of an incomparably rich spiritual life. Thus, they have bequeathed historians only some cave paintings, some wooden of stone implements, the cremated remains of a distant ancestor, and myths and legends born in the mists of time.

The first occupants of Australia are thought to have originated somewhere in India. Driven by a thirst for new horizons, they migrated on foot and by raft, reaching Ceylon, Malaysia, New Guinea and, finally, Australia. At the time, the land masses and islands of modern South-East Asia were closer together. A few families established themselves on the north-east coast of the continent. Over successive millenia, other perpetual nomads set out in search of food and territory, spreading along the coasts and down the river systems towards the interior and the southern side of the continent. These were less arid times and survival was guaranteed by the relative abundance of game (especially kangaroos) and edible plants. There was no competition from wild beasts or more aggressive human groups. Tribes felt a spiritual and physical bond to their hunting territory. They co-existed in peace, having no chieftains, no iron weapons and no military organization. From a historical point of view, this lack of aggression is one of the Aborigines' more intriguing characteristics. When the Europeans arrived at the end of the 18th century, there were about 300,000 Aborigines, divided into more than 500 tribes. In 1930 their numbers were estimated at 61,000 (plus 18,000 part-Aborigines) and today there are around 200,000 (mostly of mixed race).

A LATE DISCOVERY

Another paradox of Australian prehistory lay in the fact that nearby Asia exhibited almost no interest at all in the huge, empty continent to the south. About 16,000 years ago, melting ice caused a rise in sea levels and made travel across the Indonesian archipelago difficult. The Malays, who had set out 4000 years ago to conquer Indonesia, never reached New Guinea, much less Australia. We can only assume that the Chinese, Indians and Moslem or Buddhist merchants, who controlled maritime commerce in this part of the globe until the arrival of the Portuguese and the Dutch, were too occupied with military and political problems in their own countries to be bothered with Australia. However, Asia did know of Australia's existence. The discovery, in 1879, of a 14th-century jade statuette near Darwin suggests that a Chinese fleet may have reached the area at the beginning of the 15th century. We also know that people from Macassar in the Celebes used to fish along Australia's northern coast for that prized Chinese delicacy, the *sea cucumber*.

In Europe, Terra Australis Incognita had long existed in legend. Since the earliest times, people had suspected the existence of a continent large enough to 'balance' the known countries of the northern hemisphere. The great navigators of the late 16th century were keen to solve the mystery. From then on, the Portuguese regularly plied the waters of the Indonesian archipelago as far as New Guinea. French navigators also sailed the area. In 1606, a Spaniard, Luis Vaez de Torres, negotiated the strait which bears his name, between the tip of modern Queensland and New Guinea. Credit for the official discovery of Australia by a European goes to Dutchman Willem Jansz who, in 1606, sailed into the Gulf of Carpenteria, sighting the Australian coast near the top of the Cape York Peninsula. He charted the coast under the impression that it formed part of New Guinea. Ten years later, in 1616, Dirck Hartog unintentionally landed on the coast of Western Australia.

In 1636, Anthony van Diemen was appointed Governor-General of the Dutch East Indies, the jewel in the Dutch crown. Van Diemen organized several expeditions to the south under the command of Abel Tasman. In 1642 Tasman discovered the island which would first be named Van Diemen's Land, in honour of his patron, and later, Tasmania. He sailed on eastward and also discovered New Zealand. On a second voyage, Tasman sighted the northern coast of Australia.

Then the British entered upon the scene. The pirate William Dampier explored the north-west of the continent in 1688 and again in 1699. A revival of French interest, when Louis de Bougainville sighted the Great Barrier Reef in 1766, spurred the British on to put an end to speculation and the covetousness of other nations. James Cook, the first hero in the conquest of Australia, left London aboard the *Endeavour* in 1768. On April 29, 1770, he dropped anchor in Botany Bay, before following the coast northwards. On August 22, 1770 he claimed the eastern seabord in the name of the British Crown, naming it New South Wales.

In the course of two subsequent voyages across the Pacific, Cook solved the mystery of Terra Australis, but his discovery of a

Building a population:
Convicts, emancipists, exclusionists and bushrangers

Australia needed a workforce in order to develop its new territory. Between 1788 and 1840 (1852 in Tasmania), almost 130,000 convicts were transported to Australia. A further 30,000 were taken to Western Australia before transportation there ceased in 1868. Free settlers were welcome and, between 1830 and 1840, 173,000 had migrated from Britain. The arrival of the new immigrants accentuated the characteristics of the Australian population. There was racial homogeneity (by 1850 the majority of the 405,000 colonists were of Anglo-Saxon origin), and socio-political divergence. On the one side were the emancipists, freed convicts, often of working-class Irish origin, and whose living conditions in the bush created an ill-defined 'Australianness' which is still evident today. On the other side there were the exclusionists, officials, military officers and free settlers who clung to their British middle-class way of life.

Social conflict was inevitable and a new character appeared on the scene: the bushranger. The bushranger was a highway bandit, a Robin Hood of the bush; he usually ended his days hanging by the neck at the end of a rope. However, the excesses of the colonial police caused the people of the bush to identify with him. Ben Hall and Ned Kelly were the best-known bushrangers and, in time, they both became Australian folk heros.

veritable Australian continent aroused little interest in London. At the time, Britain had other problems: the North American colonies were in revolt. In 1783, all 13 colonies there became independent. The immediate result was the closure of the American penal settlements which had been accepting the unruly overflow from British prisons. Thoughts in London turned to Cook and Botany Bay. In January 1787, the British Parliament authorized the departure for New South Wales of the first shipment of convicts.

THE FOUNDING OF A COLONY: SETTLEMENT AND EXPLORATION

The First Fleet, under the command of Captain Arthur Phillip, consisted of two warships and nine transports. On board were some 800 convicts, 200 of them women, a handful of children and 200 soldiers. On January 18, 1788, eight months after leaving England, Phillip dropped anchor in Botany Bay but, finding his anchorage too exposed, he sailed north and entered an inlet which he named Sydney Cove in honour of British Home Secretary Lord Sydney. On January 26, 1788, the convicts and their guard disembarked. The Union Jack was hoisted, a toast was offered to the king's health, and they set to work.

The early days were difficult: illness, a scarcity of food, and isolation drained the little colony. Tensions later developed between the emancipists and the exclusionists (see box for definition of these terms). Between 1790 and 1820, the colony had an additional problem to deal with: it contained four times as many men as women and most of the latter were former prostitutes. To make matters worse, alcohol was almost flowing in the streets: rum became the local currency and the soldiers in charge of maintaining order in the colony were known as the Rum Corps.

In 1801, the colony at last found some direction thanks to the efforts of John MacArthur, a wealthy member of the colonial

Gold fever.

aristocracy who had introduced the merino sheep to New South Wales. In 1802, MacArthur took samples of merino wool to England and, in 1807, shipped out the first commercial quantities. His success and the lack of suitable pastures near Sydney caused sheep breeders to look further afield. The barrier of the Blue Mountains was soon crossed. The wide, fertile plains to the west were invaded by 'squatters' who lost no time in driving out the dingoes (wild dogs) and Aborigines. Within 30 years they had founded a formidable wool industry, the country's first economic breakthrough.

Explorers and detachments of soldiers opened the way for the sheep breeders. Between 1801 and 1803, Matthew Flinders became the first man to circumnavigate Australia. In 1826, Edmund Lockyer led a detachment of 44 men to the site of Albany in Western Australia. There he raised the Union Jack, annexing Western Australia to the British Crown. The state capital, Perth, was founded by James Stirling in 1829. In the same year, Charles Sturt discovered the Murray River: Australia's principal water-course. The new colony of South Australia (the colonizers didn't have much imagination) was proclaimed in 1834 and a site for its capital, Adelaide, chosen in 1836. In 1835, John Batman sailed from his birthplace in Tasmania, which had been colonized since the turn of the century, and bartered with the local Aborigines for land on the site of present-day Melbourne. Soon after, in 1851, the Port

Phillip District separated from New South Wales to become the Colony of Victoria. The colonization of vast pastures in northern New South Wales led, in 1859, to the establishment of the separate state of Queensland. All that remained was the red heart of the central Australian desert. The men who set out, despite the heat and the immense emptiness of the desert, to conquer Australia's last frontier were imbued with a kind of mystical faith, an all-powerful patriotism, an intense scientific curiosity and a down-to-earth awareness of the realities of the bush.

Between 1837 and 1840, George Grey traveled northwards and discovered the Murchinson and Gascoyne rivers. In 1841, Edward Eyre completed the first crossing of the continent from Adelaide to Albany and, in 1844, Charles Sturt led a second expedition to the centre of Australia, in search of an inland sea. In 1848, the Prussian-born explorer, Ludwig Leichhardt, disappeared while attempting to cross Australia from east to west. In 1860, John McDouall Stuart reached the centre of Australia and disproved once and for all the myth of an inland sea stretching north to the Timor Sea. A year later, another expedition ended in tragedy, when Robert Burke and William Wills perished after having crossed the continent from south to north. Finally, in 1870, John Forrest led an expedition which crossed the western half of the continent from Perth to Adelaide.

THE GOLD RUSHES

On February 12, 1851, gold was discovered at Summerhill Creek, a few miles north of Bathurst in New South Wales, followed in September by further discoveries at Ballarat, not far from Melbourne. Gold fever spread throughout the peaceful colony, leading to a sizable influx of new immigrants who formed a previously absent Australian middle class. Within 10 years the population had doubled to over 1 million inhabitants. The newer arrivals were richer, more enterprising, better educated and more 'civilized' than the first waves of settlers. They also introduced new political ideas which spread quickly in the bush and led, in 1854, to the only revolt in Australian history, the short-lived insurrection at Eureka Stockade.

By 1854, the amount of gold being discovered had decreased. In contrast, the license fee for miners had increased and was being collected in a particularly brutal manner by the colonial police. A new slogan appeared in mining camps: 'no taxation without representation'. On November 30, 1854, in a move aimed at asserting their claims, the diggers, led by Peter Lalor, took up arms and barricaded themselves in the stockade at Eureka near Ballarat. They then proclaimed the 'Republic of Victoria' and raised the blue Southern Cross flag, swearing by it that they would defend their rights and their freedom. On December 2, thirsty in the southern heat, many of the insurgents deserted the stockade for the town's pubs. Police and soldiers attacked the remainder at about 4.30 on the morning of December 3. It was all over in a matter of minutes. Six soldiers and 30 miners, 10 of them Irishmen, were dead.

Although this insurrection had achieved little on its own, the British had not forgotten the aftermath of similar conflicts in

America. Two years later, the four eastern colonies were granted their own parliamentary governments, based on the British model. The symbolic importance of the Eureka stockade has remained engraved on the Australian subconscious. Even today, Australian republicans have adopted the blue and white flag of the Ballarat miners as the symbol of their cause.

In the latter part of the 1850s, the most important colonies—New South Wales, South Australia, Victoria and Tasmania—devised constitutions for themselves, which were among the most democratic in the world at the time. Universal (white) male suffrage and the secret ballot were adopted. Queensland and Western Australia soon followed suit. In 1894, South Australia became the first Australian colony, and the first state in the world to give women the vote. By 1902, the franchise had been extended to women nationally.

Gold attracted not only the British and Irish: Americans, Germans and Chinese (especially) arrived in droves. In 1857, one Victorian male in seven was Chinese. The Americans, often from the south, urged the gold diggers to make known their dislike of the 'yellow hordes'. On July 4, American Independence Day, two important anti-Chinese riots took place. The deep-set racist feelings which typified the times built up until the first federal parliament introduced a law in 1901 aimed at preventing all coloured migration to Australia. This law, known as the 'White Australia Policy', was retained by all future governments until 1973, when it was disowned officially by the Whitlam Labor government.

THE ERA OF GREAT INDUSTRIAL CONQUESTS

The second half of the 19th century was a period of great economic development for Australia. The economy diversified; communications developed; the first unions won unique social advantages for their members; Sydney was connected to Melbourne by telegraph in 1858, to London by cable in 1872, to Adelaide by train in 1888. Between 1870 and 1890, 10,000 mi/16,000 km of railways were built. In Melbourne, in 1850, building workers demanded eight-hour work days for eight shillings a day. They were successful in 1855.

Then everything collapsed. In the early 1890s, the prices of wool, wheat and metals crashed, panic set in among financial circles, unemployment appeared and earlier social gains came under threat. The unions responded with widespread strikes involving tens of thousands of workers. The strikers lost but their leaders decided to continue the fight, just as they had in Britain. The Australian Labor Party was formed. Politics moved from the age of great men to the age of great parties.

AN INDEPENDENT FEDERAL AUSTRALIA

No doubt fearing the worst (an American-style republic), politicians introduced a system tailored to the geographic, economic, social and cultural situation of the country. Australia was to be independent without severing the ties binding it to the British

Crown. A draft constitution was approved by referendum in the six colonies and ratified by the British Parliament in Westminster. The Commonwealth of Australia was proclaimed on January 1, 1901. The six founding colonies became the six states to which was added the Northern Territory. The British King acquired the title King of Australia. The Southern Cross and the Union Jack were united on the new flag and Canberra was made the federal capital, located in an independent Capital Territory midway between Sydney and Melbourne.

In 1901, Australia had a population of 4 million, 87 percent born in Australia. Its economy was based on the export of raw materials (mainly minerals and wool) and the importation of finished goods, principally from Britain. Political life became more structured: a conservative coalition, the Liberal Party, was formed to counter the Labor Party, which defended the workers and unions, and alternating governments of these two parties have characterized Australian political life ever since (see 'Elections and political parties' p. 44).

The Labor Party tends to be elected in difficult times (during the two World Wars, the Depression), or when urgent reforms need to be introduced. For the remainder of the time, the Liberals are left to manage prosperity as discreetly as possible. However, political arguments have taken second place to the rapid progress of legislation for social reform (a minimum wage was introduced in 1907) which, in turn, has been facilitated by Australia's strict immigration policy.

When World War I began in 1914, Australian volunteers rushed to defend the 'mother country', Great Britain, and its allies. A country of 5 million people, Australia sent more than 330,000 soldiers or 11.2 percent of its population to Europe and the Middle East. Australia's famous *diggers* (gold diggers) suffered greater losses than did United States forces: 60,000 killed, or 65 percent of all participants. The bravery of the Anzacs, a joint Australian and New Zealand expeditionary force, has become a legend. On April 25, 1915, 10,000 Australian and New Zealand soldiers lost their lives on the hills of Gallipoli in Turkey in one of the most ill-prepared military operations of the war. To emphasize the meaning of the sacrifice, Australians refused in two referendums (1916 and 1917) to introduce compulsory conscription. Anzac Day, April 25, is now the most important public holiday in the Australian calendar. Even after 70 years, it still conjures up feelings of sadness and reverence which go far beyond the simple remembrance of a military defeat.

ECONOMIC CRISIS
AND THE JAPANESE INVASION

In the period between the two World Wars, Australia closely resembled the rest of the western world. It experienced a period of prosperity, followed by the Depression of the 1930s which brought the country to its knees. One Australian in three was out of work. Unemployment brought suffering and even starvation to Australia. The generations affected by the crisis still find it difficult to accept their children's apathy and indifference to strengthening their position in society. Another consequence of the crisis has been a reinforcing of the idea that the main function of the state is to protect the well-being of its citizens. From 1945 until 1974, when world-wide inflation threatened the international economic balance, successive governments (mainly Liberal) managed to keep the unemployment rate below 2 percent.

The start of World War II saw more or less the same scenario as in 1914, albeit with less enthusiasm: volunteers were sent to Europe and the Middle East. However, in 1941 war came closer. The Japanese turned the Pacific into a battlefield. Hawaii, Singapore, New Guinea and the Solomon Islands all suffered. In 1942, the Japanese bombed Darwin, Broome and Wyndham. Japanese pocket submarines entered Sydney Harbour and sank a ferry. This time conscription was approved and the Labor Prime Minister John Curtin turned for help to the other great Pacific power, the United States. General MacArthur set up his head-quarters in Melbourne and Australian and American forces slowly began retaking Japanese positions, with considerable loss of life.

THE GOLDEN AGE

After the war, Australia remained focused on Asia and the Pacific. Japan became one of its major trading partners, as did the United States. In order to make use of the continent's fabulous mineral riches, the government admitted 2 million immigrants between 1945 and 1966. Most were Europeans, but not all were Anglo-Saxons. Italians and Greeks in particular arrived in great numbers. This was Australia's Golden Age. Its standard of living became one of the highest in the world. The Olympic Games in Melbourne in 1956 bore witness to a prosperous, balanced and peaceful society. The country was led by an entrenched prime minister, Robert Menzies, who was re-elected continuously from 1949 until he retired in 1966. Fearful of the communist threat from within and without, Menzies sent troops to Korea (1950-53) and Vietnam (1965-72). In 1951, he even tried to pass a law making the tiny Australian Communist Party illegal. The law was passed by Parliament, annulled by the High Court of Australia and rejected at a referendum which allowed Australians once more to reaffirm their attachment to all kinds of freedoms. Another important referendum was held during this period: in 1967 a clear majority of white Australians voted to give Australian citizenship to the Aborigines.

AUSTRALIA'S SECOND WIND

Menzies was succeeded by a series of Liberal prime ministers, all of whom espoused strong pro-American views. During the Vietnam War, Prime Minister Harold Holt assured United States President Lyndon B. Johnson that Australia would go 'all the way with LBJ'. In 1972, after 23 years in power, the conservative coalition was ousted at the polls by Gough Whitlam's Labor Party. A whirlwind swept through the country. The final troops were withdrawn from Vietnam, diplomatic relations were established with the People's Republic of China, the White Australia Policy was abandoned, ancestral land was returned to the Aborigines and a system of universal health care was introduced. Alas, it was a case of too many reforms introduced too quickly. Inflation and unemployment made worse by the international recession, a virulent anti-Labor campaign in the press and a controversial use of vice-regal powers by the Queen's representative, Governor-General Sir John Kerr, ended with the dismissal of Prime Minister Whitlam and the installation in his place of opposition leader Malcolm Fraser. Called upon to ratify or reject this solution at parliamentary elections, the Australian people approved Malcolm Fraser; he was re-elected to lead the country in three subsequent elections.

In 1983, the situation changed again. A growing conflict between opponents and supporters of a giant hydro-electric scheme in Tasmania, the latter supported by the Liberal government, led to the election of Labor Party moderate Bob Hawke. Hawke was re-elected in 1985.

AUSTRALIA TODAY

Australia is a federal, constitutional monarchy. Its institutions are based largely on those of Great Britain and the United States.

THE STATE

Institutions

The head of state is the Governor-General, the representative of Queen Elizabeth II whose official title in the Antipodes is Queen of Australia. The Governor-General does not exercise political power but instead a series of left-over constitutional powers, such as the right to convene, prorogue and dissolve the Parliament, to ratify laws, to swear in government ministers and to act as commander of the armed forces. Like the Queen in Britain, he can exercise his powers only on the recommendation of the elected majority in the Lower House.

At the federal level, Parliament consists of the House of Representatives, similar to the British House of Commons, and the Senate, based directly on its American counterpart. The party or coalition which holds the majority of seats in the House of Representatives is asked by the Governor-General to form a federal government, under the leadership of a Prime Minister. The Prime Minister is responsible to Parliament. House of Representatives elections are held every three years.

The Senate represents the states and contains 10 members from each, plus two from each territory. State senators are elected for six years, territorial senators for three. They have, among other things, the power to block implementation of the budget, and thereby the operation of government. Unlike their American counterparts, members of both houses are obliged to vote along party lines.

Another federal institution inspired by the example of the United States is the High Court of Australia. Based on the model of the United States Supreme Court, it possesses the same kinds of powers.

The head of government at the state level is the Premier, the equivalent of the governor of an American state. Local government and municipal authorities operate in much the same manner as elsewhere in the world. Where federal, state and local government policies conflict, federal policy prevails.

Elections and political parties

Voting is compulsory and the law provides penalties for those who do not avail themselves of their electoral rights. The electoral system at all levels is that of preferential proportional voting, undoubtedly the most complicated system in the Western World. Candidates can be ranked in order of the voter's preference or by political party.

Three major political parties are represented in the various parliaments: the *Australian Labor Party,* the socialist, reformist party representing the workers; the *Liberal Party of Australia,* comparable to the British Conservative Party, being more sympathetic to business interests; and the *National Party* (formerly the Country Party), the Liberal Party's ally and federal coalition partner.

The Labor Party shares almost the same percentage of the vote as the conservative coalition. The handful of votes separating the major parties demonstrates wealthy and stable Australia's resistance to any change, even a minor one which might upset the firm national consensus. For 60 of the 80 or so years since federation, Australians have chosen conservative governments.

Several smaller parties of varying importance vie to break the grip of the 'Big Three' on the Australian political scene: the *Australian Democrats,* a centrist party of independents, represented in the Senate; the *Communist Party,* a party whose influence and effectiveness are minimal; and, a recent newcomer, the *Nuclear Disarmament Party,* representing significant ecological and anti-nuclear interests. It succeeded in having one of its members elected to the Senate in 1985.

THE POWER OF THE UNIONS

The unions in Australia form a real power on the political, economic and social scene. Like the British trade unions, they represent all branches of industry and are so powerful that in certain areas of employment one must be a member of the appropriate trade union in order to get a job. In 1983, 3 million Australian workers (55 percent of the working population) belonged to one of the country's 319 trade unions. These unions are amalgamated at a federal level in a single organization, the all-powerful Australian Council of Trade Unions (ACTU).

Australian trade unions demonstrate their political muscle in different ways. On the one hand, they control, or rather nurture, the labor movement—Prime Minister Bob Hawke was for a long time President of the ACTU. On the other hand, they intervene directly in the life of the country, not only in 'traditional' areas, such as pay claims, but also in the areas of ecology and foreign policy. Take the famous (or notorious) black bans and green bans, for example.

Black bans are boycotts by all unions against countries which jeopardize the national interest by their actions, or which need a lesson in human rights. Thus, in 1973-74, the unions decided to institute black bans against France for carrying out atmospheric

Road trains used for long-distance transport.

nuclear testing in the Pacific. Post office workers refused to handle French mail, dock workers refused to unload French ships, and so on.

Green bans, on the other hand, are implemented on the local scene only. They occur when unionists refuse to work on a site which threatens to upset the ecological balance of an area or suburb. The *cause célèbre* in this category is the green ban placed on the exploitation of uranium deposits. The ban gives support to the Aboriginal movement which is anxious to protect sacred ancestral sites where most of these deposits are to be found. Green bans have also allowed residents of Sydney to preserve a historic section of their city and may yet be successful in guarding the Great Barrier Reef from predatory petroleum exploration companies.

THE FACE OF THE ECONOMY

The phrase 'the lucky country', coined by Australian historian Donald Horne, sums up the fortunes and the difficulties experienced by the Australian economy. The fortunes are to be found in Australia's enormous primary industry resources (minerals and agricultural products). The difficulties relate to the inability of Australian society to divorce itself from a system of economic management which is downright colonial.

The system has two main stumbling blocks: firstly, the fluctuations in world demand for primary products and in international exchange rates and regulations leave the Australian econ-

omy very vulnerable to the ups and downs of international circum
stances. Secondly, Australia has yet to build a broad industrial base
being content instead to refine certain products for export and to
import any technology it needs.

AGRICULTURE

Although the area of the country under cultivation is relatively
small (62 percent of the total surface area), agriculture plays a
major part in the national economy. It brings in a good third of
export earnings. Before World War I, the Australian economy was
based on sheep breeding and the export of raw wool to Great
Britain and Europe; although the economy is now more diversified
Australia still produces more than one-third of the world's wool
Australia is also a major cattle producer.

Another important source of revenue is cereals, wheat in
particular, but barley, maize, oats and rice are also cultivated
widely. Sugar cane is the fourth 'big gun' of the Australian
agricultural industry which also provides 60 percent of the nation's
tobacco as well as cotton, fruit (especially apples from Tasmania
and tropical fruit from Queensland), vegetables and wine.

NATURAL RESOURCES

Exactly 100 years after the Gold Rush, successive discoveries
of untold mineral deposits have placed Australia among the world's
leading producers of a number of minerals of which the most
important are: iron, coal, and bauxite, not to mention lead, zinc,
copper, nickel, mineral sands, manganese and rare and precious
metals, such as gold. Australia also produces nearly 80 percent of
its petroleum needs and sufficient natural gas to feed the continent's
five main cities. The country's remaining energy needs are met by
coal and by the giant Snowy Mountains Hydro-electric Scheme in
south-east New South Wales. With nearly 300,000 tons of extract-
able uranium, Australia has the largest reserves in the world but, to
date, Australians have refused categorically to allow the construction of nuclear facilities on their soil. On the other hand, the
development of new forms of energy is encouraged. There is no
shortage of sunlight, nor of the wind which has turned windmills in
the bush for decades. The north-west coast experiences the
strongest tides in the world and seems the ideal location for tidal
power stations.

TRADE

If Australia's trade structure has scarcely changed since the
early days of the colony (export of raw materials, import of finished
products), its trading partners certainly have. Before Federation,
70 percent of Australia's exports went to Great Britain as opposed
to 4 percent in 1984. Since Federation, imports from Great Britain
have dropped from 50 percent to 7 percent. Australia's main trading
partner is now Japan, followed by the EEC and the United States.
However, because of a worldwide surplus of the products which
make up the bulk of Australia's exports, accompanied by falling
prices for those products, and despite a protectionist trade policy

which imposes high taxes on imported goods, the trade balance has not been in Australia's favour in recent times.

STANDARD OF LIVING

In 1986 Australia had an average per capita income equivalent to US$16,536. However, this income is far more widely spread throughout the community than in most western countries. There are few poor in Australia, except for the Aborigines and other clearly defined sectors of the populace, and only a handful of the very rich. Most people belong to the huge middle class, with jobs ranging from skilled worker to managing director: 90 percent of the working population declares a total taxable income of between A$4000 and A$24,000. Australians work an average 35.6 hours per week and have between three and four weeks paid vacation per year. In the public-service sector, men can retire at 65 and women at 60. There is no obligatory retirement age.

EDUCATION

Australia's separation of church and state in the realm of education was accomplished in the 19th century, when legislators voted to establish and finance a secular system of education controlled by the state. But the influence of the English-style fee-based denominational schools is still strong today—one Australian in four is educated at a fee-based school (called private schools in Australia as in the United States). One Australian in five is educated in a Catholic school in this predominantly Protestant country. The number of students attending fee-based schools has been growing steadily in recent years. Despite the high standards of the majority of state-run schools, numerous members of the Australian middle class (especially successful immigrants) value the terribly British' veneer that a fee-based school education bestows. It is true that to succeed, at least in public life, it is almost a prerequisite to have attended one of the more prestigious schools, such as Geelong Grammar School near Melbourne, where Prince Charles completed his secondary studies. Imagine wearing a boater, blazer, tie and long trousers (boys), or a round-brimmed hat and white gloves (girls) when it's 104 °F/40 °C in the shade!

School is compulsory between ages six and 16. At the end of secondary school (called high school as in the US), pupils must pass the Higher School Certificate (HSC) examination in order to be admitted to one of Australia's 19 free universities. A quota system, based on the level of marks (grades) obtained at the HSC, regulates the numbers of students admitted to particular university faculties.

Primary school children in the bush enjoy an education system unique in the world, the School of the Air. The sons and daughters of graziers or miners receive lessons daily by radio from more than a dozen centres, each broadcasting over a radius of several hundred miles and using the Flying Doctor network (see p. 196). For their secondary education, these children will leave their families to attend high school in a 'nearby' city—often more than 100 miles away—in order to mix with others of their own age.

WHO ARE THE AUSTRALIANS?

Australia has a population of 16 million, a population density of less than one per square mile (a little over two per square kilometre). As it happens, this figure does not accurately reflect the population distribution because Australia is the most urbanized country on earth, with 86 percent of its inhabitants living in urban areas.

WHERE DO THEY LIVE?

Almost half of the Australian population lives in the two largest cities: Sydney and Melbourne. Sydney has 3.3 million inhabitants, or 21 percent of the Australian population, while Melbourne (2.9 million inhabitants) accounts for almost 20 percent. If you add to these figures the populations of Brisbane (1.1 million), Adelaide and Perth (a little under 1 million each), it quickly becomes evident that close to 10 million Australians live in the five state capitals. Seven further population centres, Hobart (173,000), Darwin (63,000), Canberra (256,000), Newcastle (414,000), Wollongong (235,000), Geelong (143,000) and the Gold Coast (192,000) add another 1.5 million or so. Of the 5 million Australians who do not congregate in one of the large centres, many live in the large rural towns of northern Queensland or the Murray River valley.

The geographical distribution of the population is similarly out of balance: 80 percent of Australians live within the Cairns-Sydney-Adelaide 'boomerang', between the coast and the mountains. Perth, in the south-west of the continent, is the only other significant population centre. Scarcely 2 million Australians live in the outback. Working as farmers and miners, they are responsible for two-thirds of the country's wealth. Australia's population is also notable for its slow growth. Given a birth rate which has stabilized at the 1975-76 level and an average immigration of 50,000 people per year, statisticians estimate that, by the year 2000, there will still be no more than 18 million Australians. Finally, contrary to popular belief, there are not more men than women in Australia: since 1983 Australian women have slightly outnumbered Australian men.

Aboriginal children of central Australia.

WHERE DO THEY COME FROM?

Another fundamental characteristic of Australia lies in the fact that, until very recently, its population was among the whitest and most Anglo-Saxon on the planet. In the past, unlike the United States, Australia was not regarded as a land of promise for immigrants from all over Europe, nor was it a land of slavery.

In 1890, every second Australian was an immigrant. As a result of a selective immigration policy, 50 percent of these came from England, 12 percent were from Scotland and a whole 25 percent were from Ireland, leaving only 13 percent from other countries. The significant Irish minority (working-class, Catholic and anti-British) soon found itself at loggerheads with the Protestant, middle-class and colonialist English. The Eureka Stockade uprising of 1854 was Irish-inspired, and the Australian Labor Party has traditionally been close to the Roman Catholic Church and fiercely nationalistic.

After World War II, the need for economic growth meant opening the floodgates to non-English-speaking immigrants. Between 1945 and 1985, 3.9 million immigrants took up residence in Australia, half of them from continental Europe (80 percent stayed). Between 1947 and 1952, Australia also acquired more than 170,000 refugees from Eastern Europe: Yugoslavs, Poles, Hungarians, Czechs and people from Baltic countries. As a result, the population doubled in 30 years.

In order to avoid the racial problems that beset some other countries, Australia avoided any colour mix in its population by not introducing slavery, by ignoring the Aborigines, and by hermetically sealing its borders to foreign non-whites from 1901 to 1973 under the *Commonwealth Immigration Act*. The only Asian minorities who succeeded in infiltrating Australia until then were the Chinese, the 'Afghans' (anyone from the Indian sub-continent) and the Japanese. At the time of the Gold Rush, the Chinese represented up to 12 percent of all miners. The Afghan camel drivers came from Asia in the 19th century to breed the herds of imported camels needed at the time to provide a means of transport in desert areas. The Japanese came as pearl fishermen to Broome in Western Australia.

In 1973 the doors opened wide and selection of immigrants on the basis of race was abolished. There was no major influx of foreigners until the United States withdrew its forces from Indochina in the aftermath of the Vietnam War: since April 1975, Australia has accepted more than 80,000 Indochinese refugees, giving its population the highest percentage of these refugees of any country in the world. The challenge was considerable when the Cambodian 'boat people' arrived directly on Australia's northern shores, creating legal and health problems never experienced before for local and federal authorities. They had the job of integrating this group of people, with their own traditions, language and culture, into a society where attitudes to integration were rigid, to say the least, especially in a time of economic difficulties and high unemployment. The all-powerful unions did not look favourably upon the 'flood' of workers with a reputation for hard work and docility. In addition, the annual intake of Asian refugees meant reducing traditional European immigrant numbers.

For better or worse, immigration statistics show that the scales have swung. In 1983, 43 percent of immigrants came from Europe but 38 percent also came from Asia (most of the remainder were from New Zealand). Thus, if the main body of migrants is still British, second place (in front of New Zealanders) goes to those classified as 'other Asians', or Indochinese. The Thais, Indonesians and Filipinos represent national groups more important than the Italians, Greeks and Germans who had held top ranking in the past. The statistics are largely borne out by the faces to be seen in city streets. The composition of the population has altered visibly over the last dozen years, and for the first time in its history, Australia is well on the way to becoming a multi-racial society.

THE AUSTRALIAN WAY OF LIFE

The final important feature of the Australian population is its social and cultural homogeneity. Two centuries of prosperity and peace have made Australia the paradise of the middle class. Except for certain famous and long-established pastoral families, some all-powerful industrialists, the Aborigines, a few 'poor whites' and some more or less voluntary martyrs of the consumer society, the vast majority of Australians belong to a single socio-cultural type. This type has nothing to do with the pioneer in the bush or the horseman in the desert. Whatever his geographical origins, the average Australian lives a comfortable suburban life. He has his own house (70 percent of Australians do) with a garden as its crowning glory. He drives to the office (there are over 8 million cars), and spends the rest of his time sitting in front of the TV set, at the beach, at a football or cricket match, or in the pub. He has plenty of leisure time: the average Australian work week was 35.6 hours in 1984 (45 in the agricultural sector, 37 in industry and 34 in the Public Service).

The basic homogeneity of the Australian population does, however, conceal certain contradictions affecting the future of a people whose main potential has yet to be realized. The vastness of

---

Jeremy Bentham's vision of Utopia

The founding of Australia was a social experiment, an attempt to create a latter-day Utopia—a *dreamtime* come to life (see p. 55). It was born out of an idea of happiness on earth, not only as a possibility, but as the destiny of mankind. Jeremy Bentham (d. 1832), an English moralist, expressed his doctrine of utilitarianism as 'the greatest happiness for the greatest number'. It was partly because of Bentham's condemnation of the overcrowding in English prisons that the British Parliament decided to establish a penal colony at Sydney in 1788. Bentham also drew up the designs for a model prison that was tried out successfully in Port Arthur, Tasmania.

Today Bentham's philosophy lives on in Australia in the terms of a welfare state that believes in equality for all and the enjoyment of life. As in other Western societies, equality is relative: there are rich and poor, privileged and unprivileged, but these differences are less accentuated than in many other countries. Attempts are being made to close the existing gaps, especially between the whites and Aborigines, and Australians are justifiably proud of their tangible material success and happiness.

the continent remains to be conquered, its history to be written, the forging of a new civilization to be completed. Three societies exist side-by-side in Australia. In the heart of the country are the Aborigines, remnants of a prehistoric past, revering their own spiritual values rather than the prevailing materialism which holds nothing for them. In the outback the descendants of the early pioneers work in extremely harsh conditions to produce the country's essential resources. These are stolid people, courageous, proud and self-reliant. Along the coastal strip an enormous middle class plays its part in the drama. Its particular ideology can be summed up in the phrase, 'work to live, don't live to work'. This classless society extols a sort of hedonistic ideal, a search for happiness and comfort in a conscientious application of Bentham's doctrine of utilitarianism: 'the greatest happiness for the greatest number'.

RELIGION

Australia was never a refuge for victims of religious persecution. Today, formal religion there plays more of an institutional and moral role than a spiritual one. Be that as it may, in a country with total religious freedom, at the 1981 census 76.4 percent of the population declared themselves to be Christians: 26.1 percent were members of the Church of England (headed by Queen Elizabeth II), 26 percent Roman Catholic (mainly Irish and Italian families), 4.4 percent Presbyterian, 3.4 percent Methodist, and 2.9 percent Orthodox (mostly Greek). Some 14 other religions are also represented in Australia, among them Judaism, Islam and Buddhism. Large numbers of Aborigines retain the Animist beliefs of their ancestors.

Religious influences are especially noticeable in two areas: education (one Australian child in four goes to a church school) and in the Puritan approach to such social issues as the opening hours of pubs. The law guarantees the individual's right to get drunk at home but not in public, an attitude that comes as a strange contrast in a society which is otherwise free of such complexes.

THE ABORIGINES

It is difficult to cover a subject which merits an entire book of its own in just a few pages but a few essentials can be set down. First of all a warning: do not regard the Aborigines as a tourist attraction. Their main desire is to be left in peace, and they have been protected for some years now by laws preventing intrusive tourism. As a result, only the autonomous Aboriginal councils on the reserves of the Northern Territory, Western Australia and Queensland, where the last full-blood Aborigines retain their traditions more or less intact, can give permission for tourists to enter their territory. Such permission is very difficult to obtain, not least because it is hard to contact those who are responsible. On the other hand, there's nothing to prevent you from admiring the amazing works of art which the Aborigines have given the world—astoundingly beautiful rock paintings in outback caves and more easily accessible bark paintings or carved wooden figures in city galleries.

Ceremonial body painting on Bathurst Island.

Any Aborigines you are likely to meet will probably belong to detribalized, part-Aboriginal groups located in settlements close to urbanized areas of central and northern Australia. These are the people most affected by the ravages of poverty, illness and alcoholism resulting from detribalization and the loss of their own land. The result is a pitiful spectacle seemingly without solution, and one for which modern society is largely responsible. However, there are hopeful signs, mostly in the realization by Aborigines that they hold their destiny in their own hands, and that the struggle for dignity is worthwhile. White Australia for its part seems finally to appreciate the magnitude of the problem and is intent on finding the ways and means of resolving it.

You will nevertheless meet well-adjusted Aborigines on the cattle stations in the outback. Often half-caste 'stockmen' (cow-boys), they find themselves at home in a job and an environment which they love, where they are relatively well integrated among white cattlemen who respect their skills in the bush.

Who are the Aborigines?

Aboriginal civilization reflects the same strange and solitary beauty as the desert in which it developed. It represents a life which is poor in material terms, but rich spiritually, enduring because of the traditions on which it is founded. It is a civilization which had adapted completely, as long as 40,000 years ago, to an environment which no other race of people knew until the arrival of the Europeans in the 18th century.

When the Europeans arrived, there were between 300,000 and 500,000 Aborigines on the Australian continent divided into 500 or

600 tribes and speaking between 300 and 500 languages. Each tribe was defined by the territory in which it hunted. A spiritual and emotional bond gave the tribe the inalienable right to utilize the land, but not to own it. The size of such hunting territories varied from several hundred square miles to scores of thousands. The people had nothing to fear from predatory animals or cold for the most part—their only problem was food. The Aborigines are among the few races on earth not to have domesticated their environment, practiced agriculture or raised animals. The reason lies partly in the fact that the indigenous species of plants do not lend themselves to cultivation, and that the Aborigines' only domestic animal was the dingo, a wild dog which had accompanied them from Asia. In humid and, therefore, fertile conditions, the edible plants and game were exploited by a scattered population which hunted and gathered with an innate respect for the environment, believing that nature did not belong to mankind, but rather that mankind belonged to nature.

True Aborigines are nomads who carry with them an absolute minimum of possessions. In family groups of 20 to 40 persons, they cover between 7-13 mi/12-20 km per day over their tribal territory. The men walk in front, each armed with a wooden spear (often made more effective by making a pointed stone tip and using a throwing stick called a *woomera*) or a boomerang, a weapon invented over 10,000 years ago. The women follow on behind, carrying their indispensable possessions—sticks for digging, stone axes, bark dishes and perhaps one young child. Birth control based on abstention, abortion or infanticide is a basic element contributing to the equilibrium between the tribe and its territory.

The men are very capable hunters and fishers. They bring to the camp kangaroos, koalas, wombats, lizards and fish, which are cooked in an earthen oven, the fire lit by rubbing together two pieces of dry wood. The meat diet is supplemented by the women who use their digging sticks to unearth eggs, roots, insects, rodents and larvae (*witchetty* grubs). They also gather fruit and edible leaves, and winnow dry grass in their bark dishes before grinding the resulting seeds between two stones to make them edible. The only other problem is water, or the lack of it. If a river or lake is dry, the Aborigines know how to find water in tree trunks or how to extract it from frogs. In this way they can survive, whereas a modern-day European would die of thirst within a short time. Each evening a new camp is set up around fires kept alight all night to ward off mosquitoes. The people sleep in the open if the night is clear or in a cave or shelter *(wurley)* made of boughs, leaves and plaited grass during the rainy season. In marshy or colder areas, the Aborigines construct raised huts or stone shelters. Only the tribes in the south-west of the country, where winters can be chilly, wear clothing made from sewn kangaroo skins.

Aborigines are extremely skilled at weaving, knotting and plaiting belts, baskets, bags, mats and nets, and making fishing lines from hair or plant fibres. Those tribes which live near lakes or on the sea build rafts and bark canoes. On ceremonial occasions men, women and children may wear necklaces, headbands or belts of feathers, shells, dyed seeds or animal teeth, and have patterns painted on their skin in coloured earth. Ritual scarring of the skin is also practiced.

The most spiritual people on earth

Stone Age civilization is very rich at the social, spiritual and artistic levels. For their part, the Aborigines devised one of the most complicated kinship systems in human history, guaranteeing each individual a definite place in the tribal system, and regulating precisely family relationships and rights to hunting territory. These ancient codes of conduct gave rise to an egalitarian society (the only marked social distinction is that between the sexes) that is both peace-loving and without individual rulers. Decisions are made at tribal gatherings after the old people have been consulted. As there is no written tradition, old people act as guardians of the laws, traditions and cultural and religious heritage of the group. Their religion is not based on written texts, priests or churches. A sacred place may be a circle of rocks in the desert, a tree or *billabong* (pond). The Aborigines believe in the existence of two worlds: the physical world and an invisible, spirit world called *dreamtime* which constantly influences the physical world, giving it its life force. The spirits inhabiting dreamtime materialized in order to populate the sterile, empty earth, forming the environment and creating plants, animals and tribes, their laws, beliefs and territories. Thus, humans came to share life and nature with the animals, plants and other natural phenomena. Each tribe and family grouping can trace its origins and those of the most minute feature of the environment back to a totemic ancestor or to a mythological event in the dreamtime. This overall totemism of their environment explains why the Aborigines did not set out to control nature, other human beings or the weather. It is impossible for them to behave in such a way because the eternal spirit world does not tolerate it.

The cultural inheritance of the tribe is handed down from generation to generation in its legends, complicated initiation rituals, magic and art. In a society where the present and the past, the known and the unknown are fundamentally linked, magic plays a very important role and affects every aspect of tribal life. The best-known example of Aboriginal magic is the ceremony of *pointing the bone*. During the ceremony, the *kadaicha* man points a piece of bone in the direction of an individual guilty of having infringed tribal law. Convinced of his own guilt, the individual will simply die within a couple of days. Nothing can be done to prevent such a death.

Aboriginal art is simultaneously symbolic, and related to religious practices and magic. Every important stage in the life of the individual within the tribe is marked by an initiation ceremony. During the ceremony, each person plays a role related to a personal totem. At a *corroboree,* dancers decorate their bodies with elaborate painted designs and with feather or down accessories. The dancing is accompanied by chanting, hand-clapping and the throbbing note of the *didgeridoo,* a long hollow wooden tube into which the player blows.

Totemic legends also provide inspiration for paintings and stone or wooden figures. The 'x-ray' technique is especially remarkable. Here the artist draws not only the outline and external features of an animal, but also its internal structure—skeleton, organs and the like. The artist's materials and 'canvas' are supplied by nature itself: ochre or charcoal on pieces of bark or the walls of a cave. Equally fascinating are the enormous abstract designs set out directly on the ground on ceremonial occasions, the true art of a people who have never needed museums. Aborigines of the past have left engravings in stone, using techniques completely forgotten today, and in wood, such as the famous funeral carvings of the Tiwi people on Melville and Bathurst islands. The wooden implements which they use and those which are sold to tourists are decorated at the tip with animal or floral motifs.

The Aborigines and colonization

Writing at the close of the 17th century, the buccaneer and explorer William Dampier declared the Aborigines to be the 'ugliest savages' he had ever seen. Unfortunately this attitude was widespread among the colonizers of Australia. The 'noble savage' was of little interest to the neo-Darwinians who regarded the Aborigines as being among the most primitive and lowly races on earth. Of course the colonizers did not spare a thought for the rightful occupants of the country they were appropriating. Like the kangaroos and the eucalyptus trees, the Aborigines had to make way for sheep. Unlike the North American Indians, the Aborigines were incapable of defending themselves.

The Aboriginal population in the Colony of Victoria fell in the first 30 years from 10,000 to 2000. In Tasmania, 73 years after the founding of Hobart, not one of the original 5000 Aboriginal inhabitants of the island remained. Today, only 4000 mixed-race Tasmanian Aborigines can claim to belong to the Aboriginal 'nation'. In the darkest hours of Australia's 'conquest of the West', the colonizers put a price on the ears of Aborigines, who were subsequently shot and poisoned by professional hunters. The remainder were at the mercy of the laws of nature, especially those governed by infectious diseases such as smallpox, syphilis and measles. Perhaps the most insidious 'disease' to afflict the Aborigines was more of a spiritual illness: by depriving the tribes of their ancestral territories, the colonizers also took away the Aborigines' reason to live to the point where many simply died. Alcohol claimed many more.

The British government and the churches, although aware of the problem, could propose only one solution: assimilation. A system of missions and reserves was established in 1838 to settle the nomads, dress them, feed them and convert them to Christianity. The reserves, which for the most part were nowhere near the territories of the tribes assigned to them, were administered by missionaries. Regulations aimed at isolating each population came into force in order to prevent interbreeding from becoming widespread.

Around 1930, tales of violent clashes and atrocities occurring in central Australia, along with the alarming figures provided by the census, galvanized public opinion. Improvements in medicine and sanitation have made it possible to check the decline in the Aboriginal population and even to reverse the trend. Extensive tracts of land have been returned to Aboriginal ownership in the Northern Territory and South Australia.

The future

A referendum held in all the states in 1967 gave the Aborigines the equivalent of Australian citizenship. They gained the right to vote, freedom of movement, access to social security benefits and to be included in the National Census figures. The federal government administers Aboriginal affairs and has assumed certain of the states' rights in this area. There is a Federal Minister and a Department for Aboriginal Affairs. In 1972, to make the point that they still considered themselves strangers in their own country, a group of Aborigines opened a 'tent embassy' on the lawn in front of Parliament in Canberra. The first really effective steps at improving their lot were taken in the same year by the newly elected Whitlam government which recognized absolute Aboriginal rights to the reserves in the Northern Territory. This policy was supported by Whitlam's successor, Malcolm Fraser. The law guaranteeing ownership of the 96,500sq mi/250,000sq km of reserves in the territory was passed by Parliament on January 26, 1977, at the instigation of the Fraser government. Consultative bodies were set up, substantial sums allocated to social programs (health, housing, education, legal services), and government financial backing was given to Aborigines to develop their own self-help projects, commercial as well as social.

The problems remaining to be resolved are considerable. The 200,000 Australians of Aboriginal origin, a third of whom are full-bloods, represent slightly more than one percent of the Australian population, but they have an infant mortality rate five times greater than the national average and an unemployment rate of around 50 percent. In addition, the scourge of alcoholism is far from under control. Another difficulty lies in the presence of important mineral deposits beneath Aboriginal reserves. The Aborigines do not own the sub-soil and the conflicts between tribal groups and the mining companies are difficult to resolve for all parties.

The Northern Territory and South Australia have made considerable efforts on behalf of their Aboriginal populations. There remains a lot to be done in Western Australia and (especially) Queensland, where the state government resists any 'interference' from Canberra, but hope is at hand. White Australians, whose attitude until now has ranged from open hostility to complete indifference, seem to be prepared to give their black compatriots a chance. The federal government is steadfast in its endeavours to help Aborigines take their place in the Australian community and, for the first time ever, bases its actions on the 'recognition of the fundamental rights of the Aborigines to preserve their racial identity and their traditional way of life, or to choose a way of life which is wholly or partly European'.

This principle is completely in accord with the aspirations of the Aborigines who are convinced, and can say so with dignity and courage, that their need, their sole requirement and their only hope are enshrined in the freedom to manage their own affairs. The progress of the Aborigines towards autonomy and decentralization has taken two routes. On the one hand there are the out-stations, permanent camps established on former tribal sites. These offer permanent housing and water-wells, and will, in time, have shops, schools, pharmacies, garages, and the like. Out-stations allow Aboriginal communities to practice certain of their traditional activities, such as fishing, hunting and crafts, without being totally cut off from the more 'assimilable' features of western civilization.

The other route towards autonomy and decentralization is that of the land councils. These self-regulating bodies bring members of the community together at a local level to protect their land rights (territorial claims, negotiations with mining companies, etc.). In 1981 the separate land councils amalgamated into a national federation, which fights for recognition, in Australia and abroad, of a 'nation of the Australian Aboriginal people'.

AUSTRALIAN CULTURE

Is there such a thing as a truly Australian culture? Australia sees itself as a kind of province of a vast Anglo-Saxon domain, both in terms of its civilization and its culture. The country finds itself in a bind between British and American ideals: Victorian England gave Australia a strong belief in the importance of civilization in a hostile world, and instilled a curious aversion to the natural environment in the minds of early settlers. The first colonizers and their descendants did their utmost to turn their piece of desert into an outpost of 'green Albion', complete with manicured (and sunscorched) lawns. The American, or rather Californian, inheritance has been the 'civilization of leisure' concept but unlike Americans, Australians value work more for its material benefits than for any inherent moral or spiritual value.

The explanation for this state of affairs may be that Australians tend to live for the present. Theirs is a society which is sound in mind and body but which lacks a certain amount of imagination. The tried and true is preferred to the innovative. Nowhere is this phenomenon more evident than in the urbanization of rural areas. Mining towns in the outback are modeled down to the last detail on the residential areas of the capital cities in the south. The only difference is that roads in the outback end in the desert, whereas in the coastal cities they end at the sea. Houses are usually spacious, single-storey and comfortable, but lacking any distinctive style. Those buildings which do stand out are the pub, the church, the bank, the supermarket and, in the bush, grain silos. Streets are wide and lined with telegraph poles. Their most important resident is the used-car salesman, who announces his presence with billboards and multi-coloured banners. The man in the street often wears shorts and a vest/undershirt, while women wear short dresses. Their suntanned children are a picture of health.

Sports

Each centre of population (i.e., a group of houses clustered around a pub), even in the depths of the bush, has its own golf course, football and cricket ground, tennis courts, race-course and public swimming pool, evidence of the importance of sports in Australian life. Australia has won some impressive victories in sports as varied as tennis (Sedgman, Hoad, Cooper, Fraser, Emerson, Laver, Newcombe, Roche, Goolagong and Cash), motor racing (Brabham, Jones), swimming (Rose, Wenden, Fraser, Gould), athletics (Clarke, Elliot, De Castella), not to mention golf, cricket, yachting, squash, equestrianism and, last but not least, Australian Rules football. At the 1956 Olympic Games in Melbourne, Australia won 35 medals, 13 of them gold.

ncreasing numbers of young Australians have also taken up surfing.

The arts

Long isolated at the edge of the vast and powerful British Empire, white Australian culture has suffered from a lack of self-confidence, regularly preferring British or American productions to those based on its own folklore. It has been the victim of a kind of cultural imperialism.

Recently (starting with the Whitlam Labor government in the early 1970s), Australia has begun to assert its political and cultural autonomy; to reaffirm its *ocker*—distinctively Australian—values; to rediscover its myths and local heros (bushranger Ned Kelly, racehorse Phar Lap); to reinstate its creative past. At the same time, a 'culture industry' has been established, with governmental and public backing. In the space of a few years, a new generation of film makers produced *Mad Max, Picnic at Hanging Rock* and *Crocodile Dundee*. Australian stars, who originally had no other ambition than to appeal to their Australian audience, won international acclaim. The world has been bowled over by the freshness, energy and professionalism of movie director Peter Weir, writers Colleen McCullough, Frank Moorhouse and Nancy Cato, the rock band AC/DC, and the implacable determination of Rupert Murdoch, whose media empire embraces three continents. However, success has introduced a dilemma for creative Australians: do they stay in Australia or go abroad? Staying at home means that their work is guaranteed the 'made in Australia' label but the temptations of Hollywood (Peter Weir), London (AC/DC) or Paris (Helmut Newton) beckon.

Literature

The first books on Australia were the shipboard logs of the great navigators and the scientists who accompanied them on their voyages (James Cook and Joseph Banks, for example). The first colonial administrators also penned reports, and in the manner of the times these contained a good deal of British condescension towards the strange colony they were endeavouring to civilize. Until the 1880s, Australian literature, even that written by native-born authors, was merely a lifeless and provincial reflection of its British counterpart. Charles Harpur, a poet, was the first person to express an interest in specifically Australian people and experiences in *The Bushranger* (1853).

The Golden Age of Australian literature coincided with the wave of nationalism sweeping through Australia at the close of the 19th century. The finest specimens were published in Australia's greatest journal, the pre-war *Bulletin*. The themes treated in the *Bulletin* were typically Australian nationalistic, egalitarian and even republican. They dealt with the bush, its folklore and inhabitants, from the drover to the bushranger, from the digger to the swagman (a man who travels the outback living on occasional earnings or gifts of money and food): a far cry from the fine gentlemen of London. The most famous names from this era, and perhaps in all Australian literature, are Banjo Paterson (d. 1941), composer of Australia's 'other' national anthem, *Waltzing Matilda*; Henry Lawson (d. 1922) whose novels, such as *While the Billy Boils,* echo the great themes of the bush, spiced with republican sentiments; and Joseph Furphy (d. 1912), who wrote under the pen name of

Tom Collins and gave us his famous, aggressively Australian *Such Is Life*. Colonial Australia, its bushrangers and convicts fill the books of Rolf Boldrewood, John Stanley James (pen name Juliar Thomas) and Marcus Clarke, who was the author of *For the Term of His Natural Life,* which was made into the television series of the same name. Even the American author Mark Twain was impressed by the beauty of early Australia. On a visit to Sydney in 1895, he remarked of the harbour that it was 'the darling of Sydney and the wonder of the world'.

The populist and 'typically Australian' tradition also inspired more contemporary writers, such as Vance Palmer, Frank Dalby Davison, Frank Hardy and Xavier Herbert. Herbert's books *Capricornia* and *Poor Fellow My Country* are *the* great Australian novels dealing with Aborigines. Finally there are the works of Patrick White, 1973 winner of the Nobel Prize for Literature. The high standard of White's writing proves that there is no longer anything provincial about Australian literature.

Other authors have gained a worldwide reputation without being obviously Australian: former war correspondent Alan Moorhead; Morris West and Thomas Keneally, two best-selling international writers; and Colleen McCullough whose novel *The Thorn Birds* has broken sales records all over the world. Women novelists play a particularly important role in Australian literature: Daisy Bates who lived among the Aborigines for 25 years, well-known feminist Germaine Greer, Ethel Robertson who wrote under the pen name Henry Handel Richardson, Joan Lindsay and Nancy Cato are only a few. Two authors above all represent the 1980s: Frank Moorhouse *(The Americans, Baby)* and Peter Carey *(Illywhacker).*

Visual arts

Although not so well known abroad, Australian painting is of world-class standard (for a description of Aboriginal art, see pp. 55-56). Local Australian artists, like writers, excel at realistic descriptions of their environment, especially bush landscapes and scenes from daily life. The best-known landscape artists from the end of the 19th century belonged to the Heidelberg School (Heidelberg near Melbourne, not in Germany). They include Tom Roberts, Arthur Streeton, Frederick McCubbin and Charles Conder, and their paintings can be seen in any Australian gallery. A second, contemporary wave of artists, less academic in their approach, has refined the expression of the ambiguous relationship between the Australian people and their environment. They accentuate the feeling of loneliness which emanates from the desolate spendour of the bush, to which symbolic figures like Ned Kelly add a surreal dimension. The main proponents of this style are Sidney Nolan, Russell Drysdale, William Dobell, Arthur Boyd, Bob Dickerson, Albert Tucker, Ian Fairweather, Fred Williams, John Olson, Charles Blackman, Peter Booth and Brett Whiteley.

Australian architecture, on the other hand, is still searching for a style and talent of its own. The continent's architectural successes, at least in the monumental area, have been the work of foreign architects: the American Walter Burley Griffin who designed Canberra, the Austrian/Australian Harry Seidler who designed Sydney's Australia Square, and the Dane Joern Utzon who created the Sydney Opera House. Two Australian architects rank with the

Aboriginal crafts.

former? Robin Boyd, who was more of a theoretician, and Philip Cox, whose modern buildings are quite exceptional.

Performing arts

Classical music has always enjoyed an appreciative audience in Australia because of the prestige and refinement of the civilization it represents. Numerous concert halls attest the success of tours by internationally famous artists and local orchestras which are of a very high standard. Opera and ballet are also popular. Australian composers may be little appreciated outside a small circle of devotees but better known, especially in Europe and the United States, are the Australian Ballet, choreographer Robert Helpmann, lyric singers Nellie Melba (after whom the dessert, Peach Melba, was named), Joan Hammond, Sylvia Fisher and Joan Sutherland.

On another level entirely, Australian folk music boasts a rich tradition and is sufficiently original not to be mistaken for the English, Scottish or Irish ballads which inspired it. It also has little in common with American country or folk music. Typical bush characters have an honoured place in this music, side-by-side with the struggling unionist or the itinerant worker crying, from job to job, for his imaginary family.

Developments in popular music have electrified the Australian music scene. Performers such as Helen Reddy and Olivia Newton-John have become international stars. Rock groups that have made their mark on the international scene include AC/DC, Angels, Cold Chisel, Men at Work, Split Enz, Air Supply, Mental as Anything, Mondo Rock, Rose Tatoo, Midnight Oil and INXS. Scores of groups perform every evening at venues in all big cities. The music of rock groups performing in pubs and local halls is 100 percent raw energy.

Film

Australia's recent output in the world of film has been nothing short of remarkable. Although between 1906 and 1970 the Australian film industry produced nearly 400 films, starting in the 1930s, the British and, especially, American competition forced many Australian production houses to specialize in documentaries and, in the 1950s, in television advertising.

In the 1970s the federal government gave a boost to the national film industry by establishing an organization, the Australian Film Corporation, to promote local fiction production. The Corporation gave birth to similar bodies in South Australia, Victoria and New South Wales. These were augmented in 1973 by the creation, in Sydney, of the Australian Film and Television School. By establishing important (and since abandoned) tax shelters, the government also encouraged public investment in the film industry.

The results were not long in coming: from 1975, films such as *Caddie, Picnic at Hanging Rock* and *Sunday Too Far Away* received enthusiastic acclaim in Australia and abroad. They were followed by other successful productions including *Gallipoli, Breaker Morant, The Year of Living Dangerously* and a number of films of Aboriginal inspiration such as *Stormboy* and *The Last Wave*. Australia also specializes in powerful action films, like *Mad Max* and *Razorback*. Freshness and wide-open spaces account for the success of directors like Peter Weir, George Miller, Paul Cox, Tim Burstall, Tony Buckley, Bruce Beresford and Fred Schepisi. Hollywood itself has honoured directors Weir and Beresford, and actors and actresses such as Mel Gibson, Bryan Brown and Olivia Newton-John. Other well-known names around California include Robert Stigwood, the producer of *Saturday Night Fever* and *Grease,* and Rupert Murdoch, the new owner of Fox Studios.

The media

The communications industry of Australia is booming. There is complete freedom of the press; newspapers which have enjoyed uninterrupted publication for 150 years; dailies with circulation figures approaching 500,000 in cities of fewer than 3 million inhabitants; total daily sales of 400 per 1000 people nationwide; hundreds of radio stations; more than 100 television stations reaching 98 percent of the population; journalists whose reputations are legend throughout the world; and press barons among the most powerful anywhere. There are several high-quality dailies, such as *The Age* in Melbourne, *The Sydney Morning Herald,* the major country dailies, and *The Australian,* the only national daily. Visitors will discover an enormous amount of practical information (theatre programs, restaurant guides, etc.) in the papers. The local and regional news, the sports pages and the classified advertisements alone are worth the price of the paper (40 to 50 cents for a 30-page daily). Also worth reading are two weeklies: the *National Times* and the *Bulletin,* one of the oldest and most prestigious names of the Australian press. In addition to Australian material, it includes the American weekly, *Newsweek.*

When it comes to television and radio, praise must go to the efforts of the Australian Broadcasting Corporation, the equivalent of the BBC, for raising general standards. Commercial television (three channels in both Sydney and Melbourne) is less encouraging, consisting mainly of low-quality American series interrupted every five minutes by plagiarized American advertisements. ABC-TV, on the other hand, relies a lot on BBC programs and offers more cultural and often academic viewing.

Australian television is not, however, without originality. For some years now, all channels have been obliged to include a certain amount of Australian content in their programming, some of it of very good quality. The private networks have commissioned and produced excellent Australian series. Sports broadcasts, especially cricket, are always very professional. Sydney and Melbourne, both of which have large non-English-speaking minorities, were the first cities to introduce foreign language television with Channel 28. Its programs, often of a very high standard, are imported from all over the world and are shown with English subtitles.

Commercial radio is ever-present. When you're driving, the patter of the next local station will tell you long before the appearance of houses, that your goal is at hand. For the many Australians who live in the bush, radio remains their only contact with the outside world, and the warmth of the announcer's voice is often worth more to them than the news reports he provides or the tunes on the Top 40.

SYDNEY

Founded in 1788 by a handful of convicts under the command of Captain Arthur Phillip, Sydney was Australia's first settlement in the first colony of New South Wales. The city has served as a model for other Australian cities ever since. The five capital cities all sit comfortably south of the 26th parallel, sheltered on the coast from the extreme heat and the drought of the interior. Whether they lie directly on the coast, on a coastal river or closer to a low range of hills, all the capitals have been built according to the same plan: a city centre (the business district) serving commerce and culture; the river shoreline containing the main port and the industrial areas; and the suburbs which stretch for scores of miles, enclosing the centre. Sydney is the archetypal Australian city, the most spectacular and the most exciting. It has more of a 'city' feel about it than the others, and unique features which set it apart. As the cradle of white Australian civilization, Sydney has the longest history, the largest population (3.3 million), a better climate and, above all, superb surroundings. Sydney ranks among the world's greatest seaside cities alongside San Francisco, with which it is regularly compared.

Sydney is totally and intimately a waterside city. Port Jackson (the mouth of the Parramatta River) around which the city is built, unveils more of itself at each bend; the hollow of each hill reveals another angle, another level, original and surprising. Joined by the impressive Sydney Harbour Bridge, the two halves of the city are never far from the sea. The Pacific can be glimpsed from this or that street, between two houses, from a bridge, from one of the innumerable coves and small bays which branch off the harbour, or from the harbour, a voyage of discovery in itself.

In Sydney, the beach is never far away and the concept of leisure suits its inhabitants like a glove. Work slots in somewhere between the beach and the pub. Many locals actually travel to work by boat, arriving and departing from Circular (semi-circular in fact) Quay. From there, ferries service some of the city suburbs.

On Sundays, the harbour is alive with colour from the spinnakers of yachts as they dart among ferries, container ships, windsurfers and ships of the Royal Australian Navy. Sydney Harbour is the most important port in Australia, after the ore-

The Sydney Opera House on the bay.

loading ports of the north-west. Sydney's brick warehouses, its wooden jetties, its cranes and its cosmopolitan population of sailors from all over the world contribute to the city's unique atmosphere

For the last 20 years, this undisputed capital of the South Pacific has set about voluntarily polishing its image. The Sydney Opera House with its full sails of sparkling tiles and its smoked glass stands in defiance of the artistic isolation which Australia has complained of since the times of the convicts. Another successful venture has been the renovation of the historic Rocks area between the city centre—or City—and the bridge. Sydney is also proud of its international cuisine, its museums and theatres, its department stores and its parks. Its red-light district, King Cross, is the only place of its kind in Australia.

Sydney is there for the taking and Sydneysiders will delight in showing you the other side of their favourite city. They will guide you into typical turn-of-the-century neighbourhoods, take you to the popular beaches, invite you to parties or take you sailing on their yachts, in one of the most beautiful harbours on earth.

▬▬ PRACTICAL INFORMATION

Telephone area code: 02.
Map coordinates refer to the map pp. 68-69.

Access

Plane

Sydney's international airport is connected by numerous direct flights to all the major capitals of the world. There is a regular bus service, the *Airport Express,* which takes 30 min. to reach Circular Quay and also stops elsewhere in the city. Tel: 290 2988.

International airlines

Air New Zealand, 115 Pitt St., City (A3). Tel: 234 4122.
British Airways, 64 Castlereagh St., City (B3). Tel: 232 1777.
Canadian Pacific Airlines, 62 Pitt St., City (B3). Tel: 27 3077.
Continental Airlines, 83 Clarence St., City (A3). Tel: 232 8222.
Qantas Airways, International Centre, George St., City (A3). Tel: 236 3636
United Airlines, 14 Martin Plaza, City (A3). Tel: 237 8742.

Domestic airlines

Air New South Wales, 8 Bent St., City (B3). Tel: 268 1894.
Ansett Airlines, Oxford and Riley St., Darlinghurst (B5). Tel: 268 1555.
Australian Airlines, 70 Hunter St., City (B3). Tel: 693 3333.
East-West Airlines, 54 Carrington St., City (A3). Tel: 219 5111.

Bus

There are daily connections between Sydney, Melbourne, Brisbane Canberra and Adelaide.
AAT Kings Tours, 46 Kent Rd., Mascot. Tel: 669 5444.
Ansett-Pioneer, corner of Oxford and Riley Sts., Darlinghurst (B5). Tel: 268 1881.
Greyhound Australia, corner of Oxford and Riley Sts., Darlinghurst (B5). Tel: 268 1414.

Train

Sydney is connected to Brisbane, Melbourne, Canberra, Adelaide, Alice Springs and Perth by daily trains.

Central Train Station, Eddy St., City (A6). Information and reservations for long-distance trips: 11-13 York St., City (A4). Tel: 217 8812.

Getting around Sydney

On foot

Sydney extends some 60 mi/100 km from north to south. The central city on the other hand is relatively compact—most of the interesting areas and monuments are located within about 4 sq mi/9 sq km. To get your bearings in the centre, remember that the bridge, Circular Quay and the Opera House are on the northern side of the city (see map pp. 68-69) and that the main streets run north/south.

Bus, ferry and train

Of all the cities in Australia, Sydney has by far the best public transport system—buses, ferries and trains serve both the metropolitan area and the suburbs. The Urban Transit Authority (UTA) publishes a very detailed but almost incomprehensible guide to its services. It will be of little use to the occasional visitor. The only real way to get around is to go to Circular Quay, which is a main crossroads for bus, ferry and train services, and ask an employee of the UTA who will politely put you on the right track. Go ahead and board one of the blue and white ferries, if only for the trip out and back. You will explore the bays and inlets of the harbour, discovering the other side of Sydney, the warehouses and working-class suburbs, the areas where Sydneysiders live. While on the subject of ferries, don't forget that each January there is an extremely popular event in the Festival of Sydney: the Great Ferryboat Race. A half-dozen or so of the UTA's finest craft start and finish at the bridge in a race around the harbour.

   The UTA offers two discount fares on all its services: the *Day Rover,* valid for one day (after 9am during the week and all day at the weekend), and the *Weekly Rover,* valid for seven days. Tel: train 2 0942; bus 2 0543; ferry and general UTA services 29 2622.

A general guide called *Sydney by Public Transport* is produced by Gregory's. Considered indispensable, even by Sydneysiders, it is sold at virtually every newsstand and bookshop in the city.

Taxis

Taxis are numerous and relatively inexpensive. The main radio-controlled taxis are:

Combined Taxis. Tel: 332 8888.

RSL Cabs. Tel: 699 0144.

Legion Cabs. Tel: 2 0918.

Car rental

Renting a car to explore Sydney is an excellent idea as long as you are used to driving on the left-hand side of the road and expert in the art of reading city maps. If not, it's best to leave the driving to someone who knows the city. The major car rental companies have offices at the airport and in the big hotels. There is a complete listing in the Yellow Pages of the phone book. The following are the head offices of the main companies:

Avis, 163 Mitchell Rd., Alexandria. Tel: 519 5300.

Budget, 93 William St., Kings Cross (C5). Tel: 339 8811.

Hertz, corner of William and Riley Sts., City (B5). Tel: 357 6621.

Letz, 110 Darlinghurst Rd., Kings Cross (C5). Tel: 331 3099.

Thrifty, 85 William St., Kings Cross (C5). Tel: 357 5399.

Boat

One way to enjoy magnificent Port Jackson is to rent a yacht. On Saturdays and Sundays, hundreds of boats, ranging from windsurfers to 12-metre America's Cup yachts, fill the harbour. There is, however, one rule that must be observed: the hydrofoils which run a regular passenger service between the city and Manly, a suburb located where the ocean and the

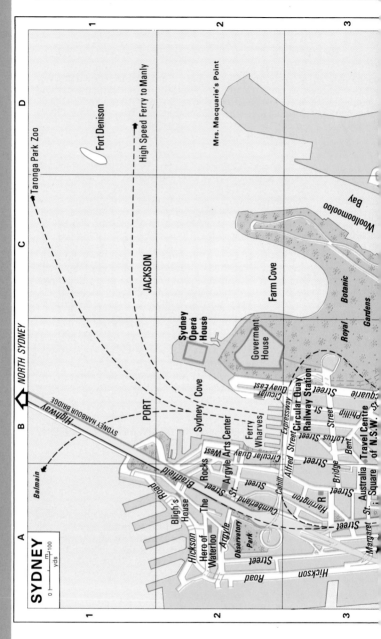

harbour meet, have absolute priority, even over yachts. For boat renta
contact **Walton's Hire Boats,** The Esplanade, Balmoral Beach. Te
969 6006. Prices are reasonable and the boats well maintained.

Organized trips
Sydney Explorer. An excellent service devised by the New South Wale
Tourism Commission, it consists of an 11 mi/18 km bus tour around the cit
for less than A$10. You can get on or off the bus at any of the 20 stops e

route, and can repeat any section of the tour you like. **UTA Travel Centre,** 11 York St., City (A4). Tel: 297 6143.

Captain Cook Cruise. A cruiser on the harbour, offering commentary and lunch. Very professional. You have the choice of six routes, with a great range of prices: from a simple 1.5 hour harbour tour to a supper cruise at night. **Captain Cook Cruise,** Jetty No 6, Circular Quay (B2). Tel: 27 4416.

Another alternative is to take a bus and ferry tour with the UTA, going by one means to Manly and back by the other (Sun. only).

Heliflite. Helicopter tours, over the city and harbour, further inland or along the coast. Tel: 634 7281.

Useful addresses

Map coordinates refer to the map pp. 68-69.

Tourist information

Sydney Visitor's Bureau, 100 Market St., City (A4). Tel: 232 1377. Specializes mostly in business trips and conferences.

Tourist Information Centre, Martin Plaza, between Castlereagh and Elizabeth Sts., City (B4). Tel: 235 2424.

Travel Centre of New South Wales, 16 Spring St., City (B3). Tel: 231 4444. Open 8.30am to 5pm Mon. to Fri. Well stocked with brochures and free maps of Sydney and NSW. Also operates as travel agency. The staff are especially courteous and efficient.

Consulates

American Consulate-General, corner of Elizabeth and Park Sts., City (B5). Tel: 264 7044.

British Consulate-General, Gold Fields House, 1 Alfred St., Circular Quay (B3). Tel: 27 7521.

Canadian Consulate-General, AMP Centre, 50 Bridge St., City (B3). Tel: 231 6522.

Post office

General Post Office (GPO), Martin Plaza, between George and Pitt Sts., City (A4). Tel: 230 7013. The GPO handles telegrams, stamps and international phone calls.

Automobile club

Royal Automobile Club of Australia, 89 Macquarie St., City (A3). Tel: 27 5656.

Accommodation

Map coordinates refer to the map pp. 68-69. Coordinates containing a second letter indicate specific location on the map.

There is no shortage of accommodation in Sydney. All categories of hotel are represented. The following is a selected list.

International-standard hotels

Those located in the City cater more for the business traveler, while those in Kings Cross and nearby Potts Point cater more for the tourist.

In the City

▲▲▲▲ **The Boulevard,** 90 William St. (C5-b). Tel: 357 2277. 270 rooms, 15 suites.

▲▲▲▲ **Hotel Inter-Continental Sydney,** 117 Macquarie St. (A4). Tel: 230 0200. Well-situated near GPO, this hotel offers many amenities. 531 rooms, 88 suites.

▲▲▲▲ **Menzies,** 14 Carrington St. (A3-j). Tel: 2 0232. The oldest of Sydney's fine hotels. 432 rooms, 13 suites.

▲▲▲▲ **Regent Hotel,** 199 George St. (A3-R). Tel: 238 0000. A modern hotel situated between the city centre and the Rocks area. 578 rooms, 42 suites, 6 restaurants.

▲▲▲▲ **Sheraton-Wentworth,** 61-101 Phillip St. (B3-a). Tel: 230 0700. This is the business traveler's hotel in Sydney but tourists are also welcome. 485 rooms, 33 suites.

▲▲▲▲ **Sydney Hilton,** 259 Pitt St. (A4-g). Tel: 266 0610. 582 rooms, 37 suites.

In Kings Cross

▲▲▲▲ **Gazebo Ramada Inn,** 2 Elizabeth Bay Rd. (D4-i). Tel: 358 1999. 394 rooms, 6 suites.

▲▲▲▲ **Hyatt Kingsgate,** corner of Victoria St. and Kings Cross Rd. (C5-c). Tel: 357 2233. 389 rooms, 9 suites.

▲▲▲▲ **Sebel Town House,** 23 Elizabeth Bay Rd. (D4-k). Tel: 358 3244. Motel, 160 rooms, 30 suites.

▲▲▲▲ **Top of the Cross Travelodge,** 110 Darlinghurst Rd. (C5-e). Tel: 33 0911. Motel, 96 rooms.

First-class hotels

▲▲▲ **Cambridge Inn,** Riley St., City (B5). Tel: 212 1111. 136 rooms.

▲▲▲ **Chevron,** 81 Macleay St., Potts Point (D4-f). Tel: 358 5429. 183 rooms, 24 suites.

▲▲▲ **Hampton Court,** 9 Bayswater Rd., Kings Cross (C5-d). Tel: 357 2711. 126 rooms.

▲▲▲ **Sheraton Motor Hotel,** 40 Macleay St., Potts Point (D4-m). Tel: 358 1955. Motel, 47 rooms, 22 suites.

▲▲▲ **Zebra Hyde Park,** 271 Elizabeth St., City (B4). Tel: 264 6001. Motel, 80 rooms, 6 suites.

Moderately priced and inexpensive hotels

It is possible to find inexpensive 'private hotels' or guest-houses in the City and around Kings Cross, but they're often full. In the suburbs further from the City and especially near the beaches, there is no such problem and you can enjoy the famous hospitality of an Australian pub just 20 minutes from Sydney by bus or ferry.

▲▲ **Canberra Oriental,** 223 Victoria St., Kings Cross (C5-h). Tel: 358 3155. 206 rooms.

▲▲ **Grand Hotel,** 30 Hunter St., City (B3). Tel: 232 3755. Pub, 19 rooms.

▲▲ **Imperial,** 221 Darlinghurst Rd., Kings Cross (C5). Tel: 331 4051. 100 rooms, 10 suites.

▲ **Sydney Youth Hostel,** (members only), 28 Ross St., Forest Lodge. Tel: 692 0747. 30 beds. Very close to Sydney University.

On the beach

▲▲ **Manly Pacific International Hotel,** 55 North Steyne, Manly (D1 east). Tel: 977 7666.

▲ **Thelellen Beach Inn,** 2 Campbell Parade, Bondi (D6 east). Tel: 30 5333. Pleasant guest house, situated on Australia's most famous beach.

You will also find numerous inexpensive pubs, motels and guest houses all along the coast.

Food

Map coordinates refer to the map pp. 68-69.

In Sydney, as in the other cities, all the world's cuisines are represented. However Sydney's speciality is seafood, especially oysters, with a taste to delight the most discerning connoisseur. With very few exceptions, it is not necessary to dress up to eat out but shorts, sandals or tennis shoes are not welcome in the better restaurants. Prices can vary from about A$50 per person in the best restaurants, A$20 to A$40 in very good restaurants, and from A$4 to A$10 for a meal in a pub or BYO (Bring Your Own alcohol). Restaurant information can be found in Leo Schofield's *Good Food Guide,* published locally by the *Sydney Morning Herald.*

Elegant restaurants

Sydney's (and possibly Australia's) two most expensive restaurants are located outside the city, in surroundings which complement the cuisine to perfection.

The Berowra Waters Inn, Berowra Waters. Tel: 456 1027. Situated about 25 mi/40 km (one hour by road) from Sydney along the Pacific Highway to Newcastle, this restaurant stands on the banks of the Berowra River. The food, service and decor are outstanding. There is a wide choice of seafood and an excellent French and Australian wine list. Open for lunch and dinner on Wed., Sat. and Sun. Reservations essential.

Glenella, 56 Govett's Leap Rd., Blackheath. Tel: (047) 87 8352. This restaurant is located in the heart of the Blue Mountains, 72 mi/116 km (2.5 hours by road) from Sydney, along the Great Western Highway towards Bathurst. Excellent French-Australian food in a castle-hotel setting. Overnight accommodation is available. Phone for reservations.

French

French restaurants are numerous and popular in Sydney. The best of them do not neccessarily have French-born chefs.

Bagatelle, 117 Riley St., East Sydney (B5). Tel: 357 5675. Simple and tasty nouvelle cuisine. Close to the city, well regarded.

Claude's French Restaurant, 10 Oxford St., Woollahra (D6 east). Tel: 331 2325. Be sure to bring your own wine.

Pegrum's, corner of Gurner and Cambridge Sts., Paddington (D6). Tel: 357 4776. Fashionable and expensive.

Percy's, corner of Oxford St. and Moore Park Rd., Paddington (D6). Tel: 33 3377. Elegance and style in a fashionable area of Sydney.

Puligny's, 240 Military Rd., Neutral Bay. Tel: 908 2552. Famous for its decor, service, fish and desserts.

The Verandah, 13 Kellett St., Kings Cross (C5). Tel: 358 4112. Louisiana-style French food.

Italian

Local Italian restaurants offer good, inexpensive food, as well as first-class regional specialities.

Atlanta, 41 Crown St., Woolloomooloo (B4). Tel: 33 6467. Situated between Kings Cross and the city, this is an unpretentious, excellent and inexpensive BYO, and a haunt for young people on their way to or from the pub.

Beppi's, corner of Yurong and Stanley Sts., East Sydney (B6). Tel: 357 4558. Simple cuisine, sophisticated surroundings.

D'Arcy's, 92 Hargrave St., Paddington (D6). Tel: 32 3706. One of Sydney's fashionable restaurants and rightly so.

Il Fiasco, 38 Bayswater Rd., Kings Cross (D5). Tel: 358 1881. Restaurant and disco, the last word in chic in Sydney.

La Rustica, 435 Parramatta Rd., Leichhardt. Tel: 569 5824. In Sydney's Italian quarter. Good food and not too expensive.

La Strada, 95 Macleay St., Potts Point (D4). Tel: 358 1160. The place in Sydney where local and international stars congregate.

Oriental

Chinese

There are numerous Chinese restaurants (thanks to the refugees, Vietnamese restaurants are now also beginning to appear) in Sydney's Chinatown in Dixon St., near Central Station (A6). Also worth recommending:

Imperial Peking, corner of Know and Bay Sts., Double Bay. Tel: 326 2957. Cantonese and Pekinese cuisine.

Japanese

Suntory, 529 Kent St., City (A5). Tel: 267 2990.

Seafood

Doyles on the Beach, Watsons Bay. Tel: 337 2007. The restaurant does not take reservations, but is one of Sydney's most famous. It is situated on the beach, with a unique view down the harbour, and

City tour bus.

offers fish cooked in the 'fish and chips' style. About 30 minutes from the city.

Fishwives, 457 Elizabeth St., Surry Hills (A6). Tel: 699 5594. Excellent food and pleasant atmosphere.

The Grape Escape, 139 Blues Point Rd., McMahons Point. Tel: 929 6268. Lobsters, excellent wine list, 1850s decor, jazz.

The Contented Sole, 156 Hall St., Bondi (D1 east). Tel: 30 6261. Very elaborate seafood platter in a sophisticated atmosphere. BYO.

With a view

Bennelong and Harbour restaurants, Sydney Opera House (B2). Tel: 241 1371. Sydney's most prestigious address. From the **Bennelong,** a very smart restaurant, and the **Harbour,** a coffee and snack shop, you can admire the view before the show.

The Summit, 47th floor, Australia Square, George St., City (A3). Tel: 27 9777.

Sydney Tower Restaurant, Centrepoint, corner of Market and Pitt Sts., City (A4). Tel: 233 3722.

Situated high above the city, these two restaurants offer views over the harbour and the city. Among the most stunning views you'll ever see.

Pubs

Map coordinates refer to the map pp. 68-69.

New South Wales has the most liberal drinking laws in Australia. Pubs can open in summer from 11am until 11pm and along the harbour some open from 6am until 6pm. The beers have different names depending on their size (middy, pot, schooner—see 'Guide to Australian English, p. 200), but you'll be given the medium-size if you just ask for a *'glass of beer'*. If you'd rather keep a clear head, especially when the temperature climbs to over 90 °F/35 °C, the *lemon squash* served with ice is deliciously thirst-quenching. The regular drinkers in Sydney pubs range from building workers in their undershirts to clerks and casually dressed couples. A typical (but fast disappearing) sight in Sydney's pubs is the tiled walls. According to some people this makes them easier to clean, but, according to others their 'hospital' appearance plays on the consciences of those still imbued with a little good old-fashioned Australian Puritanism. The following is a selection of the most popular or most attractive Sydney pubs.

In the Rocks *(A2)*

The **Hero of Waterloo,** 81 Lower Fort St., and the **Lord Nelson,** 19 Kent St. (two of Australia's oldest pubs); the **Mercantile,** 25 George St. N., and the **Orient** on Argyle St. are the most lively in Sydney, especially on a Friday evening.

In Paddington *(D6)*

The **Four in Hand,** 105 Sutherland St., the **Lord Dudley,** the **Royal** and the **Rose and Crown,** all on Glenmore Rd., are typical of this former working-class area which has now become one of the most trendy in the city.

In Balmain *(A1 west)*

The **London Hotel** on Darling St. A classic pub in an historical area.

In the City

The **Marble Bar** at the **Hilton** (A4-g). This fabulous bar was part of the original 1900 hotel which occupied the site of the present ultra-modern Hilton complex. The bar has been completely rebuilt (including the extraordinary Baroque decoration, marble columns, provocative paintings and giant mirrors) and is one of the most popular meeting-places in the city.

In Surry Hills *(B6)*

The **Evening Star,** 370 Elizabeth St., is the watering hole for journalists.

On the beach

The **Watsons Bay Hotel** at Watsons Bay, close to **Doyle's** restaurant, has a magnificent beer garden where a sun-bronzed and relaxed crowd gather at the end of a day at the beach.

The most popular beach pubs (at Bondi, Manly etc.) often have rock bands in the evenings. Their live music is very popular, especially with the surfing set. Programs are given in the daily papers, and most fully in the Friday *Sydney Morning Herald.*

Shopping

Map coordinates refer to the map pp. 68-69.

Most shops are open from 8.30am until 5.30pm during the week (9pm on Thurs.) and from 8.30 until noon on Sat. Department stores offering much the same goods as their overseas counterparts are **David Jones** (in the City) and **Grace Brothers** (in the City and south of it, near Sydney University). **Woolworths** and **Coles** (similar to Woolworths) have branches in the city and almost all suburbs. More typically Australian are the shopping arcades, full of small boutiques (A4). The earliest of them date from around 1900 like **The Strand,** between George and Pitt Sts., while the more modern, air-conditioned arcades (**Centrepoint, MLC Tower** between Pitt and Castlereagh Sts.) serve as a welcome haven from the heat on a hot summer's day. **Knox St.,** in up-market Double Bay, is Sydney's equivalent of New York's Fifth Ave., or London's Knightsbridge. The suburbs are the domain of the giant shopping centres, the most successful being **Birkenhead Point** at Drummoyne. It is an Australian version of San Francisco's Pier 33, as is **Pier One** under the Harbour Bridge on the southern shore (B1), offering boutiques, restaurants, games for the children etc. Another interesting complex is the **Argyle Arts Centre** in the Rocks (A2), a historic warehouse area which offers a wide choice of Australian arts and crafts shops. On a Saturday morning, make a visit to Sydney's main market, **Paddy's Market**, near the Chinatown (Haymarket) area (A5).

Aboriginal art

There is a greater choice in Alice Springs, but it is still worth visiting one or two galleries in Sydney, just to familiarize yourself with the different styles and prices.

Aboriginal Arts Centre, 7 Walker Lane, Paddington (D6). Tel: 357 6839.

Bush Church Aid Society, 135 Bathurst St., City (A5). Tel: 264 3164.

Antiques

Australian antiques include very fine collections of furniture, arts and crafts from the early Australian period (19th century), plus Art Nouveau and Art Deco.

You can find unique and very inexpensive pieces at **Op Shops,** clothing and furniture shops operated by the **Salvation Army** or similar organizations, or at the flea markets held every Sat., especially in Paddington and Balmain. Among the most highly thought of antique shops are:

Anne Schofield, 36 Queen St., Woollahra (D6 east). Tel: 32 1326.

Copeland and de Soos, 66 Queen St., Woollahra (D6 east). Tel: 32 5288.

The Antique Centre, 531 South Dowling St., Surry Hills (C6). Tel: 33 3244. This is a veritable supermarket of second-hand and antique wares.

Art galleries

The main commercial galleries are located in the Paddington-Woollahra area. They exhibit contemporary as well as traditional Australian works.

Barry Stern Galleries, 19 Glenmore Rd., Paddington (C6). Tel: 331 4676.

Holdsworth Gallery, 86 Holdsworth St., Woollahra (D6 east). Tel: 32 1364.

Robin Gibson Gallery, 278 Liverpool St., Darlinghurst (C5). Tel: 331 6692.

Rudy Komon Art Gallery, 124 Jersey Rd., Woollahra (D6 east). Tel: 32 2533.

You can also admire an excellent collection of works by Australian and overseas artists at the **Art Gallery of NSW,** Art Gallery Rd., The Domain (B-C4). Tel: 221 2656. See p. 80.

Opals

Even if your budget doesn't run to the purchase of a beautifully cut or mounted stone (several hundred dollars or more, depending on the cut and quality of the stone), you should still have a look through one of the numerous shops specializing in the famous Australian opals. There you can at least dream and perhaps buy a stone or fragment of opal embedded in the original rock. These cost from A$10 up. Don't forget your plane ticket or passport—they will entitle you to a 20 percent discount.

The Opal Skymine, level 6, Australia Square, George St., City (A3). Tel: 27 9912. Reproduction opal mine and boutique.

E. Gregory Sherman, 67 Castlereagh St., City (B3). Tel: 233 6355.

Flame Opals, 119 George St., The Rocks (A2). Tel: 27 3446.

Gemtec Australia, 250 Pitt St., City (A4). Tel: 267 7939

Opals Australia, 20 Bond St., City (A3). Tel: 233 1288.

Sports

Map coordinates refer to the map pp. 68-69.

Melbourne, more than Sydney, is the sport capital of Australia. However, this does not prevent Sydneysiders from following and playing all manner of sports. Here, as in the rest of Australia, summer cricket (from October to March), tennis, golf and horse racing are all very popular, but the real favourites are Rugby League football, surfing and boating.

Rugby League football

This is played from February through September by a dozen teams representing different areas of the city. It is Sydney's main winter sport and is advertised regularly in the press.

Surf lifesaving carnivals

The most popular beaches in Sydney and the rest of Australia are patrolled by highly trained volunteer lifeguards who look after the safety of bathers. Lifesavers belong to surf lifesaving clubs and are experts at most seaside sports: swimming, sand sprinting, surfing and surfboat handling. These boats, propelled by muscular rowers, are designed to cut through or to ride the Pacific breakers. *Surf carnivals,* held by these clubs from November through March, include surfing, surfboat and beach sprint competitions. Don't miss them. Programs can be found in the newspapers, or you can phone 699 1982 for information.

Yachting regattas

The most famous and spectacular boat race is without a doubt, the Sydney to Hobart Yacht Race which attracts competitors from all over the world. Since it first started in 1945, the 680 nautical mile race which begins at 11am on the day after Christmas each year has drawn thousands of spectators to the harbour to cheer on their favourite yacht or skipper.

Golf and tennis

If you fancy a round of golf in Sydney, it will cost you between A$10 and A$15 at a private club, such as the **NSW Golf Club,** Henry Rd., La Perouse. Tel: 661 4455. Otherwise, you can pay less than A$6 for 18 holes at a municipal course, such as **Bondi Golf Links,** Military Rd., North Bondi. Tel: 30 1981. If you prefer tennis, there is no shortage of courts. You'll pay between A$3.50 and A$10 to hire a court for an hour. For tennis information contact **NSW Tennis Assoc.,** 30 Alma Rd., Paddington (D6). Tel: 331 4144.

Entertainment and cultural life

Map coordinates refer to the map pp. 68-69.

Performing arts

The **Sydney Opera House** (B2) is famous not only for its architecture (see p. 80) but also for the programs it presents: ballet, theatre, opera and concerts by overseas as well as Australian performers. International standard. Programs and information can be obtained by phoning 250 7111 or 2 0525.

Other less grand venues also present high-quality programs:

Theatre Royal, MLC Centre, King St., City (A4). Tel: 231 6111. There you may catch a play by David Williamson, one of Australia's most popular contemporary playwrights.

Her Majesty's, Quay St., City (A6). Tel: 212 1066. Musical comedies.

Nimrod, Seymour Centre, corner of Cleveland St. and City Rd. Darlington (near Sydney University). Tel: 692 0555. High-quality avant-garde theatre.

Cinemas

Commercial cinemas are not very numerous but are generally very spacious, with enormous screens. American films arrive very quickly, sometimes even before they're shown in the United States, and there is also an 'art and experimental' circuit. Programs are advertised in the daily papers.

Festivals and celebrations

Aside from great sporting occasions and days commemorating patriotic events, the following are Sydney's main festivities:

The Festival of Sydney

Held each January. Theatre, music and exhibitions in the parks around the

A newspaper stand in Sydney.

City. Usually free. Firework display and the Great Ferryboat Race. Program in the daily papers.

Chinese New Year
Held at the end of January or during February in Chinatown (Dixon St., near the Central Station, A6). Dragon dance, firecrackers, music.

Highland Gathering of the Clans
Held on January 1, at Wentworth Park, Glebe. Sydney's Scottish community revels in all its splendour.

The Royal Easter Show
Starts 10 days before Easter, at Sydney Showground, Moore Park. A high-powered agricultural show with drum majorettes, equestrian competitions, etc.

The City to Surf
Famous footrace, held in August through the streets from the city to Bondi Beach.

Nightlife
Map coordinates refer to the map pp. 68-69.

True to its cosmopolitan reputation, Sydney swings at night and not only in Kings Cross.

Discotheques
Open until 3am, closed on Sun. All tastes are catered for.

Kinselas, 383 Bourke St., Darlinghurst (C5) Tel: 331 3100. Very popular, stage shows.

Rogues, 10 Oxford St., Darlinghurst (B5). Tel: 33 6924. One of the more sophisticated of Sydney's discos.

Hip-Hop, 11 Oxford St., Darlinghurst (B5). Tel: 332 2568. Very 'in'.

Tivoli, 652 George St., City (A6). Tel: 267 5499. Live music.

Cauldron, 207 Darlinghurst Rd., Darlinghurst (C6). Tel: 331 1523. Good place to meet people.

Arthurs, 155 Victoria St., Potts Point (C4). Tel: 358 5097. Tiny disco.

Live rock
Every evening between 30 and 50 pubs offer live music. For details, see the *'Gig Guide'* in the *Daily Telegraph* or the blue *'Metro'* supplement in Friday's *Sydney Morning Herald.*

Live jazz
The Regent, Don Burrows Room, 199 George St., City (A3-R). Tel: 238 0000.

The Stoned Crow, 39 Willoughby Rd., Crows Nest. Tel: 43 4882.

▬▬ GETTING TO KNOW SYDNEY

Because of its natural beauty and the attractions it has to offer, Sydney is the only Australian city which completely lends itself to tourism in the traditional sense. You should set aside at least three days to explore the harbour, the city, Kings Cross, the Rocks, Paddington and Balmain. Top it all off with a day at the beach.

The harbour

An attraction in its own right, the harbour also provides an ideal way to explore Sydney from aboard a ferry, a yacht or day cruiser (see pp. 67-70).

The City

The City, and especially the northern end near Circular Quay, is the most civilized place in Australia, if by 'civilized' you mean offering a kind of natural urban patina: weathered stone, greying buildings, 100-year-old fig trees, streets obviously following the slope of hills, bustling crowds and newspaper vendors always there when you want the latest edition. There's nothing here that you wouldn't find in any major European or American city, but at the end of your trip or after several weeks in the bush, these familiar sights will take on a certain charm.

Start your stroll around the City by visiting the 48th floor of **Australia Square Tower** in George St. (A3) or the top of **Sydney Tower** on Market St. between Elizabeth and George (A-B4). Both are *open 10am to 10pm every day of the year except Christmas Day.* Sydney Tower, which rises to 1000 ft/305 m, is the highest structure in the South Pacific. Its summit is reached by high-speed elevator and consists of an observation platform and two revolving restaurants. It offers splendid panoramic views over Sydney and its endless suburbs. **George Street***** is the main thoroughfare through the City district which stretches 1.5 mi/2.5 km north-south between Circular Quay and Central Station, and much the same distance east-west, from Darling Harbour to the Royal Botanic Gardens. **Martin Plaza** is a pedestrian zone which slopes from Macquarie St. to George St. more or less dividing the northern business area from the stores, theatres and cinemas to the south.

Strictly speaking, Sydney does not have the beauty of London, New York or San Francisco. Apart from the Opera House, the buildings are neither original in style nor elegant. However, its charm derives from the juxtaposition of styles that have developed over the last 200 years: Victorian, fin de siècle, art nouveau, art deco and post-Bauhaus. Brown stone, brick and concrete, wrought-iron balconies, sharp 1930s angles and early 1960s green plastic panels coexist as in **Macquarie St.** (B3), between Bent and Bridge Sts., opposite the **Royal Botanic Gardens.** Sydney is the 1930s capital of Australia; the **Harbour Bridge**** was opened in 1932. The **Queen Victoria Buildings*** in George St. are also eyecatching, having

ecently been renovated in the great Rococo tradition. End your visit to the
ity with a leisurely stroll through one of the parks on its eastern side: **Hyde
ark, The Domain** or the very beautiful **Royal Botanic Gardens** (B-C, 3-4).
ollow Mrs Macquaries Rd. to Mrs Macquaries Point, at the northern end
f the gardens. The view to the west over the Opera House, the bridge and
he City is superb.

he Rocks

he Rocks area is situated at the foot of the Sydney Harbour Bridge, at the
orth-western end of George St. (A2). It was here, in 1788, that the First
leet set up its encampment. This soon attracted the usual mixture of
eople found in port-side areas all over the world. The dilapidated state of
his part of the city, following the partial leveling of some sections during
he plague of 1900 and of others prior to the construction of the bridge and
he expressway in 1957, led in 1970 to the NSW government's decision
unique in Australia) to preserve, renovate and develop the Rocks as the
cradle of the nation'. Fifteen years later, their plan was crowned with
uccess, not only from the tourist's point of view, but also at a basic,
uman level. The organization in charge of the project set out to retain the
ocial character of the area, at the same time permitting limited, integrated
igh-rise building construction. The shops, art galleries, museums and
estaurants in renovated former warehouses, and the famous Rocks pubs
ave made the area one of Sydney's major tourist attractions. The section
orth of the entrance to the bridge is particularly original: the *Hickson Road
ocks,* the pubs with ships' funnels in the background and the striking view
f the city from **Observatory Hill**★★ make an extended visit to the Rocks
orthwhile. Activities in the Rocks usually continue until late at night,
specially at the weekend. Information: **Rocks Visitors Centre,** 104
eorge St. Tel: 27 4972.

ings Cross

ocated at the upper end of William St. (C5), 20 minutes by foot from the
ty, Kings Cross may remind you of London's Soho or New York's 42nd
treet. By Australian standards, where the Victorian credo remains 'do
hat you like but do it in your own home', **Darlinghurst Rd.** is without a
oubt the most 'Bohemian' street in the country. It survived the influx of
merican servicemen on leave from Vietnam during the 1960s who found
 more orderly, more hygienic and more 'American' than either Saigon or
angkok. Today, with its 24-hour bars, nightclubs, sex-shops, pharmacies
nd pizzerias, Kings Cross remains the meeting place of a cross-section of
umanity: hippies, punks, prostitutes, uniformed sailors, farmers (with felt
ats down to their eyebrows), truckies (who don't hesitate to park their 10-
on trucks in front of their favourite night-spot), and Japanese who gaze
own from their double-decker tourist buses.

addington★★

o the east of the city, Paddington and Woollahra are typical of the inner
uburbs around all large Australian cities. There you can see splendid multi-
torey terrace houses, magnificent wrought-iron verandas and balconies.
he area, which was home to the middle class at the end of the 19th
entury, later became that of the early Anglo-Saxon working class and, just
fter World War II, European immigrants. In the last 20 years, a new
eneration of wealthy, young, energetic executives and television stars
ave bought ever more expensive houses there, renovating them in the
xisting style of the area: quiet, charming and full of character. Padding-
on—with its hills, lofty views of the harbour, hundred-year-old trees, res-
aurants, galleries, pubs and Saturday flea market—has been the more
opular of these two neighbourhoods.

almain★★

almain, on the other side of Darling Harbour to the west of the city, was
ke Paddington 20 years ago, before the *trendies,* fashionable young
eople, moved in. There used to be a large working-class and immigrant

population here, stretching back decades. All groups still come together a
the **flea market** on Sat. mornings in the neo-Gothic church in Darling St
or at the **London Hotel.** A stroll through Balmain will convey the ambienc
of this harbour-side suburb. A ferry from Circular Quay to Darling St. Wha
will take you past the container-ship docks and drop you at the foot c
Darling Street★★. You can walk along this busy street into the heart c
Balmain and return from there by bus to the city. If you decide to go by bu
and return by ferry, wait until evening and admire the city and Harbou
Bridge from the wharf or the deck of the ferry.

The beaches

Set aside a fine summer day to enjoy Sydney's fabulous beaches. They ca
be divided into two groups: those to the south of Port Jackson—Bond
Tamarama, Coogee (*less than 6 mi/10 km from the city*)—and those to th
north—Manly *(9 mi/15 km)*, Curl Curl *(13 mi/20 km)*, Dee Wh
(14 mi/21 km), Mona Vale *(19 mi/30 km)* and Palm Beach *(28 mi/44 km*
There are numerous other beaches in between, on both sides of th
harbour and around its foreshores. The southern beaches, especially thos
which can be reached by bus from Circular Quay, are the most popula
Bondi (pronounced bon-dye) is probably Australia's best-known beach. T
the north, **Manly** is easily reached by ferry or hydrofoil from Circular Quay
Lady Jane Beach in the harbour itself is an official nudist beach. Mos
beaches are protected from sharks by nets, and regular boat and plan
patrols. Flags designate areas for body surfers and surfboard riders.

▬▬ WHAT TO SEE

Sydney Opera House★★★

Bennelong Point, City (B2). Tel: 2 0588. *Tours daily 8am to 4pm, excep
Sat.*
It is to Danish architect Joern Utzon that Australians owe their fines
example of architecture. The Sydney Opera House was completed in 197;
its construction financed in part by a NSW state lottery. Queen Elizabeth
declared the building open at a ceremony worthy of a royal weddinç
Although thought to be a little aggressive by some critics, it is a monumer
to modern architecture. If you don't have time to attend a performance, a
least set aside A$2.50 and an hour for a tour. Tickets reserved for oversea
visitors on the 9am and 9.30am tours can be purchased in the main ha
(See also 'Performing arts' p. 76.)

Australian Museum

Corner of William and College Sts., City (B5). Tel: 339 8111. *Open Tues. t
Sat. 10am to 5pm, Mon. and Sun. noon to 5pm.*
Natural history, fish, Aboriginal and Melanesian art, one gallery devoted t
the Australian desert.

Art Gallery of New South Wales★★★

Art Gallery Rd., The Domain (B4). Tel: 221 2100. *Open Mon. to Sat. 10a
to 5pm, Sun. noon to 5pm.*
Very representative collection of works by post-Renaissance Europea
artists, Australian artists from the beginning of the 19th century, as well a
Aboriginal arts and crafts from thousands of years ago.

Elizabeth Bay House★

7 Onslow Ave., Elizabeth Bay (D4). Tel: 358 2344. *Open Tues. to Fri. 10a
to 4pm, Sat. 10am to 5pm and Sun. noon to 5pm.*
Middle-class mansion built in 1832 and very well restored, especially th
beautiful internal staircase. Views over the harbour, historical exhibition:

Vaucluse House★

Wentworth Rd., Vaucluse. Tel: 337 1957. *Open daily 10am to 4pm.*
The house is located in the wealthy suburb of Vaucluse and is one c
Australia's first great homes, built in 1827 by William Wentworth. Bot
interior and exterior are Early Australian, the gardens are magnificent an
the furnishings first-class.

Colonial House Museum
53 Lower Fort St., Dawes Point. Tel: 276 0008. *Open daily 10am to 5pm.* Two-storey terrace house dating from 1880 and restored down to the last detail.

Zoological parks

Before going off to the bush to view them in their natural habitat, you can see kangaroos, koalas, emus and wombats, not to mention lions and elephants, at **Taronga Park Zoo and Aquarium,** Bradleys Head Rd., Mosman. Tel: 969 2777. The nicest way to get there is to take a direct ferry from Circular Quay.

Koalas are the speciality at **Koala Park,** 84 Castle Hill Rd., West Pennant Hills, about 25 mi/40 km from the city, north of Parramatta on Highway No 55. Tel: 875 2777.

If you're lucky and have the patience, you might also see kangaroos in the **Ku-Ring-Gai Chase National Park★★,** 15 mi/24 km north of Sydney on the Pacific Highway. Tel: 450 1880. This 37,000 acre/15,000 ha park is a paradise for bushwalkers. You might end your walking day with dinner at Berowra Waters on the return journey (see 'Food' p. 71).

SYDNEY TO BRISBANE:
NEW ENGLAND
AND THE GOLD COAST

I n 1813, 25 years after the first convicts had arrived at Botany Bay, one of Australia's first great visionaries, William Wentworth, took part in the expedition which discovered a way across the Blue Mountains of the Great Dividing Range. The mountains had been a barrier between the colonists and limitless plains which were well suited to sheep farming and the production of wool.

Although wool is still important to the Australian economy, the influx of the tourist trade and the development of the wine industry in recent years have added new life to the strip of land between the ocean and the Great Dividing Range. The inland southern area between Sydney and Brisbane, called New England, is lush, green and a centre for sheep, cattle and horse breeding as well as the principal area for the production of fine Australian wines. The coastal area is one of endless, white-sand beaches with a view of the inland mountains and a sapphire sea all the way from Newcastle to the Gold Coast—and Surfers Paradise—just to the south of Brisbane.

THE NEW ENGLAND AND PACIFIC HIGHWAYS

Traveling north from Sydney, there are two major routes to Brisbane. The New England Highway (Highway No 15), follows an inland route 646 mi/1040 km long, while the Pacific Highway (Highway No 1), stretches along the coast for 637 mi/1025 km.

▬▬▬ THE NEW ENGLAND HIGHWAY

The discreet, restful charm of the New England countryside will remind visitors of the north-eastern United States. The region alternates between plateaux and long valley plains, subject to harsh winters and vividly coloured autumns. The New England highway begins at **Newcastle,** once a centre for the production of coal which brought prosperity to the region in the early industrial age. From there, the highway passes through the **Hunter Valley★★**, 100 mi/160 km north of Sydney. Although most of the vineyards are concentrated around Pokolbin, **Cessnock★** offers the best choice of accommodation and is the commercial centre of the area. The main wineries are generally open from 9am to 5pm for tastings and wine tours and several of them include restaurants (Saxonvale Happy Valley

ungerford Hills, and Wyndham Estate). Other well-known wineries
clude: Tamburlaine, Tyrell's and Rothbury Estate.

etween the Hunter Valley and Brisbane, the main towns along the route
re **Tamworth**★★ (280 mi/451 km from Sydney), Australia's Nashville and
ountry-music capital, and **Armidale** (350 mi/564 km), the location of one
f the country's most beautiful universities. Other small towns, such as
uswellbrook (183 mi/293 km), **Scone** (187 mi/299 km) and **Uralla**
37 mi/543 km) are quite typical of this pastoral region, where the towns
ong the highway usually consist of 20 or 30 picturesque Victorian houses,
ree or four pubs with cast-iron verandas, a stout bank, two churches of
fferent religions, a golf course, a central bus and train station, stockyards,
service station and the inevitable used-car lot. As you drive, you will
ncounter herds of cattle and flocks of sheep being escorted along by a
andful of genuine stockmen (cowboys). If you stop the car (and you may
ave to if the animals are on the road), these cowboys will be only too glad
o have a chat with you. At **Glen Innes** (62 mi/100 km north of Armidale)
ou turn east and join up with the Pacific Highway at **Grafton,** before
eading for the Gold Coast in Queensland (see p. 85).

Accommodation and food
Country pubs in this region are very hospitable and the food is first-rate.

In Cessnock:
▲▲ **Cumberland Motor Inn,** 57 Cumberland St. Tel: (049) 90 6633.
29 rooms.

In Tamworth:
▲ **Good Companions Hotel,** 9 Brisbane St. Tel: (067) 66 2850.

In Armidale:
▲ **Royal Hotel,** corner of Marsh and Beardy Sts. Tel: (067) 72 2259.
18 rooms.

In Grafton:
▲▲ **Camden Lodge,** 17 Villiers St. Tel: (066) 42 1822. 29 rooms,
1 suite.

THE PACIFIC HIGHWAY

ne coast and the magnificent New South Wales beaches which border the
acific Highway will appeal to the visitor in search of peace and quiet, as
ey have not been exploited to the same extent as the Gold Coast (see
85). The first of the resort towns south of the Gold Coast is **Port
acquarie,** with a marine and dolphin park (King Neptune Reserve) as well
s the Sea Acres Sanctuary, a 741-acre/300-ha wildlife reserve. The hard-
ore surfing fraternity which scorns Surfers Paradise likes to gather near
offs Harbour (363 mi/580 km north of Sydney), remarkable not only for
s surf but also for its 33-ft/10-m high Big Banana (you can visit a banana
antation and sample banana dishes of all kinds from 8:30am to 5:30pm,
ee of charge). The best surf in the area is to be enjoyed at **Byron Bay**★★
25 mi/840 km), which also has a nature sanctuary, The Everglades,
mous for its water lilies.

ne hinterland, in the hills of the Great Dividing Range, enjoys a perfect
icroclimate. This region (particularly around the town of **Bellingen**★★,
56 mi/570 km north of Sydney) has become home to writers, artists and
tired luminaries. It's easy to see why.

Accommodation
There are numerous hotels and motels along the Pacific Highway. A
few recommendations:

In Port Macquarie
▲▲ **Country Comfort,** corner of Buller and Hollingwood Sts.
Tel: (065) 83 2955. 60 rooms.

In Coffs Harbour
▲▲ **Zebra Coffs Harbour,** 27 Grafton St. Tel: (066) 52 1588.
46 rooms.

In Byron Bay

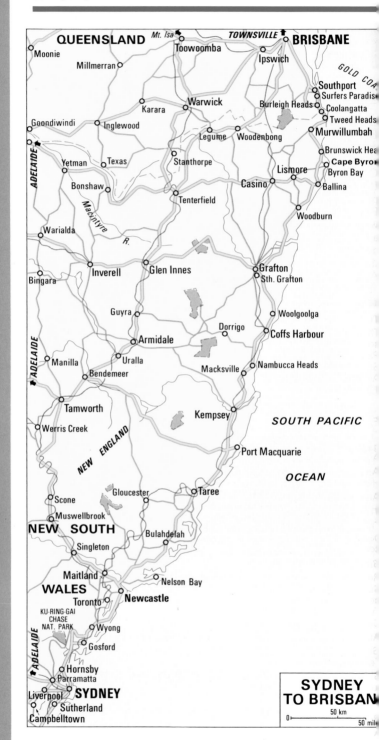

QUEENSLAND   Mt. Isa   TOWNSVILLE   BRISBANE
Moonie
Millmerran
Toowoomba
Ipswich
GOLD COA
Warwick
Karara
Southport
Surfers Paradis
Burleigh Heads   Coolangatta
Tweed Heads
Goondiwindi   Inglewood
Legume   Woodenbong
Murwillumbah
Yetman   Texas
Stanthorpe
Brunswick Hea
Cape Byro
Lismore   Byron Bay
Casino
Ballina
Bonshaw
Tenterfield
Woodburn
Warialda
Mackintyre R.
Inverell   Glen Innes
Grafton
Sth. Grafton
Bingara
Guyra
Woolgoolga
Dorrigo   Coffs Harbour
Armidale
Manilla   Uralla
Macksville   Nambucca Heads
Bendemeer
Tamworth
Kempsey
SOUTH PACIFIC
Werris Creek
NEW ENGLAND
Port Macquarie
OCEAN
Gloucester   Taree
Scone
Muswellbrook
NEW   SOUTH   Bulahdelah
Singleton
Maitland
Nelson Bay
WALES
Toronto   Newcastle
KU-RING-GAI
CHASE
NAT. PARK   Wyong
Gosford
Hornsby
Parramatta
Liverpool   SYDNEY
Sutherland
Campbelltown
ADELAIDE
ADELAIDE
ADELAIDE

SYDNEY
TO BRISBAN
0 ——— 50 km
50 mile

▲▲ **Byron Motor Lodge,** corner of Lawson and Butler Sts. Tel: (066) 85 6522. 14 rooms, 2 suites.
In Bellingen
▲▲ **Bellinger Valley Inn,** Dorrigo Rd. Tel: (066) 55 1599. 20 rooms.

THE GOLD COAST

To the European or American tourist familiar with the Costa Brava, the Costa Smeralda or Hawaii, a visit to Surfers Paradise may seem superfluous. The Gold Coast is deliberately and unashamedly commercial, popular and fairly crowded. In a sense, the Gold Coast, even more than Canberra, is the capital of Australia. It is as anarchic and overpopulated as the federal capital is carefully planned, bureaucratic, distinguished and unfrequented. Surfers Paradise, an anti-Canberra, is the only place in Australia where you will find a real regional, social and cultural mix. It has close to half a million inhabitants at the height of the tourist season, and belongs no more to Queensland or New South Wales (although it straddles the border) than to any other state. The Gold Coast belongs to all Australia.

PRACTICAL INFORMATION

Telephone area code: 075.

The Gold Coast stretches over 20 mi/32 km, from Southport, 44 mi/70 km south of Brisbane, to Tweed Heads, 560 mi/900 km north of Sydney on the Pacific Ocean (see map p. 84). The best-known beach on the coast, Surfers Paradise, is situated 6 mi/10 km south of Southport. Coolangatta Airport, which serves the border and the Queensland coast, is located 12 mi/20 km south of Surfers.

Access

Plane

There are direct **Australian Airlines** and **Ansett** flights between Coolangatta and Brisbane, Adelaide, Melbourne and Launceston in Tasmania. Airport bus to Surfers Paradise.

Ansett, Boundary St., Coolangatta, or Cosmopolitan Centre, Gold Coast Highway. Tel: 31 8100.

Australian Airlines, 30 Cavill Ave., Surfers Paradise. Tel: 38 1066.

Train

The daily *Gold Coast Express* deposits Sydney passengers at Murwillumbah (17-hour trip), 19 mi/30 km south of Coolangatta. A bus service connects with the coast.

Bus

Regular and frequent service to and from Brisbane (1 hour 30 min. to Surfers Paradise, 2 hours to Tweed Heads). The bus stops at all the beaches along the Pacific Highway between Southport and Coolangatta-Tweed Heads. Daily Sydney-Brisbane bus service passes through the Gold Coast, stopping at Coolangatta, Surfers and Southport (15 hours).

Ansett-Pioneer, Haulan St., Surfers Paradise. Tel: 226 1184.

Greyhound, Greyhound Terminal, Cavill Park Building, Surfers Paradise. Tel: 38 8344.

Skennars (local company only), Griffith St., Coolangatta. Tel: 36 2574. Also runs from **Islander Motel,** Surfers Paradise. Tel: 38 9944.

Getting around the Gold Coast

Bus

A local bus service with the imaginative name of *Surfside Busline* operates

5am to midnight between Coolangatta and Southport. Tel: 36 2449

Car rental

Avis, 3156 Gold Coast Highway, Surfers Paradise. Tel: 39 9388.

Budget, 24 Orchid Ave., Surfers Paradise. Tel: 36 1344.

Hertz, 3108 Gold Coast Highway, Surfers Paradise. Tel: 38 5366.

Holiday Mokes, corner of the Esplanade and Cavill Ave., Surfers Paradise. Tel: 38 3365.

Taxis

Regent Taxis. Tel: 32 8000.

Taxi Service. Tel: 36 1144.

Useful addresses

Tourist information

Queensland Government Travel Centre, 38-40 Cavill Ave., Surfers Paradise. Tel: 38 5988.

Accommodation

As tourist capital of Australia, the Gold Coast offers over 120 hotels, motels and assorted residences with prosaic names straight out of a pulp novel: Blue Skies, El Mirador, High Seas, Shelley Lodge, Bay Mist and the like. During the tourist season (over Christmas) and in winter (July to August), these hotels attract thousands of frozen southerners from Sydney and Melbourne. At these times of the year it is best to make reservations in advance. Because of the intense competition for guests, particularly in the low season (the Coast never closes), the prices at inexpensive hotels are quite affordable, especially at hotels outside Surfers.

International-standard and first-class hotels

These include the famous 30-storey hotels which give Surfers Paradise its mini-Miami character. Though good taste may be somewhat lacking at some of these establishments, they offer superb comfort, the beach starts literally at their doorstep and they are not very expensive.

▲▲▲▲ **Apollo Quality Inn,** The Esplanade, Surfers Paradise. Tel: 39 0099. Motel. 40 rooms and 80 suites on 22 floors.

▲▲▲▲ **Chateau Quality Inn,** The Esplanade, Surfers Paradise. Tel: 38 1022. Motel. 36 rooms, 108 suites.

▲▲▲▲ **Conrad International and Jupiters Casino,** Gold Coast Highway, Broadbeach. Tel: 92 1133. 622 rooms, 32 suites. Casino with floor shows (seating for 1100). Eat your heart out Las Vegas!

▲▲▲▲ **Holiday Inn,** 22 View Ave., Surfers Paradise. Tel: 22 1066. 400 rooms. American-style comfort.

▲▲▲▲ **Iluka Quality Inn,** The Esplanade, Surfers Paradise. Tel: 39 9155. Motel. 32 rooms, 80 suites.

▲▲▲ **Equinox Sun Resort,** 348 Main Beach Parade, Surfers Paradise. Tel: 38 3288. 149 rooms.

▲▲▲ **Islander Quality Inn,** Beach Rd., Surfers Paradise. Tel: 38 8000. Motel. 99 rooms, 50 suites.

▲▲▲ **The Sands,** The Esplanade, Surfers Paradise. Tel: 39 8433. 82 rooms.

Moderately priced and inexpensive hotels

The choice is enormous and the further from Surfers Paradise they are the cheaper they get.

▲▲ **Hi-Ho Holiday Homestead,** 2 Queensland Ave, Broadbeach. Tel: 38 2777. 33 rooms.

▲▲ **Sea Horse Hotel,** 2309 Gold Coast Highway, Mermaid Beach. Tel: 527 999. 19 rooms.

▲▲ **Southport Motor Inn,** 2 Barney St, Southport. Tel: 32 7922. 38 rooms, 26 suites.

▲ **Bombora Holiday Lodge,** Dutton St., Coolangatta. Tel: 36 1888. 48 rooms.

▲ **The Hub Apartments,** 21 Cavill Ave, Surfers Paradise. Tel: 31 5559.

▲ **Pihroch Holiday Flats,** 2112 Gold Coast Highway, Miami. Tel: 35 5994.

Food

Like all seaside resorts in the world, the Gold Coast offers plenty of places to eat, although 'restaurant' may not always be the appropriate term for these establishments. During the day, and between dips in the ocean, you can pick up a hamburger or pizza. **McDonald's** and **Pizza Hut,** however, are not the only fast-food outlets. There are lots of other eateries along the Gold Coast Highway or Cavill Ave., and the food is often excellent. In the evening, after the beach, you can 'dress up'. In most restaurants, dressing up means not wearing 'shorts, T-shirts or sandals (flip-flops)'. You can eat Chinese, Italian, French or Mexican food in one of the many restaurants along the coast. The cuisine is acceptable and the atmosphere pleasant but prices are somewhat high.

French

Marie La Rose, Centre Arcade, Gold Coast Highway. Tel: 39 8741.

Indian

Tandoori Taj, 3100 Gold Coast Highway, Surfers Paradise. Tel: 39 9433.

Italian

Danny's, Monte Carlo Building, 39 Orchid Ave., Surfers Paradise. Tel: 38 0311.

Mexican

Mexican Kitchen, 3094 Gold Coast Highway, Surfers Paradise. Tel: 38 4919. BYO.

Oriental

Chinese

Tein Loong, 57 Cavill Ave., Surfers Paradise. Tel: 31 5129.

Japanese

Shogun, 90 Bundall Rd., Surfers Paradise. Tel: 38 2872.

Seafood

Oskar's, Greenmount Beach, Marine Parade, Coolangatta. Tel: 36 4621. The undisputed best address on the coast.

'Trendy'

Trickett Street Brasserie, corner of Trickett St. and the Gold Coast Highway, Surfers Paradise. Tel: 38 0400.

With a view

For a little relief from the coastal heat, a pleasant restaurant in the hills overlooking the coast, with homestyle cooking is the **Bungunya,** 160 Long Rd., Eagle Heights, Tamborine Mountain. Tel: 45 1044.

Sports

The Gold Coast is also the ideal place for indulging in your favourite sports, among them:

Boating

Max Brown Sailboards. Tel: 32 7722.

Bob Legg Yachts. Tel: 39 4433.

Haddon's Hire Boats. Tel: 57 1796.

Go-kart racing

Le Mans, Pacific Highway, Coomera North. Tel: 46 6566.

Go-Kart Hire, Nerang-Broadbeach Rd., Carrara. Tel: 58 3959.

Golf

Golfers Paradise, corner of Market St. and Nerang-Broadbeach Rd. Carrara. Tel: 52 6445.

Horseback riding

Gibson's Riding Ranch, Tallebudgera Dam Rd., Burleigh Heads Tel: 33 8159.

Pubs and nightlife

The Gold Coast's reputation within Australia has much to do with its lively nightlife. Indeed, this is the only part of suburban Australia which, at least during the tourist season, does *not* close after midnight. The discos are crowded until the early hours of the morning. Young men and women cement the bonds of future friendships on the beach in the morning, in the great Australian tradition of 'boy meets girl', around a pack of ice-cold beer.

Selected addresses

Bombay Rock, corner of Ferny and Cavill Aves., Surfers Paradise Tel: 50 2400. Disco and rock.

Clancy's, Beach Rd., Surfers Paradise. Tel: 38 0790. Disco and rock.

Conrad International Hotel and Jupiters Casino, Gold Coast Highway Broadbeach. Tel: 92 1133. Open 24 hours a day.

Flashez, 3030 Gold Coast Highway, Surfers Paradise. Tel: 38 0790. Disco floor shows.

Lone Star Tavern, corner of Sunshine Blvd. and Markeri St., Mermaid Waters. Tel: 52 2500. Disco.

Melba's on the Park, 46 Cavill Ave., Surfers Paradise. Tel: 38 7411 Nightclub.

Penthouse Nightclub, Orchid Ave., Surfers Paradise. Tel: 39 0289 Restaurants and disco on four levels.

The Seagulls (Rugby football club), Gollan Drive, West Tweed Heads Tel: 36 8433. Restaurants, gambling, floor shows, rock, disco.

Twains International, The Mark Building, Orchid Ave., Surfers Paradise Tel: 38 5000. Restaurant, bar, floor shows.

Night tours

One convenient way of doing the nightly rounds of the coast, without missing any of its attractions, and of meeting the under-30s is with a 'Night Tour'. The first two tours listed below are aboard double-decker buses, the third aboard a minibus.

Buck Rogers Nite Tours. Tel: 30 5908.

Bill Rawle Night Tours. Tel: 31 5447.

Good Time Tours. Tel: 50 1455.

▬ WHAT TO SEE

The Gold Coast is 19 mi/30 km of white sand, waves rolling in from the Pacific and sunshine on tap. The famous Queensland Golden Girls are bronzed to perfection and the guys are pictures of fitness. Beware of the surf: there's nothing 'pacific' about it and the safest place to bathe is between the flags on patrolled beaches. For those in search of a family vacation, the Gold Coast also provides a number of attractions.

A surfer's paradise.

Excursions

Cades County Wet 'n' Wild, Pacific Highway, Oxenford. Tel: 53 2277. Australia's only wave pool, water slides, etc.

Currumbin Sanctuary, Gold Coast Highway, Currumbin. Tel: 34 1266. Magnificent animal sanctuary, famous for its parrots and budgerigars. A similar attraction is **Bird Gardens,** Creek Rd., Currumbin. Tel: 33 0208.

Dreamworld, Pacific Highway, Coomera. Tel: 53 1133. Disney-style amusement park.

Fisherman's Wharf, Seaworld Drive, The Spit. Tel: 32 7944. Inspired by the shopping centre of the same name in San Francisco, but slightly more down-market. Boutiques, restaurants, live entertainment.

Magic Mountain, Gold Coast Highway, Nobby's Beach. Tel: 52 2333. Almost surrealistic replica of a 'magic' mountain castle. Various attractions.

Sea World*, The Spit, Main Beach. Tel: 32 1055. An artificial lake with trained porpoises, savage sharks (including the skeleton of an enormous white shark), tropical fish, various live shows, amusement park, etc.

Wild Waters, 3808 Pacific Highway, Logan City. Tel: 209 7689. Like Cades County but a little smaller.

Flying tour

Why not take the flight of your life in a *Tiger Moth,* an open-cockpit biplane from 1942? The pilot, Bruce McGarvie, a retired Melbourne businessman, will almost touch the tops of the Surfers Paradise skyscrapers with his wing-tips and, best of all, will perform some aerobatics which will literally take your breath away.

Bruce McGarvie, **Tiger Moth Joy Rides,** PO Box 224, Broadbeach. Tel: 38 9083.

Cruises

To discover another side of the Gold Coast, take a trip on a cruiser on the lagoon at Surfers Paradise. Surfers actually owes its success to the **Nerang**

River which flows parallel to Surfers about 0.3 mi/0.5 km from the coast before turning east again at Southport on the southern side of Moreton Bay. The lagoon is home to the Gold Coast residential areas and accentuates even more the resemblance with Miami Beach. From the deck of the *Island Adventurer,* with a plastic glass of Wynns Black Label Champagne in your hand, you'll discover the *ultima Thule* of Australian suburbia: brick houses with patios costing as much as A$ 1 million. Impeccably manicured lawns planted with groves of mango trees, bread fruits and bougainvilleas slope down to the eternally blue waters of the Nerang. Supermarkets can only be reached by boat, windsurfer, outboard motorboat, yacht or priceless cabin-cruiser moored in front of the stars' mansions. Your hostess on the cruise will reel off names totally unknown outside Queensland. For many Australians, a house on the lagoon at Surfers Paradise is the ultimate reward at the end of their working lives. One can see their point.

Champagne Breakfast Cruise. Tel: 39 1355.

Chevron Princess Cruises. Tel: 39 9833.

Sir Bruce Cruises. Tel: 32 5031.

Shangri-La Cruises. Tel: 38 1444.

BRISBANE

Brisbane is the greenest city in Australia: covered with the tropical green of palm trees, bougainvilleas and frangipanis in the only large centre of population north of the 25th parallel (about the level of Miami in the Northern Hemisphere). The air is humid and warm and the mist rising from the hills in the evening gives the city a distinctly Asian character.

Brisbane is also the only state capital which is not located directly on the sea. Instead, it lies along the Brisbane River, 25 mi/40 km from its mouth on the Pacific Ocean. In 1824, the British government authorized the Governor of New South Wales, Sir Thomas Brisbane, to establish a penal settlement for 'the most hardened criminals' at Moreton Bay on a river which had recently been discovered 625 mi/1000 km north of Sydney. The river and a new settlement established upstream in 1825 soon adopted the name of the governor. In 1839, the penal settlement was closed and in 1859 Queensland separated from New South Wales and made Brisbane its capital. Today, with over one million inhabitants, Brisbane is the most densely populated of the 'small' capital cities and its city council administers one of the largest municipalities in the world. Queensland's immense natural riches, its climate—mild winters, and summers which, while humid, never reach the extreme temperatures of Melbourne or Adelaide—and its quietly dynamic lifestyle act as a magnet, attracting large numbers of southerners each year to move or invest there.

Civilized, urbane and confident in its future, Brisbane is potentially the most attractive state capital in the Commonwealth from the tourist viewpoint. Yet it is only in recent years that the city has made any real effort to attract tourists passing through on their way to the Great Barrier Reef or Surfers Paradise. The city is far from lacking in charm and could well rank just behind Sydney in terms of Australian urban success.

■■■ *PRACTICAL INFORMATION*

Telephone area code: 07.

Access

Plane

Numerous airlines fly direct to Brisbane from Europe, the Pacific and the United States. There are also direct **Ansett/Australian Airlines** flights to and from Darwin (3 hours 45 min.), Mt. Isa (2 hours 15 min.), Townsville (1 hour 35 min.), Alice Springs (2 hours 45 min.), Sydney (1 hour 15 min.) and Melbourne (1 hour 50 min.). Connecting flights are also available between Brisbane and Adelaide, Perth and other urban centres.

Ansett, 16 Ann St., City. Tel: 226 1111.

Australian Airlines, 247 Adelaide St., City. Tel: 223 3333.

East-West Airlines, corner Edward and Elizabeth Sts., City. Tel: 229 0455.

Connections with regional centres, especially the Great Barrier Reef, can be made through **Australian Airlines, Ansett, Air Queensland** (MIM House, 160 Ann St., City. Tel: 229 1311), and **Barrier Reef Airways** (Tel: 268 6255).

Skennars Airport Commuter Service (Tel: 268 5084) runs a regular bus service from Brisbane Airport to the city.

Train

Brisbane and the entire northern Queensland coast are linked to the enormous Australian railway network. The *Brisbane Express* runs daily between Brisbane and Sydney (16 hours). Further north, the *Sunlander* runs between Brisbane and Cairns six times a week (37 hours).

Queensland Railways, 305 Edward St., City. Tel: 225 0211. Tickets are also available from **Railways city booking office,** 208 Adelaide St., City. Tel: 225 0211.

Bus

Over the distances involved, there is little difference in price between the 2nd-class train fare (not including bed) and the bus fare (the bus is faster).

To/from Cairns: 727 mi/1770 km, 27 hours.
To/from Darwin via Mt. Isa: 2498 mi/4020 km, 56 hours plus connections.
To/from Sydney: 627 mi/1010 km, 17 hours.
To/from Melbourne via Dubbo: 1255 mi/2020 km, 30 hours.
To/from Adelaide via Wagga Wagga: 1268 mi/2040 km, 36 hours; connections to Perth, Alice Springs and Darwin.
To/from the Gold Coast (Surfers Paradise): more or less hourly bus service, 50 mi/80 km, slightly less than 2 hours.

Skennars, 22 Barry Parade, City. Tel: 832 1148.

Greyhound, 96 Victoria St., West End. Tel: 240 9333.

Ansett-Pioneer, Roman St., Coach Terminal. Tel: 846 3633.

Car

To/from Sydney (625 mi/1000 km), see map p. 84.
If you're coming from Sydney to Brisbane, you have the choice of two routes: coastal Highway No 1 (Pacific Highway) or inland Highway No 15 (New England Highway). These routes are detailed on pp. 82-83, in the section 'Sydney to Brisbane'.

To/from Melbourne (1060 mi/1700 km), see map pp. 118-119.
From Melbourne, take Highway No 31 (Hume Highway) as far as Seymour (62 mi/99 km north of Melbourne), then Highway No 39 (Newell Highway). You will cross the Sturt Highway from Adelaide at Narrandera (278 mi/445 km from Melbourne). Continue along the Newell Highway to Goondiwindi. From there you can take Highway No 42 (Cunningham Highway) to Brisbane. At Coonabarabran, 44 mi/70 km north of Dubbo, you can also follow Highway No 34 to link up with Highway No 15 (New England Highway) at Tamworth.

To/from Adelaide (1245 mi/1992 km), see map pp. 158-159.
All the routes pass through the richest and most populated areas of south-eastern Australia. The countryside hardly changes from east to west: low rounded hills, eucalypt forests, sheep or cattle pastures, small bush towns with 19th-century pubs. Further north along the coast, the vegetation soon becomes tropical. These routes are detailed on pp. 160-161, in the section 'Adelaide and South Australia'.

To/from the Great Barrier Reef and the north
Highway No 1 follows the coast 1117 mi/1787 km north to Cairns and beyond. As you journey north, you will pass through Bundaberg (211 mi/338 km from Brisbane), famous for its rum, before reaching Gladstone (378 mi/605 km), the gateway to the Great Barrier Reef and Heron Island (see 'The Great Barrier Reef' p. 99). Rockhampton (461 mi/738 km) will be your next stop and from there you can get to Great Keppel Island. Yeppoon, 25 mi/40 km north of Rockhampton, has recently become the most modern tourist resort on the Queensland coast, thanks to investment by a Japanese millionaire in the Iwasaki Resort. From Mackay (702 mi/1123 km), you can reach Lindeman and Brampton islands, and from Proserpine (783 mi/1252 km), Shute Harbour and the Whitsunday Group of islands. Townsville (949 mi/1518 km) is the capital of Northern Queensland and the access point for Magnetic and Orpheus islands. From Cardwell (1055 mi/1688 km) you can get to Hinchinbrook Island and at Tully (1084 mi/1735 km) you can choose between taking a boat to Dunk Island or continuing on to Cairns (1117 mi/1787 km) and taking a plane. The Cape York Peninsula stretches beyond Cairns, its most northerly point, which faces New Guinea, being 531 mi/850 km further on. The road above Cairns is better suited to four-wheel-drive vehicles.

Tourism is not the only resource that the Coral Sea coast from Brisbane to Cairns has to offer. Tropical agriculture (sugar cane and tropical fruits), cattle breeding, coal and minerals from the interior have turned the coast's major ports into expanding towns, employing more than half the state's population, an event unique in Australia. The development of the north has even led to a lively campaign in support of an independent state of North Queensland within the Commonwealth.

To/from Darwin (2470 mi/3950 km).
Driving from Brisbane to Darwin, you have a choice, at least until Mt. Isa, of two routes: Brisbane - Townsville - Mt. Isa, or Brisbane - Charleville - Longreach - Mt. Isa. The section from Mt. Isa to Darwin is covered on p. 188.

Brisbane - Mt. Isa via Townsville (1500 mi/2400 km along the coast): from Townsville the asphalt road (Highway No 78) passes through Charters Towers, Highenden, Julia Creek and Cloncurry.

Brisbane - Mt. Isa via Charleville and Longreach (1190 mi/1900 km). From Brisbane you take Highway No 54 (Warrego Highway) to Charleville, then Highway No 71 (Landsborough Highway) to Cloncurry, where you follow Highway No 78 (Flinders Highway) into Mt. Isa. This is an inland route through semi-desert and desert areas requiring that adequate safety precautions be taken (vehicle in good condition, full tool kit, spare water and fuel). There are no problems finding food and fuel as far as Mt. Isa.

Getting around Brisbane

Car rental

Avis, 275 Wickham St., Fortitude Valley. Tel: 52 9111.

Budget, corner of St. Paul's Terrace and Baxter St., Fortitude Valley. Tel: 52 0151.

Hertz, 55 Charlotte St., City. Tel: 221 6166.

Letz, 40 Lamington Ave., Eagle Farm. Tel: 268 5657.

Taxis

Ascot Taxi Service. Tel: 831 3000.

Black & White. Tel: 229 1000.

Yellow Cabs. Tel: 391 0191.

Useful addresses

Tourist information

Public transport information. Tel: 225 4444.

Queensland Government Travel Centre, 196 Adelaide St., City. Tel: 229 6900.

Consulates

British Consulate-General, 193 North Quay, City. Tel: 221 4933.

United States Consulate, 383 Wickham Terrace, City. Tel: 839 8955.

Post office

General Post Office (GPO), 261 Queens St., City. Tel: 224 1202.

Automobile club

Royal Automobile Club of Queensland (RACQ), 190-194 Edward St., City. Tel: 253 2444.

Accommodation

International-standard hotels

▲▲▲▲ **Crest International,** 106 Ann St., City. Tel: 221 7788. Centrally located, very luxurious, for business and tourist visitors. 230 rooms, 12 suites.

▲▲▲▲ **Hilton International,** Elizabeth St., City. Tel: 224 9740. Centrally located. 324 rooms, 14 suites.

▲▲▲▲ **Lennons Plaza,** 66 Queen St., City. Tel: 222 3222. One of Brisbane's highest city buildings. 120 rooms, 30 suites.

▲▲▲▲ **Sheraton,** 249 Turbot St., City. Tel: 835 3535. 414 rooms, 27 suites.

First-class hotels

▲▲▲ **Metropolitan Motor Inn,** corner of Leichhardt and Little Edward Sts., City. Tel: 221 6000. 50 rooms, 4 suites.

▲▲▲**Tower Mill Motor Inn,** 239 Wickham Terrace, City. Tel: 832 1421. Motel. Beautiful views. 69 rooms, 2 suites.

Moderately priced and inexpensive hotels

▲▲ **The Canberra,** Ann St., City. Tel: 32 0231.

▲▲ **Palace Guest House,** corner of Ann and Edward Sts., City. Tel: 229 3211. One of Australia's most spectacular hotel façades. Three storeys of wrought-iron verandas.

▲▲ **Parkview,** 128 Alice St., City. Tel: 31 2695. Motel.

▲▲ **Soho Club Motel,** 333 Wickham Terrace, City. Tel: 221 7722.

▲▲ **Wickham Terrace Motel,** 491 Wickham Terrace, City. Tel: 839 9611.

▲ **Brisbane Youth Hostel,** 15 Mitchell St., Kedron (5 mi/8 km from the city). Tel: 57 1245. 80 beds.

Food

Brisbane offers a variety of ingredients unequalled in Australia: meat from nearby farms, fish, scallops and shellfish from the river and coast, tropical fruit (paw-paws, mangos, avocados) from its gardens and plantations. The quality is first-rate, as is the preparation.

Elegant restaurants

Allegro, Central Station Plaza, City. Tel: 229 5550. European cuisine accompanied by chamber music.

Ardrossan Hall, 38 Brookes St., Bowen Hills. Tel: 52 7168. BYO. 1887 hotel transformed into a restaurant and art gallery.

Michael's, 164 Queen St., City. Tel: 229 4911. Excellent international cuisine, elegant surroundings, good cellar.

Rags, 25 Caxton St., Petrie Terrace, City. Tel: 369 4273. Post-nouvelle cuisine. Brisbane's most sophisticated address.

Ye Old Court House, Paxton St., Cleveland. Tel: 286 1386. BYO. Located 19 mi/30 km south-east of the city. Romantic setting beside Moreton Bay.

International cuisine with a view

Lennons Plazza Hotel, 66 Queen St., City. Tel: 222 3222. Smorgasbord in the Hibiscus Room on the 30th floor.

Ridge Motor Inn, 189 Leichhardt St., City. Tel: 221 5000. Magnificent restaurant.

Sheraton, 249 Turbot St., City. Tel: 835 3535. The Denisons' Room, top floor.

Chinese

Cathay, 222 Wickham St., Fortitude Valley. Tel: 52 2765. Just outside the city.

French

Baguette, 150 Racecourse Rd., Ascot. Tel: 268 6168. Elegant classic French cuisine in tropical surroundings.

La Grange, 303 Adelaide St., City. Tel: 221 5590. BYO.

Italian

Milano, 78 Queen St., City. Tel: 221 5972. Very elegant, music.

Mama Luigi's, 240 St. Pauls Terrace, Fortitude Valley. Tel: 52 2320. BYO. Very good and inexpensive.

Indian

Feroza's, 227 Given Terrace, Paddington. Tel: 369 3483. Southern Indian cuisine prepared by a Fijian chef. Delicious and inexpensive.

Mexican

Tortilla, 26 Elizabeth Arcade, City. Tel: 221 4416. Spanish-Mexican, unusual and good.

Seafood

Breakfast Creek Wharf, 192 Breakfast Creek Rd., Newstead. Tel: 52 2451. Seafood on the docks.

Gambaro's, 33 Caxton St., Petrie Terrace. Tel: 369 9500. BYO. Located in the fashionable Paddington-Red Hill area, Gambaro's offers the best mud crabs in Brisbane prepared by a family of fishermen who are equally skilled at cooking.

Markwell's Fishermen's Wharf, 237 Shore St., Cleveland Point. Tel: 286 2849. Seafood and a view over the bay. 22 mi/35 km from the city.

Special atmosphere

A pub famous for its cuisine and atmosphere is the **Breakfast Creek,** 2 Kingsford-Smith Drive, Albion. Tel: 262 5988. Situated 3 mi/5 km from the city. Barbecues in a beer garden shaded by mango trees, very pleasant.

Shopping

Brisbane boasts a mall (Queen St. Mall) and numerous shopping arcades and shopping centres. The large department stores are concentrated around Queen St. in the City and in the neighbouring suburb of Fortitude Valley.

Opals

Quilpie Opals, Lennons Plazza Building, 68 Queen St., City. Tel: 221 7369.

The Rock Shop, 193 Adelaide St., City. Tel: 229 0981.

Wool and sheepskins
Wool Exhibition Centre, Primac House, 103 Creek St., City. Tel: 223 1801.

Brisbane, long a cultural backwater, has recently made up for it with the establishment, on the Brisbane River's south bank, of the **Queensland Cultural Centre***. The Centre contains an art gallery (collections and exhibitions), several auditoria (ballet, opera, theatre, etc.), restaurants, the **Queensland Museum** and the **State Library.** For information, phone 240 7200 (Cultural Centre) or 240 6400 (performances).

Expo 88, held on the south bank of the river, right next to the Cultural Centre, was designed to accommodate some 8 million visitors between April 30 and October 30, 1988. The theme of the international exhibition: 'Leisure in the age of technology'.

Festivals
The annual **Festival of Brisbane** *(Warana Festival)* is a folkloric festival which takes place each year in late September/early October.

Queenslanders quench their thirsts by alternating glasses of cold *XXXX* (Four-X) beer with nips of *Bundaberg Rum.* Most pub buildings open out onto the balminess of the evening and cater to a varied crowd of patrons. Among them are the **Breakfast Creek** (see 'Food') and the **Paddington** (Given Terrace, Paddington). Also in Paddington are the **Caxton** and the **Prince Alfred,** both decidedly working-class, i.e., not at all tourist oriented. There are rather more sophisticated bars in the **New York Hotel** (Queen St., City) and the **Crest.** Two very popular Victorian pubs beside the Brisbane River are the **Regatta** (Coronation Drive) and the **Royal Exchange** (High St.) in Toowong, 1.3 mi/2 km from the city.

Music
If you'd like a drink accompanied by music, try the **Melbourne Hotel** (Browning St., West End, south of the river) for jazz. The **Hacienda** (394 Brunswick Rd.), the **Waterloo** (Commercial Rd.) and **Bonaparte's** (St. Pauls Terrace), all just outside the city in Fortitude Valley, have good rock music. Programs are listed in the morning *Courier Mail* or the *Telegraph,* an evening newspaper totally devoid of news. Queensland pubs are open 10am to 11pm, Mon. to Sat. and varying hours on Sun.

Dancing
Underground, corner of Hale and Caxton Sts., Paddington. Tel: 369 2633.

Sibyls, 383 Adelaide St., City. Tel: 229 2355.

New York Hotel, 69 Queen St., City. Tel: 221 0605.

Images, 24th floor, SGIO Building, City. Tel: 221 6261. Elegant, with a revolving dance floor.

▬▬ GETTING TO KNOW BRISBANE

The 37 hills on which Brisbane is built make Queensland's capital a city in which you can still breathe fresh air. The city is most typically represented by the suburb of **Paddington,** 20 minutes on foot from the city centre.

Paddington**
Start your stroll by crossing **Albert Park,** on the north-west side of the city, down to the train line. The park is shaped like a huge arena. Its slopes are covered in an immaculate grass lawn and are planted with huge clusters of bougainvilleas, hibiscus, frangipanis, palms and other species guaranteed to bring joy to the heart of tropical botanists. Follow **College Road** to the west and cross the bridge spanning the railway line. From there you will have a first-class view of the city. Once on the other side of the bridge, you are in Paddington.

Every hilly street of this inner suburb (the first residential district around the city) contains real treasures of typical Queensland colonial architecture. Brisbane has none of the brick or stone cottages, or wrought-iron terraces found in southern cities. They would not have been suited to the humid heat of tropical summers or the tornadoes that batter the city during the wet season. Brisbane suburbs are the domain of wooden houses perched on stilts and topped with corrugated-iron roofs.

The variations on this classic theme of British colonial architecture are endless. They may be elegant and elaborate, with wide verandas protected from the sun by delicate wooden trellises or slatted blinds. They may have a turret or attic surmounted by a neo-Muscovite metal cupola, surrounded by a gallery with exotic wrought-iron balcony, or be buried under the branches of frangipanis or in the shade of centuries-old mango trees. The various styles apply equally to the terrace houses lined up along the wide avenues. More modest under their triangular façades, they are often perched on the side of a hill, allowing air to circulate under their floors and cool them by a few degrees.

Under the houses, the 'cellars' formed by the stilts harbour unbelievable jumbles of split mattresses, rusty refrigerators and forgotten toys. The more 'dignified' families hide them with an additional skirt of wooden trellis, giving the house the distinguished air of a Victorian beauty clad in a crinoline. Wooden stairs lead from the front gate at street level to the sill of the usually open doorway. Behind it stretches a central corridor which divides the house and ends in a veranda on the far side. There, the two or three armchairs, which might well be screwed to the wooden floor, are reminiscent of those on the poopdeck of a ship thrusting into the wind. In the evening cool, Brisbanites can be found sitting on the top step of their stairs, glass in hand, watching the sun illuminate the last fires of a tropical sunset, while the fruit-bats go through their ballet routine against a backdrop of gilt-edged grey clouds.

Take **Ennogera Terrace** back to the city. It follows the crest of the hill and provides a splendid view of Brisbane, with some of its most beautiful elevated houses in the foreground. The **Brisbane River,** crossed by a half dozen bridges inspired by the coat-hanger style of Sydney Harbour Bridge, winds majestically around the city, through a patchwork of proud concrete and glass skyscrapers, and solid stone Victorian buildings. Huge cargo ships anchored next to the roadway load their holds with coal, sugar and meat, the products that are Queensland's answer to gold.

You return to the city via **Latrobe Terrace, Given Terrace, Caxton St.** and **Petrie Terrace.** These are the busiest and most commercial of Paddington's arteries. There you will find the shops, restaurants, galleries and pubs of this charming area.

WHAT TO SEE

Brisbane City Hall

King George Square, City. Tel: 225 4360. *Open Mon. to Fri. 9.30am to 4pm.*
A monumental 1930s building with a magnificent view of the city from its rooftop observation platform.

Miegunyah Folk Museum

31 Jordan St., Bowen Hills. *Open Tues., Wed. and weekends 10.30am to 3pm.*
A small museum dedicated to traditional local life, established in a magnificent stilt house.

Newstead House*

Breakfast Creek Rd., Newstead. *Open Mon. to Thurs. 11am to 3pm and Sun. 2pm to 5pm.*
The oldest house in Brisbane, restored as a museum.

Queensland Art Gallery

Queensland Cultural Centre, South Bank, City. Tel: 240 7303. *Open daily 10am to 5pm, Wed. 10am to 8pm.*
Australian (period and modern) and European art.

Queensland Museum

Queensland Cultural Centre, South Bank, City. Tel: 240 7555. *Open Mon to Sat. 10am to 4.45pm, Sun. 2pm to 5pm.*
A vast range of displays relating to anthropology, geology, zoology, history and technology.

Sir Thomas Brisbane Planetarium

Mt. Coot-tha Botanic Gardens. Tel. 377 5896. *Shows Wed. to Fri. 3.30pm and 7.30pm, Sat. 1.30pm, 3.30pm and 7.30pm, Sun. 1.30 and 3.30pm.*
Splendid view of the city and the largest planetarium in Australia (140 seats).

Zoological gardens

At **Bunya Park,** Bunya Rd., Eatons Hill (48 mi/77 km north of the city on Highway No 1. Tel: 264 1200) and **Lone Pine Koala Sanctuary*,** Jesmond Rd., Fig Tree Pocket (7 mi/11 km west of the city along the Centenary Highway or by ferry from Queens Wharf Rd., North Quay, City. Tel: 378 1366), you can pet koalas, wombats and kangaroos, and picnic beside the water.

THE GREAT BARRIER REEF
AND
NORTHERN QUEENSLAND

I t is no exaggeration to describe the Great Barrier Reef (see map p. 100), one of the most fabulous natural phenomena on earth, as the eighth wonder of the world. Stretching more than 1250 mi/2000 km along the coast of Queensland, from New Guinea to the Tropic of Capricorn, the reef offers the visitor unparalleled scenery, turquoise-blue waters, an underwater carpet of coral, exotic fish, birds, coconut palms and white sandy beaches—in short, everything we associate in our dreams with the tropics and the Pacific.

The Great Barrier Reef is also one of the wonders of the tourist world, thanks to first-rate facilities which combine luxury with careful integration into the natural environment. Ease of access to the reef's islands, by regular plane, helicopter or boat service from the towns on the mainland, and the very reasonable prices charged in the tourist resorts, make the Great Barrier Reef a most attractive destination for underwater sports fans, regardless of where they come from.

The reef's reputation as an international tourist attraction plays an important role in the ecological battle being fought with a number of exploration companies which covet its untapped petroleum reserves. Concerned at this threat to a marine ecosystem, as yet undisturbed, Australia has rallied international support and had the Great Barrier Reef included on the UNESCO World Heritage Listing.

WHAT IS THE GREAT BARRIER REEF?

Only to the north of Cairns does the reef form a continuous barrier. The remainder is composed of an intricate pattern of coral reefs, atolls and small islands separated by channels of varying depths. The outer edge of the reef drops vertically into the ocean to a depth of 4600 ft/1400 m near Cairns, while the inner edge, rarely more than 330 ft/100 m deep, slopes gradually down into the strip of water separating it from the mainland. The channel between the reef and the mainland grows narrower and shallower as it runs north. In 1770 Captain James Cook sailed the *Endeavour* fearlessly into this channel at its mouth near Rockhampton, little suspecting its true shape until he ran aground on a coral reef off Cooktown.

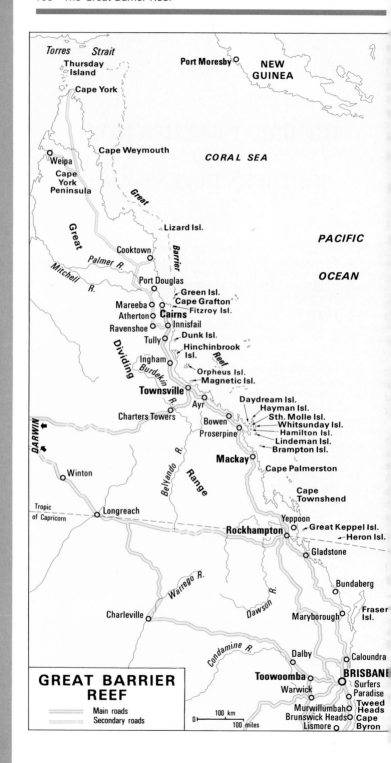

Torres   Strait
Thursday Island
Cape York
Port Moresby   NEW GUINEA

Weipa
Cape Weymouth
Cape York Peninsula

CORAL SEA

Great

Lizard Isl.

Great
Mitchell R.
Palmer R.
Cooktown
Barrier
Port Douglas
Green Isl.
Cape Grafton
Mareeba   Fitzroy Isl.
Atherton   Cairns
Ravenshoe   Innisfail
Tully   Dunk Isl.
Hinchinbrook Isl.
Ingham   Reef
Burdekin
Orpheus Isl.
Magnetic Isl.
Townsville
Ayr
Charters Towers
Bowen
Proserpine

PACIFIC

OCEAN

Dividing

Daydream Isl.
Hayman Isl.
Sth. Molle Isl.
Whitsunday Isl.
Hamilton Isl.
Lindeman Isl.
Brampton Isl.

Mackay
Cape Palmerston

Belyando R.
Range

Cape Townshend

DARWIN

Winton

Tropic of Capricorn
Longreach

Yeppoon   Great Keppel Isl.
Rockhampton   Heron Isl.
Gladstone

Warrego R.
Dawson R.

Bundaberg

Charleville
Maryborough
Fraser Isl.

Condamine R.
Dalby   Caloundra
Toowoomba   BRISBANE
Warwick   Surfers Paradise
Murwillumbah   Tweed Heads
Brunswick Heads   Cape
Lismore   Byron

GREAT BARRIER REEF

Main roads
Secondary roads

100 km
0
100 miles

The channel is scattered with over 600 islands of all sizes. The most beautiful of them have been extensively and successfully developed for tourism. Two of these developed islands, Green Island off Cairns and Heron Island off Rockhampton, are really cays (low coral islands). The other, higher, islands are actually the tops of earlier mountains which have been separated from the mainland. They may not have coral but their scenery and the comforts they offer are more than adequate for would-be Robinson Crusoes.

What is coral?

The reef has been formed over tens of thousands of years by billions of tiny marine polyps. These polyps are found all along the Australian coast between latitudes 10° and 25° south, where the water is a constant 63°F/18°C and quite shallow (about 150 ft/100 m)—ideal conditions for their development. To protect themselves, these polypes or corals secrete lime from their stomachs to form an outer skeleton. Depending on the species, the skeleton may grow from 0.5-4.5 in/1-10 cm per year. Corals emerge from their lime skeletons at night to feed, using their poisonous tentacles to 'fish' for passing plankton (this poison seems to be harmless to humans). Billions of skeletons have interwoven over countless years into gigantic underwater cathedrals which form the base of the coral reefs. A variety of algae living in the coral gives the reef its striking colours.

The reef is made of a series of coral platforms, atolls or cays ranging from tens to hundreds of yards in diameter. Most of the small islands barely rise above the surface of the ocean. Low tide unveils the rest of the reef which can stretch for hundreds of yards, intersected by a labyrinth of shallow channels.

The Great Barrier Reef can be explored on foot (tennis shoes or plastic sandals must be worn to protect the soles of your feet), in a glass-bottomed boat or by skin-diving. Its coral formations are as varied as they are spectacular: among them are impenetrable forests of antler corals; bushes of short, upright spikes; brownish, polished brain corals up to a yard across; tiny, delicate mushroom corals; fans, sponges, nodules and tentacles quivering in the clear water.

Fauna of the Great Barrier Reef

The reef is a real haven for the hundreds of birds, fish and shellfish which have always found food and shelter there. Beneath the sea the corals seem to exude strange, motionless creatures, half animal and half vegetable. There are blue and green tentacled anemones, red and black sea urchins with spines 11 in/30 cm long, and sea cucumbers, blackish, sausage-shaped animals which are prized by Chinese connoisseurs as aphrodisiacs. The crown-of-thorns starfish, the daily diet of which includes coral polyps, was a scourge of the reef in the 1970s but it seems recently to have been slowed in its destruction. It is thought that it may only attack the reef when its preferred foods, oysters and clams, have been overfished.

Firmly attached to the reef, giant clams can grow to a yard or so across; chances are small that they will hold divers prisoner in their blue and green lipped 'mouths', but it's best to be prudent and observe them from a distance. A number of the magnificent shellfish which enrapture collectors are quite able to defend themselves with poisoned barbs which cause local paralysis and excruciating pain; for this reason, be sure not to pick up living specimens.

Some sea creatures can pose serious problems for the unwary, among them sharks which sometimes come into coastal waters looking for easy prey, although no accidents have been reported in the reef area. Poisonous sea wasps, with their trailing, colourless tentacles, infest tropical Australian waters from December to March. Their sting can be fatal but they are not a major problem around Barrier Reef islands. The stonefish, however, is probably the most dangerous of all. An ugly creature, seemingly left over from prehistoric times, it can camouflage itself perfectly between clumps of coral. The 13 poisonous spines on its back can inflict a deadly sting—one more reason not to walk barefoot on the reef. Fortunately the stonefish is the only lethal species among the 1400 recorded in these waters.

The common names of some of the tiny tropical fish found here are more descriptive than a thousand scientific names: Moorish Idol, Red Emperor, Chinese Footballer, Sergeant Major, Orange Clown Fish, Fusilier, Blue Devil, Pigface, Convict Surgeonfish, etc. Other larger species, which come into coastal waters from the open sea to the delight of fishermen, include tuna, kingfish, and Australian and Spanish mackerel.

The southern part of the Great Barrier Reef is the domain of four species of turtles, the best known being the green turtle which migrates there to breed between September and March. Heron Island, one of the more developed reef islands, hosts between 500 and 700 each season. Weighing up to 450 lbs/200 kg, these green turtles can easily be observed when they come ashore between October and April to lay their eggs. After laboriously making their way up the beach, the turtles dig a hole 3 ft/1 m deep, lay from 50 to 200 eggs, fill the hole in again and return to the sea. After 10.5 weeks, the eggs hatch and the baby turtles make straight for the sea where crabs and sharks wait for those that have escaped the herons and gulls.

The reef is also a paradise for birds: noddies, terns, gulls, puffins, sea-eagles, gannets, frigate-birds and doves. Millions of them arrive to spend the northern winter (November to March) there and to breed.

■ PRACTICAL INFORMATION

Access

The more accessible areas of the Great Barrier Reef stretch from Gladstone to Cairns. The islands which have been developed for tourism are reached via 'gateways', access points on the mainland, by plane, helicopter or boat.

Other islands can be reached only by private boat. For the sake of simplicity, we have divided the mainland from south to north into the following four zones described on pp. 104-110:
— Gladstone to Great Keppel Island including Heron Island and Rockhampton.
— Mackay, Proserpine and Shute Harbour.
— The Whitsunday Island Group.

— Townsville to Cairns including Magnetic, Hinchinbrook, Orpheus, Dunk, Bedarra, Fitzroy, Green and Lizard islands.

All the towns along the coast are connected to Brisbane by Highway No 1, and by regular bus and train services. Gladstone, Rockhampton, Mackay, Proserpine, Townsville and Cairns are also connected by regular **Australian Airlines** or **Ansett** flights to Brisbane (and the rest of Australia). There are direct Ansett flights from Sydney and Brisbane to Hamilton Island (in the Whitsundays). Cairns has direct connections to Mt. Isa, Darwin and Papua New Guinea, as well as to the United States.

Accommodation and food

Accommodation on most Barrier Reef islands consists of a single resort. They are generally well appointed with numerous distractions and full dining facilities.

Useful addresses

Great Barrier Reef Marine Park Authority, PO Box 1379, Townsville, Qld 4810, publishes and distributes maps and other information concerning the area. Tel: (077) 71 2191.

Diving on the Great Barrier Reef

The reef is undoubtedly the experience of a lifetime for divers from all over the world, whether they are old hands attracted by the 3300 ft/1000 m depths on the outer edge of the reef, or just amateurs, happy enough to go snorkeling in the clear, warm waters of a shallow lagoon.

Warning: even in the best of conditions on the reef, deep water can be dangerous and divers should exercise extreme caution. At the resorts, the supervisors and diving instructors are very strict. Although a diving certificate is not compulsory, they will check your physical condition and experience before they let you depart, and may ask for a recent medical certificate or international diving certificate.

Equipment: The very strict Australian regulations forbid the use of certain kinds of cylinders that some American and British brands include. These cylinders cannot be refilled in Australia. You will have no problem renting approved equipment at any tourist resort or from the numerous diving specialists in towns on the coast. Spear-fishing is forbidden for divers equipped with air cylinders. Divers whose destination in Australia is the Great Barrier Reef are advised to contact the following organizations in advance:

Australian Underwater Federation, 24 Victoria St., New Lambton, NSW 2305, publishes a very complete guide to the Barrier Reef.

Great Barrier Reef Marine Park Authority, PO Box 1379, Townsville, Qld 4810. Tel: (077) 71 2191, issues all permits required for fishing and diving in the Marine Park area (around Heron Island).

National Parks and Wildlife Service, MLC Centre, 239 George St., Brisbane, QLD 4000. Tel: (07) 227 4111.

National Parks Ranger, Conway Ridge National Park, Shute Harbour, Qld 4802, issues permits for camping on uninhabited islands.

Numerous local companies offer diving instruction and diving cruises. The services range from equipment rental for a luxury cruise lasting several days, to a half-day's or day's diving instruction on one of the islands. Among such companies are: **Coral Sea Diving Services, Divemaster Charters, Reef Encounter, Reef Explorer, Downunder Dive and Sports** and **Whitsunday Dive Charters.** Information and reservations are available from Queensland tourist offices in Cairns or Townsville, and from the **Queensland Dive Tourism Association,** PO Box 180, Airlie Beach,

Qld 4802. Tel: (079) 46 6204. Some travel agents can also make these arrangements.

Underwater photography on the Great Barrier Reef

Underwater photography is an art in itself and requires all manner of special equipment. If your aim is merely to try out this art and to bring back some pretty photos, you will find that a watertight plastic bag (cheap!) will provide protection for your usual camera up to a depth of 10 ft/3 m. You can also use a bottom-of-the-range watertight camera. Models like the *Aquamatic* or *Minolta Weathermatic* use 110-size film, and are tough and inexpensive. If, on the other hand, you are a real underwater photography enthusiast and an especially good diver, see if you can buy (in Singapore for example) a *Nikonos* watertight and very sophisticated model (Nikon 24 × 36; interchangeable 15, 28, 35 and 80 mm lenses; non-reflex) or a *Fugica HDM*. Under water (and above it) use medium-speed film, such as *Kodachrome 64* or *Ektachrome 200*.

Warning: at depths greater than 30 ft/10 m, the water will filter out red from the spectrum. Even if your eye can compensate for this automatically, the dominant colour in your photos will be blue. A red filter will very effectively correct this problem if you open the lens halfway. Remember you need patience both underwater and when you see your films, at least until you have mastered speed, exposure and focus under the sea.

Sailing the Great Barrier Reef

Renting a boat locally, with or without crew, and going for a cruise of several days or even weeks through one of the most beautiful navigable regions on earth, is undoubtedy the best way of discovering the reef. Before you set out, read one of the sailing bibles for the area: *Cruising the Coral Coast* by Alan Lucas (Compass Publications, Sydney), or *The Yachtsman's Handbook to the Whitsunday Passage* (Whitsunday Yachting World). Yacht and boat rental firms include:

Australian Bareboat Charter, Shute Harbour Jetty, Shute Harbour, Qld 4802. Tel: local-call fee only (008) 07 5000.

Mandalay Sailing, Mandalay Road, Airlie Beach, Qld 4802. Tel: (079) 46 6679.

Queensland Yacht Charters, Shute Harbour Road, Shute Harbour, Qld 4802. Tel: local-call fee only (008) 07 5013.

Whitsunday Rent-A-Yacht, Harbour Ave., Shute Harbour, Qld 4802. Tel: local-call fee only (008) 07 5062.

Whitsunday Yachting World, Shute Harbour Jetty, Shute Harbour, Qld 4802. Tel: (079) 49 9202.

Finally, day or longer cruises are possible on quite large yachts, such as *Bacchus D, Weathers Field* and *Pegasus*. Departures are from Shute Harbour, information and rental available from the tourist office. Day cruises can also be made by launch or other motor vessels, enabling great distances to be covered quickly and in comfort.

▆▆ *GLADSTONE TO GREAT KEPPEL ISLAND*

Gladstone

Access: see general comments on access to the reef pp. 102-103.

Gladstone is situated 350 mi/562 km north of Brisbane. From Gladstone you can take a helicopter to Heron Island.

Useful addresses

Airlines

Ansett, 124 Goondoon St. Tel: (079) 72 2288.

Australian Airlines, 100 Goondoon St. Tel: (079) 72 3448.

Accommodation and food

▲▲▲ **Telford Gladstone Motor Inn,** corner of Goondoon and Yaroon Sts. Tel: (079) 72 1000. Restaurant.

▲▲ **Hi-Way Motel,** 74 Toolooa St. Tel: (079) 72 2811. Restaurant.

Heron Island

Heron Island is the most accessible and the best appointed of the reef's coral cays. It's a **National Park** of some 40 acres/16 ha, with a world-famous underwater research centre and a tourist resort capable of accommodating 220 guests. Diving equipment can be rented. The island's coral reefs can be reached on foot. Green turtles come to mate on the beaches between October and April. Its only drawback is its popularity.

Access

Helicopter from Gladstone (30 min.) **(Lloyds Helicopter Services).**

Boat from Gladstone (2.5 hrs).

Seaplane from Brisbane **(Barrier Reef Airways).**

Accommodation and food

▲▲ **Heron Island Resort,** via Gladstone, Qld 4680. Tel: (079) 78 1488. Restaurant. 22 rooms, 70 suites.

Rockhampton

Access: see general comments on access to the reef pp. 102–103.

Rockhampton is situated 413 mi/661 km north of Brisbane. With a population of 55,000 people, the dynamic and historical city of Rockhampton is the largest centre on Queensland's tropical coast. It is also the access point for the coastal tourist resorts (built with Japanese capital) at Yeppoon, 25 mi/40 km to the north, and for Great Keppel Island, where you can go by plane or boat.

Useful addresses

Tourist information

Queensland Government Travel Centre, 119 East St. Tel: (079) 27 8611.

Airlines

Ansett, 137 East St. Tel: (079) 31 0711.

Australian Airlines, 75 East St. Tel: (079) 31 0511.

Bus

Greyhound, 25 Denham St. Tel: (079) 27 7107.

Accommodation and food

▲▲▲ **Duthies Leichhardt,** corner of Bolsover and Denham Sts. Tel: (079) 27 6733. Restaurant. 127 rooms.

▲▲ **The Lodge,** 100 Gladstone Rd. Tel: (079) 27 3130.

Great Keppel Island

Great Keppel Island (3502 acres/1418 ha) has an image similar to that of the Gold Coast: white sandy beaches, discotheques and romantic rendez-vous. The island has accommodation for 320 guests, is close to the reef and offers beautiful walks in the hills.

Access

Plane from Rockhampton (25 min.) or Brisbane (2 hours).

Hydrofoil from Rosslyn Bay (15 min.): **Enterprise,** 15 Meade St., Rockhampton.

Boat from Rosslyn Bay (25 min.).

Regular bus service from Rockhampton to Rosslyn Bay: **Young's Bus Service,** 274 George St., Rockhampton. Tel: (079) 27 7000.

Accommodation and food

▲▲ **Great Keppel Island Resort,** PO Box 108, Rockhampton Qld 4700. Tel: (079) 39 1744. Restaurant. 142 rooms.

▬▬ *MACKAY, PROSERPINE AND SHUTE HARBOUR*

Mackay

Access: see general comments on access to the reef pp. 102–103.

Mackay (pop. 30,000) is situated 652 mi/1050 km from Brisbane. From Mackay you can get to Brampton Island by plane and boat, and to Lindeman Island by plane.

Useful addresses

Tourist information

Queensland Government Tourist Centre, River St. Tel: (079) 57 2292

Airlines

Ansett, 97 Victoria St. Tel: (079) 57 1571.

Australian Airlines, 105 Victoria St. Tel: (079) 57 1411.

Lindeman Aerial Services, Mackay Airport, Qld 4740. Tel: (079) 57 3226 For flights to Lindeman Island.

Accommodation and food

▲▲▲ **Coral Sands,** 40 McAlister St. Tel: (079) 51 1244. Restaurant 47 rooms.

▲▲ **Paradise Lodge,** 19 Peel St. Tel: (079) 51 1348. 12 rooms.

Proserpine

Access: see general comments on access to the reef pp. 102–103.

Proserpine (pop. 3000) is situated 737 mi/1180 km from Brisbane. From Proserpine you can get to Lindeman, Hamilton and Hayman islands by plane.

Useful addresses

Airlines

Ansett, 40 Main St. Tel: (079) 45 1433.

Australian Airlines, Main St. Tel: (079) 45 1045.

Accommodation and food

▲▲ **Prosperpine Motor Lodge,** Bruce Highway. Tel: (079) 45 1588 Restaurant. 33 rooms.

Shute Harbour—Airlie Beach[**]

Access: see general comments on access to the reef pp. 102–103.

Tourist information: **Whitsunday Tourism Association,** PO Box 83 Airlie Beach, Qld 4802. Tel: (079) 46 9133.

Located on the coast 30 mi/50 km from Proserpine, Airlie Beach and Shute Harbour are in the process of becoming major tourist centres of the northern Queensland coast. Shute Harbour is the main air and water access point for the Whitsunday group (yacht and cruiser rentals, airport, flying boat base, etc.). Airlie Beach, 6 mi/10 km away, is the 'residential district' for Shute Harbour, and offers numerous hotels, motels, restaurants, etc. The area is a first-class tourist centre, and has to date been spared the excesses of the Gold Coast.

An absolute 'must' among activities starting from Shute Harbour is a flight over the reef[***] in a small seaplane, including a landing on a reef lagoon Fantastic! Contact **Air Whitsunday,** Shute Harbour Rd., Shute Harbour Tel: (079) 46 9133.

Accommodation and food

▲▲▲ **Coral Sea Resort,** 25 Ocean View Ave., Airlie Beach. Tel: (079) 46 6458. The finest hotel in the area. Restaurant. 27 rooms.

▲ **Whitsunday Village Resort,** Shute Harbour Rd., Airlie Beach. Tel: (079) 46 6266. Restaurant. 70 rooms.

For the ultimate experience of the Great Barrier Reef, stay on a boat anchored on the reef, in a lagoon:

Sandra Reef Encounters, PO Box 56, Airlie Beach, Qld 4802. Tel: (079) 46 9133. Up to 25 people, diving equipment and instruction, access by sea-plane from Shute Harbour. Overnight stays or longer.

THE WHITSUNDAY ISLAND GROUP★★★

The island group comprising the Whitsundays and the Cumberlands, located between Bowen (to the north) and Mackay, offers the undisputed best sailing anywhere on the reef. There are 74 conventional (i.e. non-coral) islands in the group, most of them completely uninhabited. Others have successfully been developed for tourism. All the developed islands are linked by boat and/or plane with Shute Harbour on the coast.

Hayman Island★★

(11 acres/4.5 ha). The most sophisticated island in the group and the finest scenery.

Access

Helicopter from Proserpine (25 min.), boat or plane from Shute Harbour or Hamilton Island (about 2 hours in either case).

Accommodation and food

▲▲▲ **Hayman Island Resort,** via Shute Harbour, Qld 4801. Tel: (079) 46 9100. Restaurant. 164 rooms.

Daydream Island★★

(23 acres/9.5 ha). It considers itself to be Polynesian, and its covering of tropical vegetation only accentuates that impression.

Access

Boat (20 min.) from Shute Harbour. Plane from Shute Harbour or Hamilton Island.

Accommodation and food

▲▲▲ **Daydream Island Resort,** via Proserpine, Qld 4899. Tel: (079) 46 9200. Restaurant. 100 rooms.

Lindeman Island★★

(200 acres/80 ha). Famous for its golf course and for its tranquillity.

Access

Plane from Mackay or Proserpine (20-30 min.).

Accommodation and food

▲▲▲ **Lindeman Island Resort,** via Shute Harbour, Qld 4741. Tel: (079) 268 8398. Restaurant. 90 rooms.

South Molle Island★

(1000 acres/405 ha). The closest to the coast and one of the most popular islands.

Access

Boat from Shute Harbour (30 min.). Plane from Hamilton Island.

Accommodation and food

▲▲▲ **Telford South Molle,** via Shute Harbour, Qld 4800. Tel: (079) 46 9433. Restaurant. 202 rooms.

Hamilton Island

(1350 acres/548 ha). As a holiday resort, Hamilton Island has been the focal point and 'capital' of the Whitsunday group since its opening in 1984, with a runway long enough to take full-size passenger jets. It is superbly (some might say overly-equipped) and can accommodate approximately 1400 guests in its luxury hotel complex which, unfortunately, includes a 15 storey tower.

Access

Plane from Brisbane or Sydney, and boat from Shute Harbour (35 min.).

Accommodation and food

▲▲▲▲ **Hamilton Island Resort,** via Shute Harbour, Qld 4802. Tel: (079) 46 9144. Restaurant. 380 rooms.

▬▬ *TOWNSVILLE TO CAIRNS*

Townsville is situated 938 mi/1500 km from Brisbane and 1156 mi/1850 km from Cairns (see map p. 100). From Townsville, it is possible to reach Magnetic Island by boat and Dunk, Hinchinbrook and Orpheus islands by plane. From Cairns, you can reach Dunk Island by plane and Green Island by boat or plane. Half-way between Townsville and Cairns is the small town of Cardwell (100 mi/160 km north of Townsville). From there, you can reach Hinchinbrook Island, while Lizard Island, the most tropical of the developed reef islands, can be reached by plane from Cairns.

Townsville★★

With a population of 80,000, the 'capital' of North Queensland is one of Australia's most important ports and the most successful of the country's 'large' tropical cities, far ahead of Darwin. The city was founded during the gold rushes of the 1870s and its very attractive tropical colonial architecture has been well preserved. Townsville is also home to the main centre for scientific and ecological research on the Great Barrier Reef (at Turtle Bay to the south).

Useful addresses

Tourist information

Queensland Government Tourist Centre, 303 Flinders Mall. Tel: (077) 71 3077.

Airlines

Ansett, 350 Flinders Mall. Tel: (077) 81 6611.

Australian Airlines, Townsville International Hotel, Flinders Mall. Tel: (077) 81 6211.

Qantas, 280 Flinders Mall. Tel: (077) 22 6449.

Bus

Greyhound, corner of Flinders and King Sts. Tel: (077) 71 2134.

Accommodation and food

▲▲▲▲ **Barrier Reef,** off the Queensland coast between Cairns and Townsville. Tel: (612) 957 4945. A new offshore floating hotel situated in a lagoon.

▲▲▲ **Townsville International Hotel,** corner of Flinders and Stokes Sts. Tel: (077) 72 2477. Restaurant. 24 rooms.

▲▲▲ **Travelodge,** 75 The Strand. Tel: (077) 71 4255. Restaurant. 150 rooms, 3 suites.

Magnetic Island★

Largest of the northern islands—5 mi/8 km long and 12 mi/19 km wide—Magnetic Island has a permanent population of almost 2000 people. The island is a national park and bird sanctuary with a family feel about it.

Access

Boat from Townsville (35 min.): **Hayles Cruises,** 168 Flinders St., Townsville. Tel: (077) 71 6927.

Accommodation and food

The island has 350 rooms in rental bungalows, furnished accommodations and hotels, many of which have dining facilities. Among them:

▲▲▲ **The Magnetic Hotel,** The Esplanade, Picnic Bay, Magnetic Island, Qld 4816. Tel: (077) 78 5166. Restaurant. 21 rooms.

Hinchinbrook Island*

Hinchinbrook, the largest island national park in the world, covers some 99,000 acres/40,000 ha of unspoilt tropical rain forest, intersected by waterfalls, cliffs and steep hills.

Access

Boat from Cardwell (35 min.): **Tekin Cruises,** 141 Victoria St., Cardwell, Qld 4816. Tel: (070) 66 8661.

Plane from Townsville (30 min.).

Accommodation and food

▲▲▲ Hinchinbrook Island Hideaway, Hinchinbrook Island, Qld 4816. Tel: (077) 66 8585. Restaurant. 15 rooms.

Orpheus Island***

Located 50 mi/80 km to the north of Townsville, Orpheus Island is the most recently developed for tourism. It offers sophistication and tranquillity in an exquisite tropical setting. It is also a national park covering 3400 acres/1368 ha.

Access

Sea-plane or helicopter from Townsville (20 min.).

Accommodation and food

▲▲▲ Orpheus Island Resort, Private Mail Bag, Ingham, Qld 4850. Tel: (077) 77 7377. Restaurant. 25 rooms (children under 12 not accepted).

Dunk Island***

With its 6 sq mi/16 sq km, Dunk Island is probably the most popular of the Reef's Robinson Crusoe islands. Its tropical vegetation is superb, its beaches magnificent and its hotel complex is a model of understated luxury and good taste.

Access

Plane from Townsville or Cairns. Boat: the **MV Friendship.** Tel: (070) 68 7245. From Clump Point Jetty, near Tully (45 min.).

Accommodation and food

▲▲▲ Great Barrier Reef, via Townsville, Qld 4810. Tel: (070) 68 8199. Reservations through Australian Airlines. Restaurant. 141 rooms.

Bedarra Island***

Situated very close to Dunk Island, Bedarra is the most secluded and most chic of the Barrier Reef islands.

Access

From Dunk Island by boat.

Accommodation and food
▲▲▲ **Bedarra Hideaway Resort,** via Townsville, Qld 4810. Tel: (079) 68 8168. Reservations through Australian Airlines. Restaurant. 8 rooms.

Fitzroy Island★★
Another tropical paradise, consisting of an 800 acre/324 ha national park, situated to the south of Cairns. Outstanding surroundings, peace and proximity to coral reefs are its main features.

Access
Boat from Cairns (45 min.).

Accommodation and food
▲▲▲ **Fitzroy Island Resort,** PO Box 2120, Cairns, Qld 4870 Tel: (070) 51 5477. Restaurant. 5 rooms.

Green Island★★
Green Island and Heron Island to the south (see p. 105) are the only developed coral islands on the reef. Covering only 32 acres/13 ha, Green Island has less to offer than its southern counterpart but is more accessible and less developed.

Access
From Cairns: boat (Hayles Cruises) (40 min.) or plane (10 min.).

Accommodation and food
▲▲ **Green Island Reef Resort,** via Cairns, Qld 4871. Tel (070) 51 4644. Restaurant. 26 rooms.

Lizard Island★★★
Covering some 2500 acres/1000 ha, Lizard Island serves as forward base for marlin fishermen from September to December. See 'Fishing' p. 111

Access
Plane from Cairns (1 hour).

Accommodation and food
▲▲ **Lizard Island Lodge** (Resort), PO Box 2372, Cairns, Qld 4870 Tel: (070) 50 4222. Expensive relative to the amenities. Restaurant 32 rooms.

CAIRNS AND NORTHERN QUEENSLAND

Cairns (pop. 40,000) is simultaneously the gateway to the far north of Queensland (Cape York) and to Dunk, Green, Fitzroy and Lizard islands (see above). The presence of numerous Torres Strait Islanders (indigenous, but not Aboriginal, inhabitants) from the northernmost areas of the continent makes it one of the 'blackest' cities in Australia. Considered one of the world capitals for deep sea fishing (blue and black marlin), Cairns is also the meeting-place for a great number of Australia's still extant hippies, and is one of those rare Australian cities to have retained the Joseph Conrad atmosphere you expect in the British tropics. The city itself, an ideal touring base for the region, has recently invested in an enormous international airport capable of handling direct jumbo flights from Japan and the United States. As a result, hotels and Gold Coast type Aqualands are sprouting up all over.

PRACTICAL INFORMATION

Telephone area code: 070.

Useful addresses

Tourist information

Queensland Government Tourist Centre, 12 Shields St. Tel: 51 4066.

Airlines

Air Queensland (regular flights to Cape York and the rest of Queensland, including Brisbane), 62 Abbott St. Tel: 50 4222.

Ansett, 84 Lake St. Tel: 2211.

Australian Airlines, corner of Lake and Shields Sts. Tel: 50 3711.

Bus

Greyhound, 78 Grafton St. Tel: 51 3388.

Boat to Green Island

Hayles Cruises, Wharf St. Tel: 51 5644. (1 hour 20 min. by ferry or 40 min. by speed boat.)

Accommodation

▲▲▲ **Pacific International,** 43 The Esplanade. Tel: 51 7888. 176 rooms.

▲▲ **Hides Telford Hotel-Motel,** corner of Lake and Shields Sts. Tel: 51 1266. 104 rooms.

▲▲ **Tuna Towers,** 145 The Esplanade. Tel: 51 4388. 40 rooms, 20 suites.

Sports

Although the island resorts near Cairns offer a wide variety of sports, the area is particularly remarkable for fishing and diving.

Fishing

The fishing season for black or blue marlin, the best sporting fish in the world, lasts from September to mid-December. It is a very expensive sport (A$500 to A$1000 per day rental for a fully-equipped boat for a maximum 4 people), and deep-sea trips can last from one to two weeks. The sport attracts devotees (like golfer Jack Nicklaus and Britain's Prince Charles) from all over the world. The fish themselves can weigh in at 1500 lbs/680 kg or more

Information: **Marlin Marina Tourist Services,** PO Box 1542, Cairns, Qld 4870. Tel: 51 9230.

Diving

Pro-Diving Services, Marlin Jetty, Cairns, Qld 4870. Tel: 51 9915. Excursions on fully-equipped boats.

Attractions

Cape York Peninsula, to the north of Cairns, is one of the few remaining wilderness areas on earth. It contains enormous national parks, such as **Lakefield National Park** (1.3 million acres/528,000 ha) and the **Jardine River National Park** (580,685 acres/235,000 ha). Information: **Queensland National Parks and Wildlife Service,** PO Box 2066, Cairns, Qld 4870. Tel: 53 4533.

The islanders occupy huge reserves, particularly Bamaga and Thursday Island at the northernmost tip of the peninsula. The **Quinkan Ranges,** near Laura in the south of the cape, contain outstanding Aboriginal rock paintings, dating from 13,000 BC. **Cooktown** in the south and **Coen** in the north boast a certain tropical charm. Beware, however, of the dirt roads which are very rudimentary, especially above Coen. The region is open to conventional traffic only during the dry season (from August to October). Air travel **(Air Queensland)** or an organized safari in an off-road vehicle are recommended. Safari organizers include: **Kingfisher Safaris, Newlook**

Adventures, Trekabout Expeditions, Wildtrek, Oz Tours and **Kamp Ou Safaris.** A lodge, **Top of Australia Wilderness Lodge,** has been estab lished in the middle of the jungle. Information: **Air Queensland** (see 'Practical information' p. 92).

Atherton Tablelands★★★. Cairns is framed in the background by a series of plateaux upon which grow Australia's most beautiful rain forests. You can enjoy magnificent scenery, superb views of the valleys below covered with sugar cane and exotic fauna and flora. The main townships on the plateau are Mareeba, Atherton and Yungaburra—a half-day car ride not to be missed.

▬▬ OUTBACK QUEENSLAND

Outback Queensland begins to the west of the Great Dividing Range, a chain of weathered hills stretching from Cape York to Melbourne. There you will find the enormous cattle and sheep stations, ranches covering hundreds of thousands and even millions of acres. The area from Mount Isa to Birdsville (see map pp. 8-9) is especially famous for its Channel Country the rich grazing lands of the Georgina and Diamantina rivers, covered in golden pastures and eucalypts.

It is in this region, and especially along the Birdsville Track (a cattle route linking the Northern Territory with the Channel Country), that you are likely to meet *drovers*, restless cowboys with their herds of 2000 beasts heading for the pastures and markets in the south. Because of the dry conditions and the increasing cost of fuel for the *road trains* (huge trucks with up to four trailers), more and more cattle producers lead their herds 'down the Track'. You can spend a couple of days or more on a big cattle station, taking part in the exciting life of the Australian cowboy on horse motorbike or helicopter, thanks to the **Queensland Government Trave Centre,** which arranges a certain number of ranch stays. These have nothing in common with American dude ranches—this is the real thing including the dust. Best season: April to October.

This is also the season of rodeos which spring up in stations and towns all over the outback. Genuine Western flavour guaranteed. Rodeo programs are available from Queensland Government Travel Centres.

Charters Towers★★★

Situated between Townsville (80 mi/130 km away) and Mount Isa, this is the most typical of the ghost towns from the Queensland gold rush. There are beautiful colonial houses and gold mines to visit. Set aside at least one day for the trip from Townsville to Mount Isa (625 mi/1000 km of straight tarmac through the heart of the desert).

Ravenswood★, 60 mi/100 km away, is like a ghost town : half-ruined houses, cows wandering along the streets and a pub straight out of 1940s western. Worth a detour.

> **Accommodation**
>
> ▲▲ **Park Hotel,** 1 Mosman St., Charters Towers. Tel : (077) 87 1022 17 rooms, 6 suites.

Mount Isa

Mount Isa is the most important town in the region; it also has the larges copper mine in Australia. You can visit the mine, which looks as if it's part of the set for a science-fiction film, by going to the mine's Visitors' Centre any weekday at 9am or 1pm. The tour lasts 2 hours.

Useful addresses

Tourist information

Northwest Queensland Regional Tourist Association, 71 Camooweal St., Mount Isa, Qld 4825. Tel: (077) 43 7966.

Accommodation

▲▲▲ **The Overlander,** 119-127 Marian St., Mount Isa. Tel: (077) 43 5011. Inexpensive motel. Book well in advance—only 20 rooms.

SYDNEY TO MELBOURNE
VIA CANBERRA

The Hume Highway that links Sydney to Melbourne crosses through the real heartland of Australia, from sheep pastures burnt by permanent drought to the snow-covered peaks of the Great Dividing Range; from sleepy rural towns clustered about a Victorian pub to the glass and concrete of a modern capital city.

Australian legislators pre-dated the Brazilians when they decided, in 1901, to establish a capital city for the new federation in the middle of nowhere. Canberra is the perfect example of an artificial city deliberately built in the country. Politicians and geographers got together to choose a site which would meet the requirements of the new government: it had to be constitutionally and geographically separate from the six federal states, accessible from the two largest cities in the south-east, enjoy a mild climate and, above all, have its own water supply. Of the 23 sites proposed in the mountainous area of the fertile heartland, it was the Canberra Basin, 188 mi/300 km from Sydney and 406 mi/650 km from Melbourne, which finally met with the planners' approval in 1910.

THE SHEEP-FARMING COUNTRY

Goulburn★★ (132 mi/211 km from Sydney) and **Yass**★★ (185 mi/296 km) are typical rural New South Wales towns which have grown beside the main train line as a result of merino-sheep breeding. This is the area in which members of Princess Diana's family own a sheep station.

You can spend a night or more at a sheep station. Many in the area will take paying guests and you will be treated like one of the family, taking part in all the activities associated with sheep farming: shearing in spring, horseback round-ups, sheep auctions, etc. Prices are very reasonable. The addresses of two stations in the Goulburn area are given below. The Australian Tourist Commission publishes a detailed listing of the most interesting 'farm-days' (see p. 19). The tourist offices in each state can also advise you (see addresses in individual sections).

Canberra: Lake Barley Griffin with government buildings in the background.

■■■ *PRACTICAL INFORMATION*

You can explore this region by bus (**Ansett-Pioneer** and **AAT** offer tours) and even by plane. Air tours are available from Sydney in business jets and include a stay on a farm (see p. 19).

Useful addresses

Sheep stations

Berrebangalo Country Resort, Lade Vale Rd., Gunning, NSW 2581 Tel: (048) 45 1135. Margaret and Rick Otten.

Carringgal Holiday Farm, Fitzroy Falls Rd., Wildes Meadow, NSW 2577 Tel: (048) 86 4236. Mrs. Berry.

NEW SOUTH WALES

New South Wales is the only state in Australia which can offer visitors a desert safari and a trip to the snow. The north-west of the state is red-dirt country. Films like *Mad Max*, *Razorback*, and other classics of the Australian cinema were shot around **Broken Hill** (750 mi/1200 km from Sydney) and the ghost-town of **Silverton** (19 mi/30 km from Broken Hill). Other pioneer towns on the way to Broken Hill include **Lightning Ridge** (688 mi/1100 km) and **White Cliffs** (688 mi/1100 km), both famous for their opals.

The south-east, on the other hand, is the area for humid forests in summer and snow in winter. Specialized tour operators offer discovery tours to the Blue Mountains near Sydney and walking, canoe and inflatable-boat trips in the Snowy Mountains not far from Canberra. Although some skiing excursions are also offered, the skiing season is extremely short (July to September) and the snow fall unreliable.

■■■ *PRACTICAL INFORMATION*

Accommodation

▲▲ **The Lodge,** 252 Mica St., Broken Hill. Tel: (080) 88 2722. 21 rooms, 1 suite.

Useful addresses

Specialized tour operator

Wanderers Tours, PO Box 591, Broken Hill, NSW 2800.

CANBERRA

In 1910, town planners held an international competition with the intention of creating a capital city on the 91 sq mi/2366 sq km of sheep pasture which spread like a blank sheet before their eyes. The winner, American architect Walter Burley Griffin, was put in charge of the project. He set about applying contemporary theories of town planning which held that, given the dreadful chaos of the large industrial cities, new cities should be Edens planned down to the last detail. In order to do away with the problems inherent in cities, the city not only had to be situated in the countryside but there should also be no evidence that it was a city. The result was a gathering of 250,000 bureaucrats in the most densely populated rural area of Australia. Canberra is not a city. Its residents find it peaceful, quiet, unpolluted, easy to live in and a good place to raise children. It has beautiful parks, a lake, sports grounds and wide streets. However, every Friday at 4.30pm, many of them jump into their cars and, without so much as a backward glance, take off to the smoke and noise of Sydney or Melbourne.

PRACTICAL INFORMATION

Telephone area code: 062.

Access

Plane

Ansett, Australian Airlines and **East-West Airlines** offer direct flights to Canberra from Sydney and Melbourne.

Ansett, 4 Mort St. Tel: 45 6511.

Australian Airlines, Jolimont Tourist Centre, Northbourne Ave. Tel: 68 3333.

East-West Airlines, Canberra International Airport. Tel: 60 1315.

Bus

There are regular bus services to Canberra from Sydney (4.5 hours) and Melbourne (9.5 hours).

Greyhound, Jolimont Centre, Northbourne Ave. Tel: 57 2659. See chapters on Sydney and Melbourne for local addresses.

Useful addresses

Tourist information

Tourist Office: Jolimont Centre, Northbourne Ave. Tel: 49 7555.

Embassies

All of the following embassies are in the Yarralumla area on Commonwealth Ave. with the exception of the US Embassy, which is on State Circle.

Canada. Tel: 73 3844. **Great Britain.** Tel: 73 0422. **Ireland.** Tel: 73 3022. **New Zealand.** Tel: 73 3611. **USA.** Tel: 73 3711.

Accommodation

▲▲▲▲ **Canberra International,** 242 Northbourne Ave., Dickson. Tel: 47 7966. Business and tourist hotel. Attractive decor. 144 rooms. 9 suites.

▲▲▲▲ **Noahs Lakeside International,** London Circuit. Tel: 47 6244. 216 rooms. 7 suites.

▲▲▲ **Town House Motor Inn,** 60 Marcus Clarke St. Tel: 48 8011. 59 rooms. 2 suites.

▲▲ **Acacia Motor Lodge,** 65 Ainslie Ave. Tel: 49 6955. 53 rooms.

▲▲ **Tall Trees Lodge Motel,** Stephen St., Ainslie. Tel: 47 9200. 19 rooms.

Food

Canberra prides itself in matters gastronomical and offers visitors a choice of more than 200 restaurants serving the cuisines of countless nationalities. The only drawback is that there are few small, inexpensive restaurants and fewer still that are open late. The following restaurants are among the most interesting.

Elegant

Peaches, Blamey Place, Campbell. Tel: 49 7333. International cuisine.

French

The Bacchus, City Mutual Building, Hobart Place, City. Tel: 48 7939.

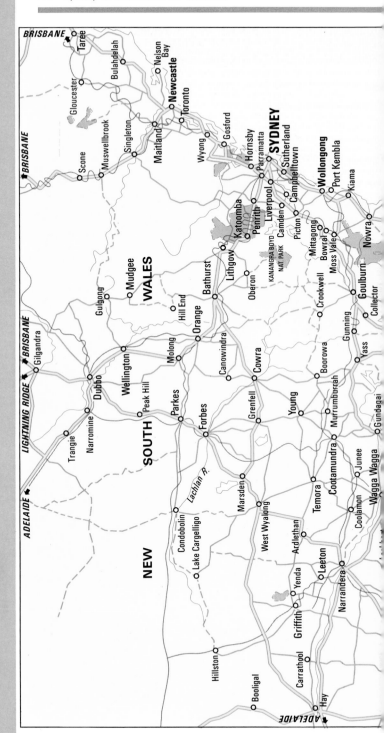

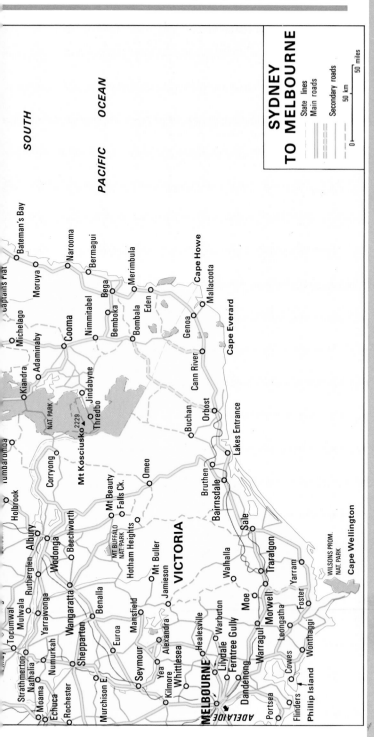

SYDNEY
TO MELBOURNE

State lines
Main roads
Secondary roads

0   50 km
0   50 miles

SOUTH

PACIFIC   OCEAN

Bateman's Bay
Narooma
Bermagui
Moruya
Captains Flat
Merimbula
Michelago
Bega
Cape Howe
Kiandra
Cooma
Nimmitabel
Bemboka
Mallacoota
Adaminaby
Bombala
Eden
Cape Everard
Jindabyne
Genoa
Thredbo
Cann River
NAT. PARK
2229
Mt Kosciusko
Buchan
Orbost
Tumbarumba
Lakes Entrance
Corryong
Omeo
Holbrook
Bruthen
Mt Beauty
Falls Ck.
Bairnsdale
MT BUFFALO
NAT. PARK
Sale
Albury
Beechworth
Rutherglen
Hotham Heights
Wodonga
Mt Buller
VICTORIA
Walhalla
Jamieson
Mulwala
Yarrawonga
Wangaratta
Benalla
Traralgon
Tocumwal
Mansfield
Moe
Yarram
Strathmerton
Euroa
Morwell
Nathalia
Numurkah
Alexandra
Warragul
Foster
Moama
Shepparton
Yea
Warburton
Leongatha
Echuca
Seymour
Healesville
Rochester
Kilmore
Lilydale
Wonthaggi
WILSONS PROM.
NAT. PARK
Murchison E.
Whittlesea
Ferntree Gully
Cape Wellington
MELBOURNE
Dandenong
Cowes
ADELAIDE
Portsea
Flinders
Phillip Island

Le Carrousel Jean-Pierre, Red Hill Lookout, Red Hill. Tel: 73 1808. Superb view over the capital and Canberra's trendiest address.

Vietnamese

Dalat, 29 Bentham St., Yarralumla. Tel: 82 4461.

Snack

The Pancake Parlour, corner of East Row and Alinga St. Tel: 47 2982 Crepes and coffee shop. Open 24 hours a day!

Nightlife

Canberra goes to bed early. Music and dancing, however, can be enjoyed at:

Ainslie Hotel, Limestone Ave., Ainslie. Jazz concerts every Friday night in the Carlton Lounge of the hotel.

Boot and Flogger, Green Square, Kingston. A pub offering rock concerts every Thursday and Saturday. Very popular.

Cafe Jax's, 131-141 City Walk, in the Mall. A good place to go to dance

Elbow room, Cobee Court Philip, near Woden Town Centre. For blues enthusiasts.

▬▬ WHAT TO SEE

Visitors should set aside at least a half day of their trip to visit the famous tourist attractions: Parliament House, the War Memorial, the High Court of Australia, the National Library and the National Gallery.

Start your tour from the top of the **Black Mountain Telecom Tower*** (640 ft/195 m). It offers a restaurant with panoramic views and a viewing platform *(open daily 9am to 10pm).* From there you can spot the city between the hills, the parks, the lake and the huge circular avenues which make up the basic urban layout of Canberra. You'll see **Lake Burley Griffin,** an artificial lake created on the Molonglo River in 1963 with water from Scrivener Dam, and the Parliamentary Triangle which forms the centre of the city. The three points of the triangle are City Hill, Capital Hill (site of the new Parliament House), and the Australian-American Memorial. Two sides of the triangle are formed by Commonwealth and Kings avenues, and its base by Constitution Avenue. This latter avenue crosses Anzac Avenue, dedicated to the Australian and New Zealand service personnel who lost their lives in World War I. Most of the sights of interest in Canberra are located within this area.

Parliament House

There are two Parliament houses: the new, modern Parliament House on Capital Hill and old Parliament House on King George Terrace, which was built in the late 1920s and resembles a large provincial railway station. Within its walls are found the House of Representatives, the Senate, the office of the Prime Minister, his ministers and the parliamentary opposition. Debates in the Chamber are open to the public and are conducted in the British tradition, presided over by a Speaker who may or may not wear a wig and black gown. Tours of Parliament House are conducted whenever the Parliament is not in session. If you want to attend a debate in the Chamber, it is best to write in advance to the Principal Attendant, **House of Representatives,** Parliament House, Canberra, ACT 2600, or to contact him personally one or two days in advance. Tel: 72 1211. The Senate, which is less prestigious, is easy to visit. Reservations can be made on the spot.

Australian National Gallery*

Parkes Place. Tel: 71 2501. *Open daily 10am to 5pm.*
Situated beside Lake Burley Griffin, this ultra-modern building houses many important Australian works (from traditional Aboriginal to contemporary

artists), as well as an excellent collection of European paintings and sculptures. Other works come from Asia, Africa and the Americas. Restaurant, coffee shop and a well-stocked shop of art books, reproductions, etc.

Australian War Memorial*

At the foot of Mt. Ainslie. *Open daily 9am to 4.45pm.* Admission is free. A monumental building dedicated to the glory of the 102,000 Australians who have died for their country. There are two storeys of relics (including several full-size bombers from World War II), arms, uniforms, photos, dioramas, paintings, etc.

High Court of Australia*

King Edward Terrace. Tel: 70 6811. *Open daily 10am to 4pm.* Located beside the lake, this building houses the other arm of federal power, the equivalent of the United States Supreme Court. After the Sydney Opera House, the structure is one of the most successful examples of modern Australian architecture. During a visit to this concrete and glass edifice, built in the sober and monumental style (complete with light wells) so beloved of American architects, tourists may be a little taken aback by the shorts and sandals of most Australian visitors. The solemnity of their surroundings seems to have little effect upon them. The High Court boasts an excellent coffee shop and is connected by a walkway to the Australian National Gallery.

National Library*

Parkes Place. Tel: 62 1111. *Open Mon. to Thurs. 9am to 10pm,* and *Thurs. to Sun. 9am to 4.45pm.*
The building, which is near the High Court beside the lake, is modern and tasteful but not outstanding. The exhibitions arranged by the National Library are usually very interesting. There is a small shop, where you can buy fine and inexpensive reproductions of 19th-century engravings in a variety of sizes.

▬ MOUNT KOSCIUSKO AND THE SNOWY MOUNTAINS

Access

Cooma can be reached by plane (**Ansett** from Sydney or **Kendall** from Melbourne), train or bus (both from Sydney).You can also drive from Sydney via Canberra or via Bega on the coast. From Melbourne you drive via Tumut (see map pp. 118-119).

Cooma

71 mi/114 km south of Canberra, Cooma is the doorway to the Snowy Mountains, the highest in Australia, and their summit, Mt. Kosciusko (7127 ft/2173 m). The rounded, fairly featureless mountains are covered in deep snow during winter (June to September) and the few patches left over in summer provide thrills for Australian tourists who have never even touched snow. At the foot of Mt. Kosciusko is the most famous and fashionable of Australia's snow resorts, **Thredbo*** (also open in summer). Here there are 44 mi/70 km of downhill and cross-country ski-runs, nine chair lifts and numerous hotels, chalets, restaurants and shops, all forming a very successful 'Alpine' village. Other resorts in the area, not far from Mt. Kosciusko, are Perisher Valley and Smiggin Holes.

Kosciusko National Park**

This park covers 1.5 million acres/630,000 ha and includes the major ski resorts in the region. Information: The Superintendant, **Kosciusko National Park,** Private Mail Bag via Cooma, NSW 2630. Tel: (648) 62 102.
The Snowy Mountains also boast Australia's largest hydroelectric and irrigation project, the **Snowy Mountains Hydroelectric Scheme.** It uses 16 dams, 7 power stations and 91 mi/145 km of tunnels to provide 5000 million kw/h of electricity a year to the neighbouring states and regulates the flow of the two largest rivers in Australia, the Murray and the Murrumbidgee.

MELBOURNE
AND RURAL VICTORIA

Founded in 1835 by Tasmanian 'squatters' John Batman and John Fawkner, Melbourne has developed so successfully that it has not quite recovered from the experience. In 1850, Victoria and its sheep breeders separated from New South Wales at a time when Melbourne's population was a mere 87,000. Ten years later, at the beginning of the Ballarat Gold Rush, the population had grown to 540,000, and had become the largest in Australia. That was the start of the continuing rivalry between Sydney and Melbourne. In 1986, the capital of Australia's smallest mainland state had more than 2.9 million inhabitants.

MELBOURNE

Melbourne is a center for finance, agriculture, intellectual and cultural activity. Its private schools, such as Geelong Grammar, where Britain's Prince Charles spent a year, and its universities are the most prestigious in the country. Its clubs are the most exclusive and its politicians the most powerful. Educated Melbournians even speak English with a different accent from the rest of Australia, and refer to themselves, in all modesty, as 'Melbourne educated'.

Just as Sydney turns to the sea, Melbourne turns resolutely to the land. It is a tough, tenacious, proud and snobbish city but its charms are not limited to those of the great middle-class. Victoria was the home of bushranger (highway bandit) Ned Kelly and the revolutionaries of the Eureka Stockade. Today, Melbourne has the third largest Greek population in the world, outside Athens and Thessaloniki.

In 1956, Melbourne hosted the Olympic Games in a stadium capable of seating 110,000 people. The stadium fills again each year at 'footy' (Australian football) Grand Final time. Melbourne is the only Australian city to have an official public holiday (first Tuesday in November) in honour of a horse race, the famous Melbourne Cup.

Twenty-first-century Melbourne.

PRACTICAL INFORMATION

Telephone area code: 03.
Map coordinates refer to the map pp. 126-127.

Access

Plane

Like Sydney, Melbourne is a centre of Australian communications. The Victorian capital is connected daily with Europe, Asia and the United States by direct international flights. Direct flights are also available linking Melbourne with all state capitals and major country centres (see p. 66).

Melbourne's Tullamarine Airport is located 13 mi/20 km from the city. There is a regular airport bus service:

Skybus, 436 Elizabeth St., City (B3). Tel: 347 8977.

International airlines

Air New Zealand, 154 Swanston St., City (B3). Tel: 654 3311.

British Airways, 330 Collins St., City (B3). Tel: 602 3000.

Canadian Pacific, 500 Collins St., City (A3). Tel: 602 6731.

Continental Airlines, 200 Queen St., City (B3). Tel: 602 5377.

Qantas, 114 William St., City (B3). Tel: 602 6026.

United Airlines, 233 Collins St., City (B3). Tel: 602 2544.

Domestic airlines

Ansett, 465 Swanston St., City (B2). Tel: 668 1211.

Australian Airlines, 50 Franklin St., City (B2). Tel: 665 1333.

East-West Airlines, 2nd floor, 230 Collins St., City (B3). Tel: 637 713.

Regional airlines

For **Kendell Airlines, Staywood Airlines, Penguin Express** (for visitors to the Fairy Penguin colony on Phillip Island) and **Murray Valley Airlines,** bookings may be made through the **Victorian Tourist Commission** (see 'Tourist information' p. 125).

Train

There are regular services between Melbourne and Sydney (13 hours), Canberra (9 hours) and Adelaide (12 hours), and connecting services to Perth, Alice Springs, Brisbane and the Queensland coast.

Victorian Railways, Railways Building, Spencer St., City (A3). Tel: 62 0771.

Bus

There are regular buses between Melbourne and Sydney (12 hours), Brisbane (24 hours), and Adelaide (11 hours), and connecting services to Perth, Darwin and Cairns.

Greyhound, corner of Swanston and Franklin Sts., City (B2). Tel: 668 2666.

Ansett-Pioneer, 465 Swanston St., City (B2). Tel: 668 2422.

Car

Melbourne is 550 mi/900 km from Sydney, 1200 mi/1900 km from Brisbane, 2500 mi/4000 km from Cairns, 450 mi/750 km from Adelaide, 2500 mi/4000 km from Darwin and 2200 mi/3500 km from Perth.

From Sydney

There are two major routes between Australia's two largest cities.

The Princes Highway (663 mi/1060 km) passes along the ocean through the cities of Wollongong (virtually an industrial satellite of Sydney), Nowra and Bega. At Eden, 30 mi/50 km from the Victorian border, the highway turns inland before rejoining the coast at Lakes Entrance on Ninety Mile Beach. It then passes through the towns of Bairnsdale, Sale and Morwell before once more turning inland and reaching Melbourne.

The Hume Highway (550 mi/900 km) is an inland route and the shortest road to Melbourne—see 'Sydney to Melbourne via Canberra' (p. 115). The routes from other cities are covered in the sections on Brisbane (p. 92), Adelaide (p. 160), the Northern Territory (pp. 187-188) and Perth (p. 173).

Climate

It should be noted that the variations between seasons are more marked in Melbourne than in the rest of the country. Summer temperatures can climb to more than 100 °F/40 °C, while winters (June to August) can be quite cold (less than 40 °F/5 °C) and very humid. Spring and autumn are most pleasant.

Getting around Melbourne

Map coordinates refer to the map pp. 126-127.

Car rental

Avis, 4 Hopkins St., Footscray. Tel: 689 6666. 400 Elizabeth St., City (B2). Tel: 663 6366.

Budget, 21 Bedford St., North Melbourne (A-B1 north). Tel: 320 6333.

Hertz, 97 Franklin St., City (B2). Tel: 699 0180.

Thrifty, 390 Elizabeth St., City (B2). Tel: 663 5200.

Taxis

Astoriataxi. Tel: 347 5511.

Silver Tops. Tel: 345 3455.

Trams

Melbourne is quite well served by a public transport system distinguished by its trams. The famous 1900-vintage green and cream trams, with their polished wooden seats, are being replaced gradually by modern, orange models which are more comfortable but not nearly so charming. There are some 201 mi/322 km of tram lines extending up to 25 mi/40 km from the city. They provide a leisurely way of discovering Melbourne.

Underground transport

Melbourne is also intensely proud of its mini-underground, the **Loop.** The first stations were opened in February 1981. **Transport Information Centre.** Tel: 617 0900.

Useful addresses

Map coordinates refer to the map pp. 126-127. Coordinates containing a second letter indicate specific location on the map.

Tourist information

Victorian Tourist Commission, 230 Collins St., City (B3). Tel: 602 9444.

Consulates

British Consulate-General, 330 Collins St., City (B3). Tel: 602 1877.

United States Consulate-General, 24 Albert Rd., South Melbourne (B6). Tel: 699 2244.

Post Office

General Post Office (GPO), corner of Elizabeth and Bourke Sts., City (B3). Tel: 609 4265. Closed weekends.

Automobile Club

Royal Automobile Club of Victoria (RACV), 123 Queen St., City (B3). Tel: 607 2211.

Accommodation

Map coordinates refer to the map pp. 126-127.

There is no shortage of hotels of all categories in Melbourne. It is best to reserve in advance, especially during public holidays or major sporting events.

International-standard hotels

▲▲▲▲ **Melbourne Hilton,** 192 Wellington Parade, East Melbourne (D4-b). Tel: 419 3311. In the grand style, well-located and modern. 387 rooms, 41 suites.

▲▲▲▲ **Menzies at the Rialto,** 425 Collins St., City (B3-a). Tel: 6 2011. An old neo-Gothic Victorian building which has been immaculately renovated. 243 rooms and suites.

▲▲▲▲ **The Regent of Melbourne,** 25 Collins St., City (C3-d). Tel: 63 0321. Ultra-modern architecture, daring interior. 325 rooms, 52 suites.

▲▲▲▲ **Rockmans Regency Hotel,** corner of Lonsdale and Exhibition Sts., City (C2). Tel: 662 3900. 185 rooms, 20 suites.

▲▲▲▲ **St. Kilda Road Travelodge,** corner of St. Kilda Rd. and Park St., South Melbourne (B6-c). Tel: 699 4833. 205 rooms.

▲▲▲▲ **Windsor Hotel,** 115 Spring St., City (C3-e). Tel: 63 0261. *The great Victorian hotel in Melbourne, if not in Australia. Grandiose, with a feeling of nostalgia.* 159 rooms, 21 suites.

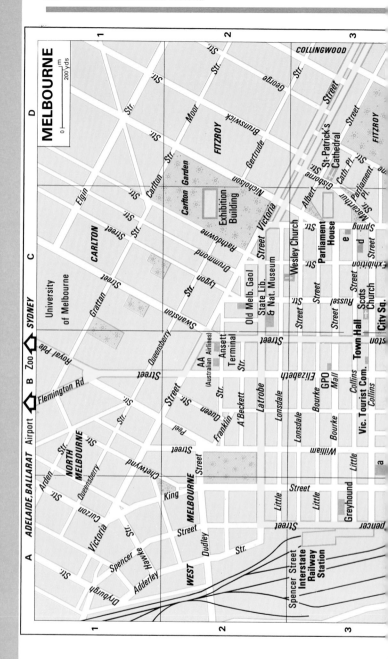

First-class hotels

▲▲▲ **Crossley Lodge,** 51 Little Bourke St., City (C3). Tel: 662 2500. 74 rooms.

The following two hotels are in Melbourne's lively Italian area.

▲▲▲ **Downtowner,** 66 Lygon St., Carlton (C2). Tel: 663 5555. 89 rooms.

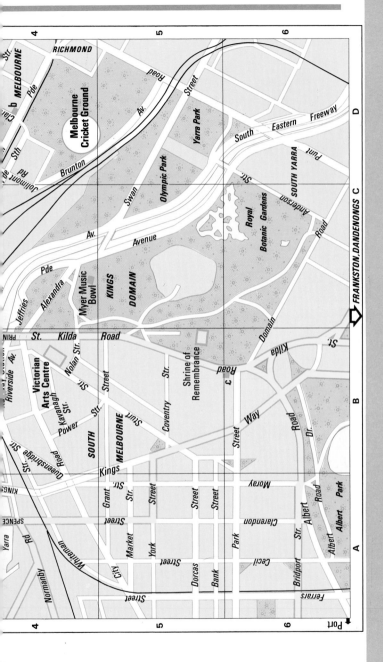

▲▲▲ **Lygon Lodge,** 220 Lygon St., Carlton (C1) . Tel: 663 6633. 66 rooms.

Inexpensive hotels

▲ **London Hotel,** 99 Elizabeth St., City (B3) . Tel: 67 6201.

▲ **Melbourne Youth Hostel,** 500 Abbotsford St., North Melbourne (A1 north) . Tel: 328 1880. 20 min. by tram from the city.

▲ **Spencer Motel,** 44 Spencer St., City (A3). Tel: 62 6991. 96 rooms

Outside the city

▲ **Linden Court Private Hotel,** 26 Acland St., St. Kilda (B6 south)
Tel: 53 4456. Situated close to St. Kilda Beach. Building classified by
the National Trust.

▲ **West End Private Hotel,** 76 Toorak Rd., South Yarra (D6 south)
Tel: 266 3155. Situated in the fashionable area of Melbourne.
12 rooms.

Food

Map coordinates refer to the map pp. 126-127.

Melbourne considers itself the gastronomic capital of Australia.
Without entering into the argument, it could be said that Melbourne did
start a fine-food wave that spread across the entire continent. There
are more than 1300 restaurants in the city, representing 60 nationalities. For more information, consult the daily *'Good Food Guide'* by
Claude Forell and Rita Ehrich in the *Age* newspaper.

Elegant restaurants

Glo Glo's, 3 Carters Ave., Toorak. Tel: 241 2615. The 'in' restaurant in
Melbourne for the rich habitués of Toorak.

Maria and Walters, 166 Rathdowne St., Carlton (C1). Tel: 347 3328.
BYO. Excellent cuisine in an intimate and luxurious atmosphere.

Stephanie's, 405 Tooronga Rd., Hawthorn East. Tel: 208 8944.
Judged the best restaurant in the country in 1985.

Chinese

The Flower Drum, 103 Little Bourke St., City (C3). Tel: 663 2531. One
of the best Chinese restaurants in Australia.

The Lotus Inn, 26 Market Lane, City. Tel: 663 4667. Excellent cuisine
at sensible prices.

French

Les Halles, 36 Swan St., Richmond (C-D5). Tel: 429 3842. BYO. Real
French cuisine at reasonable prices. Good and unpretentious.

Mietta's Melbourne, 7 Alfred Place, City (C3). Tel: 654 2366. Excellent
cuisine in the superbly restored former Naval and Military Club.

Petit Choux, 1007 High St., Armadale. Tel: 20 8515. Superb cuisine.
Quite expensive.

Tolarno, 42 Fitzroy St., St. Kilda (B6 south). Tel: 534 0521. In the only
'Bohemian' street in Melbourne. Very good and not very expensive.

Greek and Middle-Eastern

Cazablan Deli, 282 St. Kilda Rd., St. Kilda (B6). Tel: 534 7175. Middle-
Eastern specialities nicely presented. BYO.

Laikon, 272 Swan St., Richmond (D5). Tel: 428 6983. Greek. BYO.
Really inexpensive and really good, with a relaxed atmosphere.

Lambs, 100 Lygon St., Carlton (C1). Tel: 663 5636. Greek-Lebanese
cuisine at uniquely low prices. Open until 3am. BYO.

Italian

Genevieve, 233 Faraday St., Carlton (C1 north). Tel: 347 4202. BYO.
Not expensive, open late at night, near the university and a hospital, a
meeting-place for students and nurses.

Railway Hotel, 800 Nicholson St., North Fitzroy (D1). Tel: 489 8544.
An Italian 'pub'. Good, inexpensive, fun.

Tsindos Bistrot, 100 Bourke St., City (C3). Tel: 663 3076. Very good,
elegant, not too expensive.

Seafood
The Melbourne Catch, 14 McKillop St., City. Tel: 67 3638. Wide range of seafood, pleasant atmosphere.

Steaks and grill
Lazar's, 87 Johnston St., Fitzroy (D2 east). Tel: 419 2073.

Fashionable
Café Manhattan, 448 Toorak Rd., Toorak. Tel: 240 9879. A gastronomic piece of New York. BYO.

Café Neon, 276 Park St., South Melbourne (A6). Tel: 699 7301. Good and very popular.

Chalky's, 242 Lygon St., Carlton (C1). Tel: 663 6100. One room a buffet-club, the other a traditional restaurant. In summer, tables on the terrace. In the heart of Carlton.

Special atmosphere
The Colonial Tramcar Restaurant. Tel: 596 6500. Excellent cuisine in a redecorated former tram which plies the city streets.

Numerous pubs also serve very good counter lunches (lunches at the bar). Carlton, Fitzroy, North Melbourne and Richmond are the areas for inexpensive Italian, Greek and Lebanese restaurants. They usually stay open until very late at night.

Shopping
Map coordinates refer to the map pp. 126-127.

Melbourne's department stores are located on the Bourke Street Mall, a pedestrian zone (B3). Especially famous are **Myers,** the 'biggest department store in the southern hemisphere' and **David Jones,** a very 'Olde English' store with a tea shop and goods that are 'fashionable but nice'. The city's most attractive 19th-century shopping arcade, the **Royal Arcade,** is located between Bourke and Collins Sts. (B3).

Chapel St. and **Toorak Rd.** in Toorak, and **Lygon St.** in Carlton (C1) are the busiest shopping streets and offer the greatest choice among Melbourne's residential areas. Don't miss the very European **Victoria Markets,** at the top of Elizabeth St. (B3), or the smaller markets in Prahran and South Melbourne (A5).

Authentic Aboriginal arts and crafts
Aboriginal Artefacts, Art & Handicrafts, 181 Collins St., City (B3). Tel: 63 4717.

Antiques
Bruce Rutherford, 115 Collins St., City (B3). Tel: 63 3900.

Art galleries
Andrew Ivanyi, 262 Toorak Rd., South Yarra (D6 south). Tel: 241 8366.

Realities, 35 Jackson St., Toorak. Tel: 241 3312.

Tolarno, 98 River St., South Yarra (D6 south). Tel: 241 8381.

Opals
Altmann & Cherny, 120 Exhibition St., City (C3). Tel: 639 685.

Andrew Cody, 119 Swanston St., City (B3). Tel: 654 5533.

Sports
Melbourne is a world capital for competition sports.

Cricket
In summer, from October to April, the whole city follows cricket, and the MCG, built for the 1956 Olympic Games, often holds 50,000 to 80,000 spectators at matches between England and Australia.

Footy
Every Saturday in winter, from April to September, Melbourne lives for

footy (Australia football). This rapid version of rugby is very entertaining. It is played between two teams of 18 players on an oval field. 12 clubs representing 10 districts of Melbourne, the neighbouring city of Geelong and one team from Sydney compete with each other yearly for the championship. The Grand Final is played at the end of September and has attracted more than 100,000 spectators annually since the MCG was built. Loyalty to teams with names like the Tigers, the Demons, the Kangaroos and the Bombers, alienates father from son (or daughter).

The game has accounted for much of the social life of many Melbournians since the beginning of the century.

Horse racing

The Melbourne Cup, the most prestigious horse race in Australia, is the reason for declaring the first Tuesday in November a public holiday in Victoria.

Tennis

The annual **Australian Open Tennis Championship** is held at the turn of the year. It is held at the new National Tennis Centre in Flinders Park.

Entertainment and cultural life

Map coordinates refer to the map pp. 126-127.

Theatre

Melbourne, which often has full houses for Broadway and West-End productions in the traditional theatres such as **Princes Theatre, The Comedy** or **Her Majesty's,** also virtually invented experimental theatre in Australia. Numerous 'off-Broadway' theatres can be found in the inner suburbs.

La Mama, 205 Faraday St., Carlton (C1 north). Tel: 386 3583.

Universal Theatre, 19 Victoria St., Fitzroy (D2). Tel: 419 3777.

The Anthill, 199 Napier St., South Melbourne. Tel: 699 3253.

Melbourne is also the Australian capital of the theatre-restaurant. Laughs are guaranteed!

Last Laugh Restaurant, 64 Smith St., Collingwood (D3 east). Tel: 419 8600.

Comedy Café, 117 Brunswick St., Fitzroy (D2). Tel: 419 2869. BYO.

Merlin's, 135 Greeves St., Fitzroy (D2 east). Tel: 417 5399. BYO.

Nero's Fiddle, 454 Whitehorse Rd., Mitcham. Tel: 874 8065.

Concerts and exhibitions

Classical music and jazz concerts are given at the **Dallas Brooks Hall,** 300 Victoria Parade, East Melbourne (D3). Tel: 419 2288.

In summer, there are frequent rock, jazz and classical music concerts at the **Myer Music Bowl,** an open-air amphitheatre in the garden of the residence of the Governor-General of Victoria, or in one of the city's parks. There is no admission price for these concerts, held every October to May. Rock concerts are also held at **Festival Hall,** Dudley St., West Melbourne (A2). Tel: 654 5655, and the **Melbourne Sports and Entertainment Centre,** Swan St., City (C5). Tel: 429 6288.

However, the cultural heart of Melbourne is the **Victorian Arts Centre** at the top of St. Kilda Rd., beside the Yarra (B4). This enormous multi-cultural complex, topped by a 377 ft/115 m high mini-Eiffel Tower, houses a creative-arts museum (see p. 135), three theatres and a concert hall. Whereas Sydney lavished money on the exterior of its Opera House, Melbourne concentrated on the interior decor of its performance halls: unbelievable luxury, exceptional taste, outstanding acoustics and seating arrangement, superb productions. *Programs and reservations:* 617 8211.

Festivals and celebrations

Other great social events in Melbourne include the *Moomba Festival* held

Futuristic architecture in Melbourne.

during the first 10 days in March, a popular carnival which attracts surprisingly large crowds for such an otherwise apparently staid city.

The Royal Agricultural Show is held in September and gives rise to intense competition between such groups as lumberjacks or sheep shearers in a friendly atmosphere.

Pubs and nightlife

Map coordinates refer to the map pp. 126-127.

Nowhere more than in Melbourne is it important to choose the correct pub(s) in which to drink. The people of Melbourne judge a person's character by the answers to three simple questions: what school did you go to? what football team do you support on Saturday afternoon? what pub do you drink at? There are four kinds of pubs in Melbourne: the city pub where office colleagues drink; the fashionable pub where you go to mingle with people of your own milieu; the local, family pub where the barmaid calls you by your first name and does not need to ask you what you want to drink; and, finally, the pub which offers jazz or rock music.

City pubs

The city pubs are often associated with different professions.

The **John Curtin,** on Lygon St. (C2), opposite the Trades Hall, is the watering-hole for unionists and Labor-party politicians.

The **Golden Age** at 287 King St. (A3), and the **Phoenix** at 82 Flinders St. (C3) are the respective haunts of journalists from the *Age* and the *Herald* (they do not mix).

The **Central Club** in Victoria St., North Melbourne (A-B1), is open from 7am for people from the nearby city markets.

Young and Jacksons, at the top of Swanston St. (B3), attracts the suburban crowd who stop in for a quick beer before taking the train home from the nearby station. The portrait of the naked Chloé which has adorned the bar since 1908 has contributed to making it the best-known pub in Australia.

Fashionable pubs

Melbourne's fashionable pubs include the **Toorak** in Toorak Rd., reserved for the 'in' crowd who have achieved a certain social status and, at the other end of the scale, the **Albion** in Lygon St., Carlton (C1). Until recently this was the meeting-place for dropouts, artists and people looking for a fight but it has quietened down considerably.

Local pubs

The most typical local pubs are those in the inner suburbs, the 19th-century areas close to the city, where retired workers, European migrants, students and dynamic young executives live side by side. These areas include Fitzroy, which is the most cosmopolitan, Carlton, Collingwood, Richmond and North Melbourne. Closer to the sea, South Melbourne, Port Melbourne and Williamstown are less lively but more authentic. All the original working-class areas have a pub on the corner of about every major intersection. Further away, in the outer suburbs and residential areas, the pubs tend to be more modern: huge and ultra-functional.

Pubs and music

Small jazz groups (New Orleans jazz is especially popular in Melbourne) regularly play in several pubs.

Museum Hotel, 293 Latrobe St., City (A-B2). Tel: 60 1128.

Station Hotel, corner of Greville and Porter Sts., Prahran. Tel: 51 2981.

The Reef, 126 Little Collins St., City (B3). Tel: 63 4585.

Finally, as in all Australian cities, there are numerous pubs which offer evening entertainment by local groups. Programs can be found in the morning *Age* or in Thursday evening's *Herald*.

Dancing

Discotheques
All of these are rather fashionable and smart-casual dress is in order.

The Chevron, 519 St. Kilda Rd., City (B4). Tel: 51 1281, open Sun.

The Melbourne Underground, 22 King St., City (A3). Tel: 62 470.

Chasers, 386 Chapel St., South Yarra (D6 south). Tel: 241 6615.

Crystal T's, 672 Sydney Rd., Brunswick. Tel: 383 2213.

Nightclubs
Smarter than the discos.

Juliana's in the Hilton (D4).

The Club, 132 Smith St., Collingwood (D3 east).

Inflation, 60 King St., City (A3).

▄▄▄ GETTING TO KNOW MELBOURNE

More than Sydney, Melbourne requires time for visitors to adapt to its rhythm. Forget about being a tourist—travel the city by tram; feel the electric atmosphere at a football stadium; experience Melbourne's long sense of tradition along the Oxford-like banks of the Yarra River; share the simple warmth of a pub; rediscover the outdoors on the lawns of the city's splendid and extensive parks.

In spite of its size, the places of interest are relatively close to each other: the city itself; the inner suburbs (restored, cosmopolitan Victorian areas) of Carlton, Fitzroy, Collingwood and Richmond, located north-east of the Yarra; the ultra-smart shopping centres of South Yarra, Toorak and Prahran, south of the Yarra; and, between the river and the sea, the harbour and the beaches (less attractive than those in Sydney) on Port Phillip Bay.

The City

The centre of Melbourne is laid out like a checkerboard, with sides a mile long. The main artery, Swanston St., can be covered in five minutes by tram—even during the rush hour. If you stand at the beginning of Swanston St. (B3), and turn towards the south, you will see on your right the dome of Melbourne's **Flinders Street Station** (B4). On your left are the three brown-stone bell-towers of the neo-Gothic **St. Paul's Cathedral** (C3). Directly ahead, across Prince's Bridge over the Yarra, lies the **National Gallery** (B4). Beyond it is the pseudo-Aztec pyramid of the Shrine of Remembrance (B5), dedicated to those Australians who lost their lives at Gallipoli. To the north, beyond Collins St. (the main business street) and Bourke St. (the shopping street), you can see the huge sign advertising Australia's largest brewery, **Carlton United Breweries.** Its enormous structures separate the prestigious **University of Melbourne** (C1) from the City.

The buildings in the City are not very original, whether made of concrete and glass, stone or marble, but they do exude the prosperity and the respectability of Melbourne. Sometimes,though, the interiors of the banks and government buildings built prior to World War I can reach the heights of Victorian Baroque grandeur, in an orgy of marble, brass, exotic timbers and crystal. The most outstanding of these, in a more restrained and subdued style, is the reading room in the dome of the **State Library and Museum of Victoria**** (B-C2). It is open to the public and is exquisite. The museum (328 Swanston St. Tel: 669 9888) is open *10am to 5pm Mon. to Sat.,* and *2pm to 5pm on Sun.* It houses the embalmed body of race horse *Phar Lap,* a national hero and the subject of a film of the same name. Swanston St. (between Collins St. and Flinders Lane) is also the address of the **City Square** (B-C3), an American-style indoor-outdoor plaza, where, at lunchtime, stone terraces and fountains attract secretaries looking for a spot to consume their sandwiches and milkshakes, and children who enjoy splashing about in the water.

Carlton to Richmond

Located just to the north of the City (C-D1-2), **Carlton** owes its new-found prestige to the nearby University of Melbourne and to the dynamism of its large Italian community. The area is a mixture of Victorian terrace houses with fine wrought-iron balconies and modest, semi-detached cottages with corrugated-iron veranda roofs. Within a few years, the area has changed from a slightly 'tough' working-class and decidedly ethnic suburb to a relaxed, almost fashionable address for Melbourne Yuppies. Even Toorak trendies come to shop, eat and drink in Lygon St. (C1-2)—Carlton's main thoroughfare. Along with Toorak Rd., it has become one of the liveliest streets in Melbourne.

North Carlton**, on the other side of Alexandra Parade, is bordered to the west by Melbourne's oldest cemetery and by Prince's Park which contains the homeground of Carlton's Mighty Blues football team, complete with mounted policemen and 'pom-pom girls' (cheerleaders). The residential streets of North Carlton are lined with superbly restored terrace houses reflecting the calm and good taste of their current owners: university lecturers, musicians and young lawyers.

The areas Fitzroy, Collingwood and Richmond which, from north to east, link Carlton with the Yarra River are home to the Lions, Magpies and Tigers football teams respectively. Over the last decade, these suburbs have, to varying degrees, undergone the same transformation as Carlton. **Fitzroy*** (D2) and **Collingwood*** (D3) have remained essentially working-class, wearing their authenticity more discreetly than **Richmond** (D4-6) which looks across the river to Toorak and is on the point of overtaking Carlton in terms of respectability and cosmopolitan sophistication.

South of the Yarra: the wealthy areas

Toorak* and **South Yarra*** (D6 south) signify social success even more than does Vaucluse in Sydney. English gardens and stone walls conceal charming houses which reflect the days of the British Empire.

Alexandra Ave.* beside the Yarra (C-D4-6) is the epitome of the sober, elegant Victorian style. The avenue is lined with majestic oak trees, immaculate lawns and Baroque iron bridges across the river, where the rowing teams from local, prestigious private schools practice their sport. In the distance, the buildings of the city seem to belong to another world. Completing this most civilized of Australia's urban decors are the **Royal Botanic Gardens***** (C6). Next to Kew in London and Kandy in Sri Lanka, Melbourne's Botanic Gardens are among the finest English gardens in the world. There are 86 acres/35 ha of undulating, manicured lawns, lakes, romantic bridges, 19th-century kiosks, an astounding collection of more than 10,000 world plant species, adjacent oak and banyan trees, azaleas and magnolias, roses and giant ferns, firs and date-palms, willows and bamboos.

Chapel St. and Toorak Rd. are the main business streets of this aristocratic quarter. Here you will find Melbourne's most elegant restaurants, most sophisticated boutiques and most celebrated art galleries. Greville St. in Prahran is younger, more relaxed and more cosmopolitan, with an almost European feel about it.

Visitors interested in a river cruise on the Yarra should contact:

Melbourne River Cruises, Princes Walk. Tel: 63 4694.

Yarra Princess, Princes Walk. Tel: 63 1382.

Seaside Melbourne

Melbourne is the only Australian capital to have turned its back on the sea at its doorstep. The city beaches are not very inviting and the harbour, at the mouth of the Yarra, does nothing to enhance the cityscape. Only the seagulls on the grass of a football stadium are a reminder that the capital of Victoria is also one of the country's major ports. However, **St. Kilda** is not without interest. The suburb is situated at the end of St. Kilda Rd., Melbourne's main artery lined with discreet skyscrapers, luxury hotels and fine parks. It includes Fitzroy Street, Melbourne's timid answer to Sydney's Kings Cross; an amusement park (Lower Esplanade, St. Kilda. Tel: 534 0653); a Rococo theatre, the *Palais;* and an arts and crafts market along the Esplanade every Sunday. The market is not out of the ordinary but it does give the suburb an old-fashioned character reminiscent of Brighton or Eastbourne on the English coast. To the west, the Esplanade is lined with somewhat depressing 1930s houses as it turns towards the picturesque areas of Port Melbourne and the **West Gate Bridge** (famous, or rather infamous, for the alarming number of years and the loss of life involved in its construction). Then comes **Williamstown***, with terrace houses and sailors' and dockers' pubs that lend charm to the suburb.

Melbourne beaches

If you want to go swimming in Melbourne, go to the local swimming pool or be prepared to spend long but scenic hours getting to the beaches. You have the choice between the beaches of the **Mornington Peninsula** (50 to 150 mi/80 to 250 km round trip) on the twin bays of Port Phillip and Western Port to the south-east, and the surf beaches on the **Southern Ocean** (minimum 125 mi/200 km round trip) in the direction of Adelaide (see map, pp. 158-159).

Mornington Peninsula: drive past the suburban beaches of Brighton, Mordialloc and Chelsea, taking the Nepean Highway as far as **Frankston** (25 mi/40 km from Melbourne). You will then be able to choose between the coast of Port Phillip Bay and the beaches of **Rye, Rosebud** and **Sorrento** (all about 25 mi/40 km from Frankston and often crowded in summer), or the coast of Western Port Bay (38 mi/60 km from Frankston), where beaches such as **Sommers***, **Balnarring*** and **Cape Shanck** are less populated. The peninsula itself is the address of some very beautiful pastoral holdings belonging to some of the oldest families in Melbourne.

Bourke Street, Melbourne's shopping centre.

The Southern Ocean: take the Princes Highway as far as Geelong (47 mi/75 km from Melbourne), Victoria's second city (pop. 145,000). Its old Australian provincial charm is hardly affected by the establishment there of the country's leading automobile manufacturers. Turn south to **Torquay***** (14 mi/23 km from Geelong), where you will encounter the most beautiful beaches, cliffs and surf in Australia, stretching 56 mi/90 km to **Apollo Bay**** (and beyond, to Adelaide) along the Great Ocean Road***. Comparisons with Big Sur, between San Francisco and Los Angeles, are quite justified.

WHAT TO SEE

National Gallery of Victoria**

180 St. Kilda Rd., a stone's throw from the city (B4). Tel: 618 0222. *Open Tues. to Sun. 10am to 5pm.*

The National Gallery contains the greatest collection of art objects in Australia. Housed in a typical Melbourne building—huge and in exemplary taste—the gallery forms the main element of the Victorian Arts Centre.

The first level of the National Gallery is lit superbly through a stained-glass ceiling designed by Leonard French. Here, you can see exhibitions of works by contemporary Australian artists (these shows are listed in the newspapers) and a very fine collection of Asian art (don't miss the exquisite Chinese porcelains).

The second level contains the great names in painting: works by Australian artists from the 19th century to the present (Nolan, Heysen, Dobell, Friend); pre-19th-century European painting (Tiepolo, Rubens, Rembrandt, Reynolds, Gainsborough, Constable, Corot, Goya, etc.); and post-19th-century European and American art (Manet, Degas, Pissarro, Cézanne, Picasso, Pollock). Worth admiring is the remarkable collection of decorative art objects (furniture, ceramics, costumes, silverware, Mediterranean antiquities). There is also a splendid exhibition of photographs on the third level.

Banyule Gallery**

60 Buckingham Drive, Heidelberg, about 6 mi/10 km from the city. Tel: 459 7899. *Open daily 10am to 5pm, except Mon.,* when it caters for groups only.

This annex to the National Gallery houses, *in situ,* some very fine works by painters of the turn-of-the-century Australian Heidelberg School such as McCubbin, Roberts, Streeton and Conder, and their precursors, Buvelot, Nerli and Ashton. The residence in which the collection is housed was built in 1846, in the neo-Gothic style popular at the time. From its hill, it dominates the neighbouring countryside and the Yarra River.

Colony of Montsalvat**

Montsalvat, Hillcrest Avenue, Eltham, 16 mi/26 km east of the city. Tel: 439 7712.

In the same style as Banyule but more private, Montsalvat is a magnificent neo-Norman manor house built by artists themselves in the hills of Eltham, as a refuge for the Melbourne cultural aristocracy. It contains exhibitions of contemporary painting and is the setting for musical and theatrical performances of a very high calibre.

Old Melbourne Gaol and Penal Museum**

Russell St. (opposite the central police station), City (C3). Tel: 654 3628. *Open daily 10am to 5pm.*

Construction of this stone prison began in 1841. It has now been converted into a museum but was the stage, until 1929, of 104 hangings, including that of bushranger Ned Kelly in 1880. You can see the gallows (or rather the trap door) used for his execution, as well as his strange iron armour, dented by bullets, including his helmet with the eye slit that made him famous and which served as the inspiration for the well-known series of paintings by Sidney Nolan.

Como House and Rippon Lea*

Como House (1840-70), Como Ave., South Yarra (D6). Tel: 241 2550. *Open daily 10am to 5pm.*

Rippon Lea (1860-90), 192 Hotham St., Elsternwick. Tel: 523 9150. *Open daily 10am to 5pm, except in winter.*

Especially beautiful examples of high Victorian architecture, these elegant homes have been restored carefully and are surrounded by magnificent English gardens.

Melbourne Cricket Club Museum*

Yarra Park, Wellington Parade, Jolimont (D4). Tel: 63 6066. *Open Wed. morning at 10am.* Everything concerning Victoria's leading sport.

Maritime Museum

HMAS *Castemaine,* Gem Pier, Williamstown. Tel: 397 2363. *Open Sat. and Sun. 10am to 6pm.*

A naval museum on board a warship built in 1941.

Melbourne Zoo*

Royal Park. North Carlton. Tel: 347 1522. *Open daily 9am to 5pm.*

The zoo has the advantage of being located close to the city (less than 2.5 mi/4 km). Take a tram (No 18, 19 or 20 from Elizabeth St. in the city), and get off at stop No 22, opposite Carlton Stadium. Animals from all over the world, including a great variety of indigenous species (like the platypus).

▬▬ THE DANDENONGS

No Australian city would be complete without its hills. Melbourne's hills, the **Dandenongs,** are located 25 mi/40 km east of the city. There, forests such as **Sherbrooke Forest Park**** are the natural habitat of the famous lyre-bird, the Australian pheasant with a lyre-shaped tail that inspired its name. You may be lucky enough to see several specimens beneath an ash tree, a variety of eucalypt with a silvery (or ashen) trunk rising straight as a concrete column to more than 190 ft/60 m. Other lyre-birds prefer the clumps of fern trees, with their strangely tropical appearance in an undergrowth covered by snow in winter.

A further tourist attraction in the Dandenongs is **Puffing Billy,** a miniature train drawn by an old steam locomotive. Tel: 754 6876. It links the station at Belgrave—reached by a classic iron railway line—to that at Emerald Lake, a 6 mi/10 km journey through spectacular bush. On the return journey, you can watch night fall over Melbourne from the heights of Mt. Dandenong (2077 ft/633 m).

Accommodation and food

The small towns hidden in the hills, between orchards, meadows and forests, contain some excellent restaurants.

▲▲▲ **Burnham Beeches,** Sherbrooke Rd., Sherbrooke. Tel: 755 1903. This is a very elegant art deco hotel in a splendid park, with an excellent restaurant. 54 rooms, 2 suites.

Bundy's Tavern, Olinda Rd., Monbulk. Tel: 756 6122. Hungarian cuisine in a pleasant Alpine chalet atmosphere.

Coonara Springs, Coonara Rd., Olinda. Tel: 751 1043. Outstanding view, rustic-elegant atmosphere.

Mt. Rael, Yarra Glen Rd., Healesville. Tel: 62 4107. Go there for the view, and the possibility of eating outdoors on the terrace, weather permitting.

RURAL VICTORIA

Situated entirely on the moist and fertile side of the Great Dividing Range, the state of Victoria certainly deserves its reputation as Australia's 'Garden State'. Its hills, pastures and forests are greener than anywhere else on the mainland. Just like Melbourne, Victorian country towns, whether large and prosperous agricultural centres or powerful and splendidly preserved Gold Rush capitals, all bear witness to the dynamism of Victoria.

PHILLIP ISLAND AND ITS PENGUINS

Every night, since time began, hundreds of tiny Fairy Penguins have left the sea and scurried up to their burrows in the sand dunes of Summerland Beach on Phillip Island. Every night, since the invention of electricity, hundreds of silent spectators have lain on their stomachs in the sand, watching the 'penguin parade' in the glare of powerful spotlights. The penguins and the spectators feel quite at ease with each other, and a visit there is sure to please. Phillip Island is also home to 'imported' koalas and to thousands of seals. **Penguin Parade,** Summerland Beach. Tel: 56 8300.

Access

To reach Phillip Island by car, take Western Port Bay to San Remo (75 mi/120 km from Melbourne), which is connected to the island by a 2100 ft/640 m long bridge. Otherwise, take one of the numerous tour ouses operated by **AAT, Ansett** or **Australian Pacific,** 181 Flinders St., Melbourne (B4). Tel: 63 1511.

Accommodation

▲▲ **The Anchor at Cowes,** Esplanade. Tel: (059) 52 1351. Motel. 35 rooms.

▲ **Sunseeker Motor Inn,** Church St., Cowes. Tel: (059) 52 2285. 25 rooms.

WILSONS PROMONTORY

Wilsons Promontory National Park**, 156 mi/250 km east of Melbourne, owes its popularity to its magnificent beaches, its black granite cliffs, its wallabies, wombats and parrots wandering among the bungalows, and to its 124,000 acre/50,000 ha lush, virgin bush. The Promontory is a favourite rendez-vous for young Melbournians seeking the great outdoors and the 'Prom' still has enough mysterious nooks and crannies to give you the feeling of being an intrepid explorer. The view from the cliff tops along the coast is tremendous.

Access

To get to Wilsons Promontory, take the South Gippsland Highway as far as Foster (109 mi/175 km from Melbourne), and then the direct road to the park.

Accommodation

Reservations for bungalows at the park's **Tidal River** camp can be made through Victour offices.

Information: **Wilsons Promontory National Park,** Tidal River via Foster, Vic. 3960. Tel: 80 8558.

BALLARAT AND THE GOLD RUSH

It was in August 1851 that Thomas Hisock found gold on the slopes of Mt. Buninyong, a hill occupied by a few Aborigines and white shepherds, close to present-day Ballarat. The lode proved to be one of the richest in the world and within months, tens of thousands of prospectors had invaded the area and founded the town of Ballarat, destined to occupy the central stage of Australian history for many years. The town's importance rests not only on the Eureka Stockade incident in 1854 (see p. 38-39), but also on the fact that the rush to the Victorian Gold Fields in the mid–19th century saw the young colony's population triple in less than 10 years, from 400,000 to nearly 1,200,000.

The first prospectors who arrived in 1851 simply recovered the gold from the river where it lay, using the method known as panning. They would place a shovelful of alluvial dirt in a pan shaped something like a washbasin, cover it with water and sluice the dirt methodically, separating the heavier specks of gold from the rest. The dirt was washed away and soon, if the miner was lucky, only the gold remained in the bottom of the pan. After a time, however, the prospectors needed to search further afield for the gold which had been buried in the beds of former rivers thousands of years before, during volcanic eruptions. Teams of three or four miners would form to work claims smaller than 2.3sq yd/2sq m—more cramped than a grave. Mine shafts were dug through basalt, sand and volcanic slag until the alluvial deposits were reached. If Lady Luck smiled on the miners, they might recover 55 lbs/25 kg of pure gold from a single load of rubble. Then, it was back to the hole and continued digging in the blazing sun.

By 1860, however, such deposits were exhausted. The area was full of veins of gold-bearing quartz, but exploiting them needed more than determination and luck. As a result, the mines of Ballarat changed over from manual to mechanical labour. The diggers went to work for companies which could put together enough capital to buy the equipment and materials necessary for extracting, crushing and filtering the quartz. Mines such as these were in operation until 1918.

The history of the Gold Rush at the end of the 19th century is the theme of the **Sovereign Hill**** open-air museum at Ballarat (69 mi/110 km north-west of Melbourne on the Great Western Highway). There you can see an accurate, life-size reconstruction of the main street of the time, with its shops, hotels, newspaper offices, stagecoaches, crinoline-clad women, a mining camp by a gold-yielding river, where diggers in period costume demonstrate gold panning. The museum also features an underground mine. The overall concept is well thought out and the combination of

Ballarat, a legendary Gold Rush town.

authenticity and tasteful Hollywood touches has made the museum one of the most successful of its type in the world.

Gold is hitting the newspaper headlines again these days and the gold fields of Victoria and Western Australia (see p. 179) are experiencing a new gold rush by weekend diggers who spend their Saturdays and Sundays standing in rivers or in the dust of the desert, gold pan or metal detector in their hands. Nor do they toil in vain—in November 1980, a pair of hopefuls working an old mine in Victoria found a nugget weighing 66 lbs/30 kg, the *Hand of Faith* nugget, which they sold to a Las Vegas casino in early 1981 for 1 million US dollars.

The town of Ballarat itself has a current population of 57,000 and has lost nothing of its former grandeur, thanks to its many beautiful Victorian Baroque buildings.

Ballarat is the most touristic of Victoria's gold towns but there are others just as well preserved and more original within a radius of 156 mi/250 km of Melbourne. **Bendigo**★★ (94 mi/150 km from Melbourne, on the Calder Highway), especially, is Ballarat's alter ego, but there are also **Castlemaine** and **Maldon** (on the road to Bendigo), and **Stawell,** on the Great Western Highway beyond Ballarat (see map pp. 158-159).

Access

You can get to Ballarat by car (1.5 hour drive), train, bus or organized tour.
Ansett-Pioneer. Tel: (053) 342 3144.
AAT. Tel: (053) 347 5555.
Australian Pacific. Tel: (053) 63 1511.

Accommodation and food

Ballarat has lots of hotels, among them:
▲▲ **Mid City,** 19 Doveton St. North. Tel: (053) 31 1223. Motel. 71 rooms.

▲ **Provincial Hotel,** 121 Lydiard St. Tel: (053) 32 1845. 33 rooms.
Restaurants include **Dyer's Steak Stable,** Little Bridge St.
Tel: (053) 31 2850.

SNOW-CLAD VICTORIA

The highest section of the Great Dividing Range in the state of Victoria is
known as the **Victorian Alps,** although the highest mountain is less than
6200 ft/1900 m. Between June and September, the Victorian Alps receive
enough snow to support the development of a half-dozen winter-sports
resorts. These are all the more popular because they are only four to six
hours by road from Melbourne. The best equipped are:

Mt. Buffalo, 207 mi/331 km from Melbourne (4.5 hours), 5646 ft/1721 m;
for beginners. Information: (057) 55 1466.

Falls Creek, 237 mi/379 km from Melbourne (5.5 hours), 5902 ft/1799 m;
for everyone. Information: (057) 58 3224.

Mt. Buller, 151 mi/241 km from Melbourne (4 hours), 5935 ft/1809 m; the
largest ski resort in Victoria, skiing for everyone, disco, very popular.
Information: (057) 77 6077.

Mt. Hotham, 229 mi/367 km from Melbourne (6 hours), 6112 ft/1863 m;
the most isolated Victorian ski resort, excellent slopes for downhill and
cross-country skiing. Information: (057) 59 3550.

Mt. Baw Baw, 112 mi/179 km from Melbourne (3 hours), 5131 ft/1564 m;
the closest ski resort to Melbourne, for beginners and families.
Information: (056) 28 1401.

All ski resorts have hotels, motels, chalets, restaurants and ski lifts. If you
plan on spending one or more nights there, reserve as far in advance as
possible through **Victorian Tourist Bureau.** Tel: (03) 619 9444.

Numerous tour operators offer packages starting from Melbourne. Among
them are: **Hoy's Tourist Service.** Tel: (03) 59 3610; **Trekset.**
Tel: (03) 338 4266; **Wanderers Ski Holidays.** Tel: (03) 63 6003.

Information on **Baw Baw National Park:** Box 63, Rawson, Vic. 3825.
Tel: (051) 65 0381.

TASMANIA

T he green of Tasmania is the grey-green of the inevitable
eucalypts, the golden green of high pastures, the bluish-green
of the impenetrable mountain forests on the west coast. To attract
their northern cousins, Tasmanians like to emphasize the image of
a 'Holiday Isle', covered by lakes, roaring torrents, green pastures,
rural hamlets and Gothic churches.

Separated from the mainland by the 156 mi/250 km breadth of
the Bass Strait, this triangle with 188 mi/300 km of coastline barely
covers 27,000 sq mi/70,000 sq km (not even a hundredth of the
surface area of Australia). It lies in the path of the famous Roaring
Forties, the strong winds that blow at the 40th parallel south
latitude, further south than the Cape of Good Hope. The countryside is quite varied, broken by a series of hills, valleys, high plateaux
and mountains. Their sharp contours, which become more pronounced from east to west, are in stark contrast to the rounded
shapes usually associated with mountainous areas in Australia,
though the highest peak, Mt. Ossa, is only just over 5250 ft/1600 m
high. Because of its location and topography, Tasmania experiences
a temperate, relatively damp climate. The west coast, the most
mountainous, receives up to 142 in/3600 mm of rain a year and the
high plateaux are snow-covered in winter. There are numerous
lakes and rivers, filled with clear, fresh, deep-blue water.

The Aborigines had already been there for thousands of years
when Dutchman Abel Tasman 'discovered' the island in 1642. The
period from 1788 to 1901 represented a swift sweep from the
ancient, to medieval, Renaissance and new industrial age. The
island was originally named Van Diemen's Land and was annexed
to the British Crown in 1802 to prevent the French from establishing
a presence there. Hobart was established in the south in 1804 (when
the first convicts arrived) and Launceston followed in the north in
1805. More prisoners continued to arrive until transportation was
abolished in 1853 although the prison at Port Arthur was not closed
until 1877. In the meantime, attempts were being made to
exterminate the local Aborigines, or to round them up and
segregate them on offshore islands. The last full-blood Aborigine,
a woman named Truganini, died in 1876.

In 1825, Van Diemen's Land became independent from New
South Wales and in 1856, to honour the memory of its Dutch
discoverer, the colony changed its name to Tasmania. From 1901,
Tasmania's modern history has been linked to that of the British
Commonwealth which periodically rediscovers this island appen-
dage with its traditionalist inhabitants.

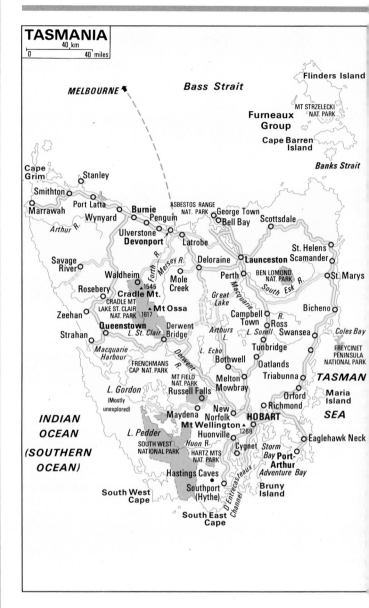

TASMANIA

0 ___ 40 km
0 ___ 40 miles

Bass Strait

MELBOURNE

Flinders Island

MT STRZELECKI NAT. PARK

Furneaux Group

Cape Barren Island

Banks Strait

Cape Grim
Stanley
Smithton
Marrawah
Port Latta
Wynyard   Burnie   ASBESTOS RANGE NAT. PARK
Penguin   George Town
Bell Bay
Scottsdale
Ulverstone
Devonport   Latrobe
Arthur R.
Savage River
Waldheim   Deloraine   Launceston   Scamander
St. Helens
Roseberry   Mole Creek   Perth   BEN LOMOND NAT. PARK   St. Marys
Cradle Mt.   ▲1545
CRADLE MT. LAKE ST. CLAIR NAT. PARK   ▲Mt Ossa   Great Lake   South Esk R.
Zeehan   1617   Campbell Town   Bicheno
Queenstown   Derwent Bridge   Ross   R.
Strahan   L. St. Clair   Arthurs L.   L. Sorell   Swansea   Coles Bay
Macquarie Harbour   L. Echo   Tunbridge   FREYCINET PENINSULA NATIONAL PARK
FRENCHMANS CAP NAT. PARK   Bothwell   Oatlands   TASMAN
L. Gordon   MT FIELD NAT. PARK   Melton   Triabunna   Maria Island
(Mostly unexplored)   Mowbray   Orford
Russell Falls   New Norfolk   Richmond   SEA
Maydena   HOBART
INDIAN OCEAN   Mt Wellington ▲
L. Pedder   1269
(SOUTHERN OCEAN)   SOUTH WEST NATIONAL PARK   Huonville   Cygnet   Storm   Port Arthur   Eaglehawk Neck
Huon R.   HARTZ MTS NAT. PARK   Bay   Adventure Bay
Hastings Caves
South West Cape   Southport (Hythe)   Bruny Island
South East Cape

The island's brutal colonial era occurred during one of the British Empire's last major attempts at expansionism. More than 67,000 convicts were transported to Tasmania and, between 1802 and 1876, the island's 3000 Aborigines were totally eliminated.

Today, with a population of 430,000, Tasmania has one of the highest unemployment rates in Australia (10.5%) and immigration alone cannot compensate for the vast numbers of young people that leave for the mainland. In order to create employment, the state took three major ecological risks by exploiting the island's forestry, mineral and hydro-electric resources.

In 1983, the commencement of work on a huge dam on the Gordon River, which was included on the UNESCO World Heritage List, led to a serious ecological-political crisis. In the federal election that resulted, Bob Hawke, an opponent of the project, was elected to the Parliament. The battle to save the island's outstanding environment still needs to be won, if only to preserve Tasmania's main industry, tourism, which attracts over 300,000 visitors per year.

Tasmania is the only state which can be covered in a few days. Its climate is pleasant, its scenery varied and its vast wilderness, cities and countryside retain the authentic flavour of an Australia which has not yet entered the 1980s.

▆▆▆ PRACTICAL INFORMATION

Access

Tasmania can be reached by boat from Melbourne or by plane from any of the major cities on the mainland, as well as from Christchurch and Auckland in New Zealand.

Boat

The only car/passenger service between Tasmania and the mainland is offered by the ferry *Abel Tasman* which connects Melbourne with Devonport on the north coast. The ferry leaves from Melbourne at 6pm on Mon., Wed., and Fri., and from Devonport at 6pm on Tues., Thurs. and Sun. The crossing takes 14.5 hours. Prices for passengers and their vehicles are very reasonable. Information and reservations:

Melbourne
Tasmanian Tourist Bureau, 256 Collins St. (B3). Tel: (03) 653 7999.

Devonport
Tasmanian Travel Bureau, 18 Rooke St. Tel: (004) 24 1526.

In Sydney or Melbourne, you can put your vehicle on a cargo ship which travels regularly to Hobart but which does not take passengers. You then fly to Hobart, coordinating your arrival with that of your vehicle. There are two ships per week between Melbourne and Hobart (30-hour voyage) and one between Sydney and Hobart (40 hours). Information and reservations:

Sydney
Tasmanian Tourist Bureau, 129 King St. (A4). Tel: (02) 233 2500.
Union Bulkships, 333 George St. (A4). Tel: (02) 2 0238.

Melbourne
Union Bulkships, 90 William St. (B3). Tel: (03) 609 1011.

Hobart
Union Bulkships, 57 Salamanca Place, Battery Point. Tel: (002) 23 4077.

Plane

Ansett and **Australian Airlines** both have daily, direct flights between Melbourne and Hobart or Launceston. Other direct flights leave from Sydney and Coolangatta on the Queensland Gold Coast. Connections to the rest of Australia are possible from Melbourne or Sydney. **East-West Airlines** offers flights from Sydney, Melbourne and Brisbane to Hobart, Devonport and Wynyard. **Ansett, Australian Airlines, Air New Zealand** and **Qantas** also fly between Hobart and Auckland and Christchurch in New Zealand.

It is advisable to arrive in Hobart and leave from Launceston, or vice versa, in order to take advantage of the very competitively priced fly/drive packages offered by the two national airlines.

Hobart
Ansett, 178 Liverpool St. Tel: (002) 38 1111.
Australian Airlines, 4 Liverpool St. Tel: (002) 38 3333.

East-West Airlines, 60 Liverpool St. Tel: (002) 38 0200.
Launceston
Ansett, 54 Brisbane St. Tel: (003) 32 5101.
Australian Airlines, 59 Brisbane St. Tel: (003) 31 4411.

Climate

Temperatures in Tasmania are considerably lower than those on the mainland. February, Hobart's hottest month, has an average temperature of 70°F/21°C, as opposed to Sydney and Melbourne's 78°F/26°C, and 84°F/29°C in the other capitals. In winter, average temperatures are between 34°F/5°C and 61°F/16°C, with snow above 3280 ft/1000 m in July-August. In both summer and winter you should come equipped for rain which falls more often in Tasmania than anywhere else in Australia.

Getting around Tasmania

Distance is no obstacle in Tasmania. If you can manage a week there, rent a car. If you have less time, combine bus, car and plane. There are no passenger trains in Tasmania.

Plane
A fast and spectacular means of discovering the island is to take a flight in a business jet. This kind of air safari, flying over the wildest parts of the island, will take you to Strahan, on the west coast, the departure point for cruises on the Gordon River. Three companies offer these flights, either from Hobart or Launceston:

Par Avion, PO Box 300, Sandy Bay. Tel: (002) 48 5390.
Scenic Air, PO Box 42, Evandale. Tel: (003) 91 8330.
Tasair, GPO Box 451E, Hobart. Tel: (002) 48 5088.

Bus
Regular bus services are provided by **Tasmanian Redline.** Between Hobart and Launceston, for example, there are 6 departures per day and the journey takes three hours.

Devonport
9 Edward St. Tel: (004) 24 2685.
Hobart
96 Harrington St. Tel: (002) 34 4577.
Launceston
112 George St. Tel: (003) 31 9177.

Tourist bus excursions are also very popular. These packages should not be scorned—the commentary by the driver-guide is often very amusing and new friendships are assured. One disadvantage: the tour pace may not necessarily be yours. Companies offering this kind of service include **Tasmanian Redline Coaches** for organized tours marketed by state tourist offices. Excursions last from a half-day to 10 or 18 days.

Car rental
Hobart
Avis, 39 Campbell St. Tel: (002) 34 4222.
Budget, 47 Liverpool St. Tel: (002) 34 5222.
Hertz, 119 Harrington St. Tel: (002) 34 5555.
Thrifty, 156 Harrington St. Tel: (002) 23 3577.
Launceston
Avis, 207 Charles St. Tel: (003) 31 1633.
Budget, 138 George St. Tel: (003) 91 8566.
Hertz, 58 Paterson St. Tel: (003) 31 2099.

Taxis
Combined Services. Tel: (003) 34 8444.

Useful addresses

Tourist information

Tasmanian Government Tourist Bureau, 80 Elizabeth St., Hobart. Tel: (002) 30 0211.

National Parks and Wildlife Service, 16 Magnet Court, Sandy Bay. Tel: (002) 30 8033.

Post office and banks

General Post Office (GPO), corner of Elizabeth and Macquarie Sts., Hobart. Tel: (002) 23 3243.

Banks are open 10am to 3pm (except the **Savings Bank of Tasmania,** open 8.30am to 5.30pm) and closed Sat. and Sun.

Automobile club

Royal Automobile Club of Tasmania, corner of Murray and Patrick Sts., Hobart. Tel: (002) 38 2200.

Attractions

If you'd like to discover Tasmania's natural wonders on a safari or a bushwalk, contact one of the following tour organizers.

Bushventures, 4 Heath Court, Kingston. Tel: (002) 29 4291. Safaris in off-road vehicles.

Craclair Tours, Box 516, PO Devonport. Tel: (004) 24 3971. Bushwalks in the Cradle Lake-Mt. Clair region.

Wilderness Tours, Arve Rd., Geeveston. Tel: (002) 97 1384. Bushwalks in the south-west.

Best season: November to May. Information and reservations: directly from the tour organizer or from Tasbureau Offices. The latter can also put you in touch with organizers of other sporting activities, such as rafting and fishing.

HOBART

Hobart (pop. 175,000), Tasmania's capital on the south coast of the island, is a Lilliput version of the larger mainland cities. It has a river mouth (the Derwent) and a bridge (the Tasman Bridge); it is close to the sea, with mountains in the background (Mt. Wellington, 4167 ft/1270 m), and mingles steep avenues, a mall and shopping arcades with its parks, Victorian areas, embryonic expressway and spreading suburbs. Above all, it has a neat and tidy, provincial atmosphere accentuated by a sky that is a lighter shade of blue than on the mainland and a deeper blue sea which reaches to the very feet of the city's modest tower blocks.

■ PRACTICAL INFORMATION

Telephone area code: 002.

Accommodation

In summer (December to February) hotels may be full. Advance booking is advisable.

International-standard and first-class hotels

▲▲▲▲ **Four Seasons Westside Motor Inn,** 156 Bathurst St. Tel: 34 6255. Central, comfortable. 140 rooms.

▲▲▲▲ **Lenna Motor Inn,** 20 Runnymede St., Battery Point. Tel: 23 2911. Located in the picturesque Battery Point district, a stylish hotel, old and well renovated. 45 rooms, 5 suites.

▲▲▲▲ **Wrest Point Federal Hotel-Casino,** 410 Sandy Bay Rd., Sandy Bay. Tel: 25 0112. Located on the waterfront a little way from

the city, this hotel was the first official casino to open in Australia. 281 rooms, 12 suites.

▲▲▲ **Southport Town House,** 167 Macquarie St. Tel: 34 4422. 108 rooms.

Moderately priced and inexpensive hotels

▲▲ **Hadleys,** 34 Murray St. Tel: 23 4355. A pub right in the centre of town, with an 'Olde English' restaurant which is one of the best in Hobart. 90 rooms.

▲▲ **Southport Motor Lodge,** 429 Sandy Bay Rd., Sandy Bay. Tel: 25 2511. 30 rooms.

▲ **Colville Cottage,** 32 Mona St., Battery Point. Tel: 23 6968. 6 rooms.

▲ **Cromwell Cottage,** 6 Cromwell St., Battery Point. Tel: 23 6734. 5 rooms.

▲ **Hobart Youth Hostel,** 54 King St., Bellerive. Tel: 44 2552. Members only.

Colville and Cromwell Cottage are very charming and well-located guest houses (bed and breakfast).

Food

By and large, Hobart is in the process of catching up with the cuisine offered on the mainland. In fact, it has a seafood restaurant which is considered the best in Australia: **Mures** (see below).

Italian

Don Camillo, 6 Magnet Court, Sandy Bay. Tel: 34 1006.

Mondo Picolo, 196 Macquarie St. Tel: 23 2362.

Seafood

J.C.'s, 160 Sandy Bay Rd., Sandy Bay. Tel: 23 6220.

Medallion, 91 Elizabeth St. Tel: 34 6018.

Milan's, 7 Beach Rd., Sandy Bay. Tel: 25 2180.

Mures, 2 Knopwood St., Battery Point. Tel: 23 6917.

Steaks and grill

The Astor Grill, 156 Macquarie St. Tel: 34 8333.

Dear Friends, 8 Brooke St., The Water Front. Tel: 23 2646.

Special atmosphere

Black Prince, 145 Elizabeth St. Tel: 34 3501. Popular among tourists.

Mr Wooby's, 65 Salamanca Place, Battery Point. Tel: 34 3466. Open until late in the evening.

Theatre-restaurant

The Rampant Bear, 13 Cromwell St., Battery Point. Tel: 23 5002.

Shopping

The **Salamanca Centre for Arts and Crafts,** 65-79 Salamanca Place, Battery Point, was established in a series of stone warehouses built in 1840. The Centre contains boutiques, galleries, restaurants and even a theatre. The craftsmanship is of a very high standard and the atmosphere somewhat tourist oriented.

On Saturday mornings an Australian-style **flea market** is held in the square opposite the elegant brown-stone buildings, behind a border of hundred-year-old plane trees.

Also tourist oriented but tasteful, the **National Trust Shop,** 25 Kirksway Place Tel: 34 9289, built in 1875, contains an information centre devoted to the historic houses and other buildings administered by the National Trust.

Tasmania, a lush island south of the Australian mainland.

Yachting regattas

Regattas are focal points of Hobart life. The Sydney-to-Hobart race (the leading yachts arrive around January 1) and the Royal Hobart Regatta (second week in February) cover the Derwent River with a mass of spinnakers, while Constitution Dock in the heart of the city takes on the atmosphere of Cowes or Bermuda.

Royal Yacht Club of Tasmania, Marleville Esplanade, Sandy Bay Tel: 23 4599.

Pubs and nightlife

Aside from the **Wrest Point Casino** (open daily 1pm to 3am or 4am), there is not much happening in the city after 5.30pm. The only people you are likely to encounter on the street will be a handful of Japanese sailors from a fishing boat anchored nearby.

Hadley's in Murray St. is the liveliest pub. The **Prince of Wales Hotel,** Hampden Rd., and the **Shipwright's Arms Hotel,** Colville St., are the Battery Point pubs. Rock music can be heard at the **St. Ives Hotel,** Sandy Bay Rd.

GETTING TO KNOW HOBART

Founded 16 years after Sydney, Hobart is the second-oldest city in Australia. Happily, it has succeeded in retaining some of its early 1900s atmosphere. The city is full of Victorian stone buildings, theatres, pubs, banks and post offices, all carefully preserved and renovated, especially along Macquarie and Davey streets. Hobart's most outstanding feature in this respect is Battery Point, to the south of the docks. Residents claim that it is the best-preserved colonial district in all Australia. They have succeeded in retaining the genuine and lively charm of an actual village without making any concessions to tourism.

Battery Point***

Battery Point owes its name to the battery of cannons installed there to protect Hobart from the French, who were Britain's traditional foe even in the Antipodes. Between 1830 and 1840, officers and high-ranking colonial administrators built elegant residences there. They were followed in the 1850s by seafarers, merchants, shipowners and shipwrights of the whaling years. The cottages from this period are more modest and the pubs have names like the Whaler's Return and the Shipwright's Arms. Battery Point has hardly changed since this era, retaining its calm atmosphere despite the influx of tourists attracted by the restaurants, galleries and antique shops. The narrow, sloping streets lead to the sea and the harbour. The Baroque residences of the nobility stand side-by-side with rows of brick corrugated-iron-roofed cottages and tiny wooden houses in pale colours of apricot, lavender blue, pink and cream. The local wrought-iron verandahs and balconies are lovingly maintained.

Arthur's Circus

Situated in the heart of the village, it must be one of the only city squares in Australia which is not square. A street bordered by 'gingerbread' houses curves around a flat, oval green, with a suburban feel to it: the atmosphere is tranquil.

Mt. Wellington**

If you want a bird's eye view of Hobart, climb the 4169 ft/1271 m up Mt Wellington (13 mi/20 km from the city); on a clear day, you can see the entire river mouth and a section of the east coast.

Tasman Bridge

The Tasman Bridge over the Derwent estuary has played a sad role in Australian history. On January 5, 1975, less than two weeks after Cyclone Tracy had destroyed Darwin, the *Lake Illawarra,* a freighter loaded with 10,000 metric tons of zinc, collided with one of the pylons of the bridge and sank, taking with it three of the 19 spans. Seven sailors and five drivers lost their lives in the accident. The bridge has now been rebuilt but is closed to traffic when large vessels are passing under it.

WHAT TO SEE

Tasmanian Museum and Art Gallery

5 Argyle St. Tel: 23 1422. *Open daily 10am to 5pm.*
The history of Tasmania, including details of its most tragic periods, especially concerning the Tasmanian Aborigines. Contemporary Australian paintings.

Van Diemen's Land Memorial Folk Museum**

103 Hampden Rd., Battery Point. Tel: 34 2791. *Open Mon. to Fri. 10am to 5pm, weekends 2pm to 5pm.*
Established in a house dating from 1836, the museum depicts the life of Tasmania's wealthiest pioneers.

Tasmanian Maritime Museum

Cromwell St., Battery Point. Tel: 23 5082. *Open daily 2pm to 4.30pm.*
Material of the seafaring history of Tasmania from the time of its discovery by Abel Tasman.

Runnymede*

61 Bay Rd., New Town. Tel: 28 1269. *Open daily 10am to 4pm, except Mon. and in July.*
Built in 1844 by a famous and rich lawyer of the period, the house has been fully restored by the National Trust.

OUTSIDE HOBART

RICHMOND

This village, 16 mi/26 km north of Hobart, attracts tourists from all over Australia to its stone bridge, built in 1823, and its Roman Catholic church, built in 1836. Both attractions are the oldest of their kind in Australia. The view of this neo-Gothic stone church, framed by the arch of the bridge, with ducks splashing about in the river in the foreground, is featured on every Tourist Office brochure. Its 'European-ness' is undeniable.

The rest of the village has been carefully restored. You can visit an 1825 prison *(open daily 9am to 5pm),* a beautiful 1888 pub with a cast-iron balcony, churches, tourist shops and houses from the 19th century.

Food

Prospect House (1830) Colebrook Main Rd. Tel: (002) 62 2207, has been converted into a restaurant and is open for lunch and dinner from Thurs. to Sat.

The pub, the **Richmond Arms,** serves excellent counter meals daily noon to 2pm, and 6pm to 7.30pm on Fri. and Sat.

PORT ARTHUR AND THE TASMAN PENINSULA

Port Arthur

The ruins of this penal colony, located 64 mi/102 km from Hobart, constitute the focal point of any visit to Tasmania and merit setting aside at least half a day. Nothing in the surroundings of Port Arthur even hints at the horrors with which some 12,500 convicts were confronted during the term of their imprisonment there between 1830 and 1877, when the prison was shut down. The sky is blue, the sea calm, the curve of the bay perfect, the lawns immaculate.

Port Arthur was a model prison as far as the colonial authorities were concerned, but a hell on earth for the convicts, not only because of the harsh discipline but also because the convicts knew that there could be no escape. The site had been carefully chosen for its virtual isolation from the rest of the colony.

The Tasman Peninsula is actually connected to the Tasmanian mainland by a narrow strip of beach, Eaglehawk Neck, which colonial authorities soon blocked off with solid chains and a dozen ferocious guard dogs. Just in case any brave souls were tempted to escape by sea, the guards circulated terrible stories of sharks in the bay. Port Arthur was also connected with Hobart by semaphore. Nineteen stations, one of which was located on a hill overlooking Eaglehawk Neck, were able to transmit news of an escape to the military authorities in the capital and receive a reply in a matter of minutes. All these measures proved extremely effective—of the 12,500 prisoners interned at Port Arthur over 47 years, only 11 succeeded in escaping.

When Port Arthur prison finally closed, there were only seven convicts within its walls. They served the remainder of their sentences in the prison in Hobart and the last of them died a free man in Launceston, in 1903. Most of the prison buildings, which formed a small town capable of accommodating 200 guards and more than 1000 prisoners at a time, were destroyed in a bush fire towards the end of the 19th century. Nothing remains of the wooden barracks nor the administrative buildings. Those which did survive were the most important buildings, of stone or brick. Today, they stand as witnesses to a cruel period which can leave no one unmoved.

The church: erected between 1834 and 1836, the church was intended for Christians of all denominations and, as a result, was never consecrated. Its wooden bell tower was destroyed in a storm in 1876. The ruins of this neo-Gothic building stand at the end of a stately lane of 100-year-old oaks.

A stone's throw from the church is **Government Cottage.** One of its most interesting features is the intricately carved pair of stone lions' heads.

The penitentiary: this exposed-brickwork building, the most imposing of any at the site, was built between 1844 and 45 as a granary and mill. In 1857, it was converted into a prison for 657 convicts. The circular **watch tower,** with its castle battlements, was built in 1835 behind the penitentiary and has been well restored.

The **asylum** and **model prison,** protected by a stand of oak trees, have been partially restored. The asylum, built between 1864 and 68 to care for the mentally ill of the colony, now houses a very interesting, small **museum.** On display is a fine scale model of the penitentiary, showing all the missing buildings. The model prison was built between 1848 and 52, using the plan of Pentonville Prison in England but with the whip being replaced by isolation and silence. Three of the wings of the cruciform building contained cells, and the fourth a chapel. Prisoners could see the sea through the bars of some cells.

A one-hour boat trip away, the **Isle of the Dead** houses the colony's cemetery for seafarers. Between 1830 and 1877, 180 free men (soldiers, officials, sailors and shipwreck victims) and 1769 convicts were buried there. Free men were entitled to the high section of the island and to solid stone tombstones (70 remain). Convicts were allocated a common pit near the water, a sailcloth winding sheet and a bed of quicklime.

The M.V. *Bundeena,* leaving from Port Arthur Jetty, Port Arthur, offers frequent daily departures during the tourist season.

The Tasman Peninsula

Other places of interest on the Tasman Peninsula are Nubeena, Premaydena (former coal mines) and the **Tasmanian Devil Park*** in Taranna (Tel: (002) 50 3230). As well as kangaroos and wombats, this private zoo houses fierce-looking Tasmanian Devils. These are marsupial carnivores, the size of a large cat, with black and white stripes and very powerful jaws. They are unique to Tasmania. The park also shows a very good film on the mysterious Tasmanian Tiger, called the Tasmanian wolf or Thylacine, another carnivorous marsupial resembling a striped wolf and supposedly extinct. Sightings of it in the inaccessible forests of the south-west are reminiscent of the legend of the Loch Ness monster.

Port Arthur, a former prison settlement, is now a vacation spot with immaculate lawns.

Accommodation

▲▲ **Four Seasons Motor Hotel,** Port Arthur. Tel: (002) 50 2102. 35 rooms.

▲▲ **Fox and Hounds,** Port Arthur. Tel: (002) 50 2217. 27 rooms.

▲▲ **Tanglewood Host Farm,** Port Arthur. Tel: (002) 50 2210. 2 rooms.

HOBART TO LAUNCESTON

There are three routes from Hobart to Launceston (see map p. 142): the coast road, the Midlands road (the most direct and most historic) and the Derwent Valley-Central Highlands road. None of the three is more than 125 mi/200 km long and all will give you the opportunity to take in the various faces of Tasmania: its quiet countryside, tiny, restored Victorian villages, isolated rural farms, densely forested mountains, rivers and lakes, desolate mountain plateaux and, never far away, the sea.

▬▬ THE COAST ROAD

If you take this route, stop in **Bicheno** (122 mi/195 km from Hobart), for its beaches, and **St. Marys** (150 mi/240 km from Hobart), for its atmosphere. There are very beautiful coastal views before you reach Orford and many hotels, motels and restaurants along the way.

▬▬ THE MIDLANDS ROAD

This route crosses the main farming regions of Tasmania (sheep, cattle, fruit), and a series of small, charming, historic towns, such as **Kempton** (29 mi/46 km from Hobart), **Oatlands** (53 mi/84 km), **Turnbridge**

(67 mi/105 km) and **Ross*** (50 mi/81 km), something like a northern version of Richmond. The stone bridge at Ross, opened in 1836, is decorated with stone arches carved by two convicts in exchange for their freedom. Ross also has three churches (Roman Catholic, Church of England and Methodist), many colonial houses and several historic pubs.

The **Ross Rodeo,** held on the first Saturday in November each year, attracts riders and spectators from all over Australia.

▬▬ THE DERWENT VALLEY AND THE CENTRAL PLATEAU

The Derwent Valley and New Norfolk

Founded in 1808, **New Norfolk** (24 mi/38 km from Hobart) is one of the oldest towns in Tasmania. It should be explored in autumn, perhaps by boat aboard the *Devil Jet* (information and tickets can be obtained from the Tasbureau Office in Hobart, or by telephoning (002) 61 2011).

You can see from the water, the town's hop-houses surrounded by hedges of poplars, its conical hop-drying sheds and its attractive farms. New Norfolk is the centre of the Tasmanian hop-growing industry. The **Hop Museum,** in an old farm on Hobart Road, is *open daily 9am to 5pm.*

The Central Plateau

The Lake Country is an area of high, bare plateaux and lakes overlooked by jagged mountain peaks. The **Cradle Mountain - Lake St. Clair National Park**** is entered from Derwent Bridge, 108 mi/173 km from Hobart on the Lyell Highway linking Hobart with the west coast. The park covers almost 321,000 acres/130,000 ha and is the most famous in Tasmania because of the spectacular 53 mi/85 km of walking trails (4 or 5 days minimum) between the lake and the mountain. Huts have been built along the various trails.

Contact the rangers in charge of the park by calling (003) 63 5187 for Cradle Mountain and (002) 89 115 for the lake.

Note: the lake can also be crossed by boat from Cynthia Bay to Narcissus Hut (M.V. **Tequila,** reservations necessary. Tel: (002) 89 1137).

Information on park can be obtained from the **National Parks and Wildlife Service** (see 'Tourist information' p. 145).

You can get back to Launceston from Derwent Bridge by following the Lake Highway (the direct route), or by following Highway No 8 via Queenstown and Zeehan, then Burnie and Devonport on the north coast. The Hobart—Queenstown—Burnie—Launceston circuit covers about 375 mi/600 km.

Queenstown

Queenstown, 160 mi/256 km from Hobart, was established at the end of the 19th century around a copper mine. The sight of the completely bare hills around the town is most unexpected in such a well-watered and densely forested area. This ecological disaster, now a tourist 'attraction', is the result of over-exploitation of the forests which, at the beginning of the century, supplied most of the town's energy needs. Bushfires and the torrential rains common in the region did the rest. Before you continue northward, make a detour through Strahan, 25 mi/41 km from Queenstown.

Strahan

This is the point of departure for a very beautiful cruise around Macquarie Harbour and along the Gordon River. You can choose between the **Gordon Explorer** (Tel: (004) 71 7179) or the **James Kelly II** (Tel: (004) 71 7187). Both offer half-day cruises with daily departures year round (twice daily in Jan. and Feb.). This cruise can be combined with a scenic flight from Launceston (see 'Getting around Tasmania' p. 144).

The Gordon River**

The Gordon River is 121 mi/193 km long and is the last of Tasmania's completely untamed rivers. It meanders through a mountainous region covered by impenetrable and virtually unexplored forests. The deep green cliffs which plunge down and are reflected in the blue-black waters of the river create a kind of temperate version of deepest Africa. **Macquarie Harbour,** a bay more than 19 mi/30 km long at the mouth of the Gordon, might have made Strahan a major port if only the channel (aptly named Hells Gates) between the bay and the ocean had been deeper. As it is, only vessels up to 10,000 metric tons and a few suicidal whales make it through. Information on the park: **National Parks and Wildlife Service** (see 'Tourist information' p. 145).

The north coast

The north coast, with the towns of **Wynyard, Burnie** and **Devonport,** and a string of very beautiful beaches, is the most populated, the wealthiest and most favoured part of Tasmania. Its proximity to Melbourne, a mere 188 mi/300 km away, on the other side of Bass Strait, may have something to do with its success.

Accommodation

Central Plateau

▲ **Cradle Mountain Lodge** (4 mi/6 km north of Waldheim). Tel: (003) 63 5187. 8 cabins.

Strahan

▲▲ **Four Seasons Strahan Inn.** Tel: (004) 71 7160. 50 rooms.

▲ **Hamers.** Tel: (004) 71 7191.

North coast

▲ **Argosy Motel,** Tarleton St., East Devonport. Tel: (004) 27 8872. 23 rooms.

▲ **Burnie Motor Lodge,** 36 Queen St., Burnie. Tel: (004) 31 1088. 24 rooms.

▲ **Southport Motel Lodge,** Bass Highway, Wynyard. Tel: (004) 42 2351.

LAUNCESTON

Launceston (pop. 85,000), the capital of northern Tasmania, was founded in 1804 at the mouth of the Tamar River, 31 mi/50 km from the sea. The city is more modern, more sophisticated and, frankly, less provincial than Hobart. It is Australia's third oldest city and is renowned for its well-preserved old homes and its beautiful parks and gardens.

▬ *PRACTICAL INFORMATION*

Telephone area code: 003.

Accommodation

Launceston has a wide range of hotels of all kinds.

International-standard and first-class hotels

▲▲▲▲ **The Launceston Country Club,** Prospect Vale, just outside the city. Tel: 44 8855. Hotel/casino. This was the first casino to be opened in the north of the island. 104 rooms.

▲▲▲ **Four Seasons Great Northern,** 3 Earl St. Tel: 31 9999. Brand new and very successful. 113 rooms.

Moderately priced and inexpensive hotels

▲▲ **Abel Tasman Motel,** 303 Hobart Rd., Kings Meadows. Tel: 44 5244. A little way from the city centre but fine if you have a car. 49 rooms.

▲▲ **The Maldon Motel,** 32 Brisbane St. Tel: 31 3979. A 'colonial' motel right in the heart of the city. 12 rooms.

▲ **Crown Hotel,** 152 Elizabeth St. Tel: 31 4137.

▲ **Launceston Youth Hostel,** 138 St. John St. Tel: 31 5839.

Food

The following restaurants are the most reliable:

The Aristocrat, corner of Paterson and Charles Sts. Tel: 31 2786. Grills and Greek food, BYO.

Clayton's Coffee Shop, 14 The Quadrant. Tel: 31 6151.

The Golden Phoenix, Trotters Lane, Prospect. Tel: 44 8766. Chinese.

Quigley's, 96 Balfour St. Tel: 31 6971. Fish and game.

Shopping

Brisbane St. is the location of the big stores. Its continuation, the Mall, is one of Australia's few non-straight streets and is bordered by small, 'arty' boutiques.

Attractions

Cruises on the Tamar River

M.V. Goondooloo, Lower Charles St., Jetty. Tel: 31 7156.

M.V. Lady Steelfox, Ritchie Mill Landing Stage.

Chairlift across Cataract Gorge

The chairlift is at First Basin, a few minutes from the city centre. Tel: 31 5915. It provides a spectacular view of the cliffs plunging down to the river and is open daily in summer, with a reduced service in winter. The 1450 ft/442 m crossing takes 6 minutes.

Nightlife

Nightlife in Launceston is livelier than in Hobart.

Music and dancing

Stiletto's (Hotel Tasman).

Astro's (Launceston Hotel).

Night Moves (Butter Factory).

Entertainment

Casino and stage shows every evening at the **Launceston Country Club** (see p. 153).

WHAT TO SEE

Clarendon House***

At Evandale, near Nile, 17 mi/27 km from Launceston. Tel: 98 6220. *Open daily 10.30am to 5pm, closed for lunch and in July.*
Built in 1838 by a rich local farmer, Clarendon House is one of the most beautiful colonial houses in Australia. Its architecture and furnishings, both in the grand style, are reminiscent of the sumptuous mansions of the Louisiana cotton barons.

Franklin House*

4 mi/6 km from Launceston on the road to the airport. Tel: 44 7824. *Open daily 9am to 5pm, closed for lunch.*
This magnificent colonial house has been restored by the National Trust.

The Cradle Mountain-Lake St Clair National Park.

The Penny Royal Complex

Paterson St. Tel: 31 6699. *Open daily 9am to 5.30pm.*
This complex comprises a fairly faithful and tasteful reconstruction of a group of workshops and mills. It includes a working hotel, the Penny Royal Watermill Motel (same address and telephone).

Queen Victoria Museum and Art Gallery

Wellington St. Tel: 31 6777. *Open Mon. to Sat. 10am to 5pm and Sun. 2pm to 5pm.*
The complex houses a fine natural history collection (including a Tasmanian Tiger), plus Aboriginal arts and crafts, tools and arms belonging to the white colonists, and paintings from the colonial era.

Rutherglen Wildlife Sanctuary

On Punchbowl Rd, south of the city. Tel: 93 6214.
Local fauna and flora in a natural setting. Magnificent rhododendron garden.

ADELAIDE AND SOUTH AUSTRALIA

Adelaide is a quiet, sleepy, and essentially Victorian city of 979,000 inhabitants, where everything seems to have been planned down to the last detail. The two men most responsible for this were Edward Gibbon Wakefield and William Light. In 1829, Wakefield hit upon the theory of 'systematic colonization'. By selling land at prices that would discourage either workers or ex-convicts, free men were encouraged to immigrate to the new, untainted provinces.

The theory, considered liberal at the time, was the basis of the foundation of Adelaide, the only Australian city that owes nothing to the importation of prisoners. The colonists of South Australia were free men, relatively rich (they had to pay their own passage), educated, reformist and somewhat idealistic. The only 'dissidents' were members of Protestant minority churches in Great Britain, mainly Scottish Methodists. South Australia was then nothing but a vast, dry plain which, in 1833, an especially optimistic explorer, Charles Sturt, had found to be 'full of promise'.

ADELAIDE

The colonists started arriving in 1836. Their first task was to choose a site for the capital of the new province. Colonel William Light, the Surveyor-General, chose the rich coastal plain on Gulf St. Vincent and, after raising the Union Jack, named the future city 'Adelaide', in honour of Queen Adelaide, wife of King William IV, and set to work. The result of his vision (commemorated by a statue erected in his honour at Montefiore Hill in North Adelaide) is a town planned to perfection, precise as a computer printout. Next to Adelaide, Melbourne is a mess, Brisbane disorganized, Perth rough-hewn and Sydney complete anarchy.

Light built his city in mile-square sections, bordered by the long avenues of North Terrace, East Terrace, South Terrace and West Terrace. Adelaide's main artery, King William St., divides the city on a north-south axis and links it to North Adelaide, the elegant, busy Victorian portion of the city, by means of a bridge across the Torrens River. Adelaide and North Adelaide are separated from the city outskirts by a ring of parks and gardens several hundred yards across. Beyond the green belt are the suburbs. They too stretch straight as a die, from the beaches of Gulf St. Vincent and the cool Adelaide Hills, all the way to Port Adelaide. Then, all of a sudden, you find yourself in the bush, with wheat fields, vineyards, forests and sheep farms. Adelaide has spared itself the mushrooming suburban sprawl typical of other Australian cities.

Intellectual and narcissistic as only a country cousin can be, Adelaide has always devoted the treasures of its imagination, as well as lots of money, to attracting the famous systematic colonizers so dear to Wakefield. South Australia has gone from being the corn silo of Australia to an industrial centre, thanks to its reserves of oil and gas. Adelaide, which was known as the City of Churches until after World War II and the 'wowser' (holier-than-thou) capital of Australia, has become a cultural centre, with its Cultural Complex and its biennial Arts Festival. The more down-to-earth souls who reach for their cricket bats at the mention of the word 'culture' are wooed by a wine festival (every other year) which shows off the quality of wines produced in the region.

The Australian Formula I Grand Prix, first staged in Adelaide in November 1985, is still a great success. Another attraction is the hotel-casino in the imposing North Terrace railway station.

Beneath its somewhat cold exterior, Adelaide is a friendly city. The Mediterranean-type climate and mass arrival of European immigrants over the last 50 years, contribute to its charm. As far as the visitor is concerned, Adelaide makes a perfect base from which to discover South Australia. The vineyards of the Barossa Valley, the opals of Coober Pedy, the kangaroos of the Flinders Ranges and the paddle-steamers on the Murray River are among the tourist riches of this often neglected state.

PRACTICAL INFORMATION

Telephone area code: 08.

Access

Adelaide, the capital of South Australia, lies at the crossroads of Australia's road, rail and air communications network.

Plane

Since 1982 Adelaide has had its own international airport, allowing direct flights from Europe, Asia and the United States. Both **Ansett** and **Australian Airlines** have direct flights to Perth, Alice Springs, Melbourne, Sydney, Brisbane, Coolangatta, etc.

Ansett, 150 North Terrace, City. Tel: 212 1111.

Australian Airlines, 144 North Terrace, City. Tel: 217 3333.

Qantas, 14 King William St., City. Tel: 237 8418.

Air tours are offered by: **Skytours,** 293 Burbridge Rd., Burkin Park. Tel: 352 3411.

There are regular buses to the city from the nearby airport.

Train

To/from Perth: the *Indian Pacific* and the *Trans Australian* (40-hour trip, daily departures except Tues. and Fri., see p. 172).
To/from Alice Springs: The *Ghan* (24-hour trip, Fri. and Tues. from May to October).
To/from Melbourne: the *Overlander* (12-hour trip, daily).
To/from Sydney (via Broken Hill): the *Alice* (24-hour trip, three times a week).
To/from Brisbane (via Sydney): the trip to Sydney takes 24 hours. Add to that another 16 hours plus changes (daily).

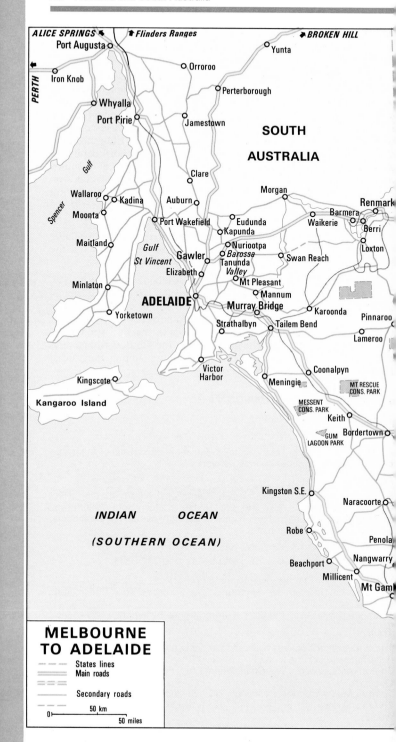

ALICE SPRINGS ◀ | ↑ Flinders Ranges | ▸ BROKEN HILL

PERTH ◀

Port Augusta

Iron Knob

Orroroo

Yunta

Perterborough

Whyalla

Port Pirie

Jamestown

SOUTH

AUSTRALIA

Gulf

Spencer

Clare

Morgan

Wallaroo Kadina

Auburn

Barmera

Renmark

Moonta

Port Wakefield

Eudunda

Waikerie

Berri

Kapunda

Loxton

Maitland

Gulf
St Vincent

Gawler

Nuriootpa
Barossa
Tanunda
Valley

Swan Reach

Elizabeth

Minlaton

ADELAIDE

Mt Pleasant

Mannum

Murray Bridge

Karoonda

Pinnaroo

Yorketown

Strathalbyn

Tailem Bend

Lameroo

Victor
Harbor

Coonalpyn

Kingscote

Meningie

MT RESCUE
CONS. PARK

Kangaroo Island

MESSENT
CONS. PARK

Keith

INDIAN   OCEAN

GUM
LAGOON PARK

Bordertown

(SOUTHERN OCEAN)

Kingston S.E.

Naracoorte

Robe

Penola

Beachport

Nangwarry

Millicent

Mt Gam

MELBOURNE
TO ADELAIDE

States lines
Main roads

Secondary roads

50 km

0

50 miles

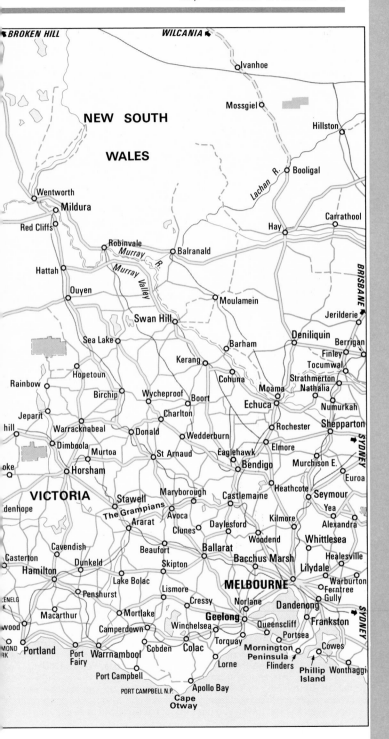

Information and tickets: **Adelaide Rail Passenger Terminal,** Keswick. Tel: 217 4111.

Bus

Greyhound, Ansett-Pioneer and **Deluxe** all offer interstate and local connections (daily).

To/from Perth: 36 hours.
To/from Alice Springs: 22 hours (more during the rainy season from November to March).
To/from Darwin (via Alice Springs): 21 hours to Alice Springs, plus 22 hours, plus changes.
To/from Melbourne (via Highway No 8): 10 hours.
To/from Sydney (via Canberra, Mildura, Renmark, Highways No 20 and 31): 24 hours.
To/from Brisbane (via Dubbo): 33 hours.

Greyhound, 111 Franklin St., City. Tel: 212 1777.

Ansett-Pioneer, 101 Franklin St. and 150 North Terrace, City. Tel: 51 2075.

Deluxe, 144 North Terrace, City. Tel: 212 2077.

Car

To the west is the road to Perth (1688 mi/2700 km away); to the north the road to Alice Springs (1063 mi/1700 km) and Darwin (2000 mi/3200 km); and to the east, three direct roads connecting Adelaide with Melbourne (469 mi/750 km), Sydney (1031 mi/1650 km) and Brisbane (1313 mi/2100 km).

To/from Perth:
See Perth and Western Australia p. 173.

To/from Alice Springs:
See Alice Springs and the Red Centre p. 193.

To/from Melbourne:
Three main roads connect Melbourne with Adelaide. All three are paved and pass through a varied countryside dotted with attractive country towns.

The most direct route (513 mi/820 km) is Highway No 8 (Western Highway in Victoria and Duke Highway in South Australia), which passes, from east to west, through the towns of **Ballarat, Horsham** and **Kaniva** in Victoria, and **Keith** and **Tailem Bend** in South Australia. All towns have hotels, restaurants, service stations, etc.

The most scenic route (575 mi/920 km) is the Princes Highway (Highway No 1), which follows Australia's most jagged and beautiful coastline. Between **Geelong** and **Warrnambool,** you would be wise to leave the Princes Highway, which turns inland, and take the Great Ocean Road, which borders the sea. A stop at **Portland** or **Mt. Gambier** is recommended.

The longest route (598 mi/957 km) is the Calder Highway and then the Sunraysia Highway (Highway No 79) which joins the Sturt Highway (Highway No 20) at Mildura, on the direct route between Adelaide and Sydney. A variation on this route, which is interesting mainly for the Murray River, is to follow the river on the Murray Valley Highway (Highway No 16). This highway can be joined from Melbourne at Kerang, via Bendigo.

To/from Sydney:
The most direct route between Sydney and Adelaide (906 mi/1450 km) involves following the Hume Highway (Highway No 31) via **Goulburn** as far as **Wagga Wagga** (305 mi/486 km from Sydney), then the Sturt Highway (Highway No 20), via the towns of **Hay** and **Mildura.** You can also follow the Murray River almost from its source, by taking the Hume Highway as far as **Albury** (363 mi/580 km from Sydney), where you join the Murray Valley Highway (No 16) heading for Echuca and Mildura. All these routes are paved and the towns you pass through have all the necessary facilities.

To/from Brisbane:
You can follow the Cunningham Highway (No 42) to **Goondiwindi,**

231 mi/370 km from Brisbane, then the Newell Highway (No 39) to **West Wyalong,** 764 mi/1223 km from Brisbane, and finally the Mid Western Highway (No 24) to **Hay** on the Sturt Highway, a total of 1400 mi/2240 km. Alternatively, take the Newell Highway (No 39) to **Dubbo** (600 mi/960 km from Brisbane), linking up with the Barrier Highway (No 32) which will take you directly to Adelaide via **Broken Hill,** a trip of 1394 mi/2230 km from Brisbane.

Getting around Adelaide

Car rental

Avis, 108 Burbridge Rd., Hilton. Tel: 354 0444.

Budget, 274 North Terrace, City. Tel: 223 1400.

Hertz, 233 Morphett St., City. Tel: 51 2856.

Bus

Metropolitan bus information. Tel: 210 1000.

Taxis

United. Tel: 223 3111.

Suburban. Tel: 211 8888.

Useful addresses

Tourist information

South Australian Government Travel Centre, 18 King William St., City. Tel: 212 1644.

Post office

General Post Office (GPO), 141 King William St., City. Tel: 216 2370.

Automobile club

Royal Automobile Association of South Australia, 41 Hindmarsh Square, City. Tel: 223 4555.

Accommodation

International-standard hotels

▲▲▲▲ **Barron Town House,** corner of Hindley and Morphett Sts., City. Tel: 211 8255. Motel, popular with business people. 68 rooms.

▲▲▲▲ **Gateway Hotel,** 147 North Terrace, City. Tel: 217 7552. Stately, centrally located. 219 rooms, 7 suites.

▲▲▲▲ **Hilton International,** 223 Victoria Square, City. Tel: 217 0711. Located in the city centre. 386 rooms.

▲▲▲▲ **Meridien Lodge,** 21 Melbourne St., North Adelaide. Tel: 267 3033. Motel located on Adelaide's liveliest street. 40 executive suites.

▲▲▲▲ **Oberoi Hotel,** 62 Brougham Place, North Adelaide. Tel: 267 3444. Located in one of Adelaide's lively areas, this splendid hotel overlooks the city and its parks.

First-class hotels

▲▲▲ **Festival Lodge,** 140 North Terrace, City. Tel: 212 7877. Centrally located. 44 rooms.

▲▲▲ **Flinders Lodge,** 27 Dequetteville Terrace, Kent Town. Tel: 332 8222. Less than 10 minutes from the city by bus or taxi, the motel is located in Adelaide's green belt. 63 rooms.

▲▲▲ **Grosvenor Hotel,** 125 North Terrace, City. Tel: 51 2962. Located opposite the main railway station, this former pub has been well renovated and is Adelaide's most pleasant hotel. 200 rooms, 28 suites.

▲▲▲ **Royal Coach,** 24 Dequetteville Terrace, Kent Town. Tel: 42 5676. A stone's throw from Flinders Lodge. 40 rooms, 2 suites.

▲▲▲ **South Park Motor Inn,** 1 South Terrace, City. Tel: 212 1277. Views over the parks. 98 rooms, 8 suites.

Moderately priced and inexpensive hotels

▲▲ **Ambassadors,** 107 King William St., City. Tel: 51 4331. Motel. A little expensive but central. 28 rooms.

▲▲ **Earl of Zetland Motel,** 44 Flinders St., City. Tel: 223 5500. 30 rooms.

▲▲ **Kent Town Lodge,** 22 Wakefield St., Kent Town. Tel: 31 7568. 40 rooms.

▲ **Adelaide Youth Hostel,** 290 Gilles St., City. Tel: 223 6077. 16 beds.

On the beach

▲▲ **Adelaide Aviators Lodge,** 728 Tapleys Hill Rd. Tel: 356 8388. 30 rooms.

▲▲ **Delmonte Lodge,** 209 The Esplanade, Henley Beach. Tel: 353 5155. 73 rooms.

Food

Adelaide claims to have the greatest number of restaurants per head (or mouth), but the state's speciality rarely figures on the most prestigious restaurant menus. It is the *pie floater*, the famous Australian meat pie served up on a bed of pea soup.

Elegant restaurants

Ayers House, 288 North Terrace, City. Tel: 224 066. First-class food, service and surroundings (colonial). Shaded seats outside.

Jarmer's, 297 Kensington Park. Tel: 322 2080. Widely thought of as the best restaurant in Adelaide.

Oberoi Hotel (see p. 161). Located on the top floor of the hotel, this restaurant offers a splendid view and good curries.

Sables, Grosvenor Hotel (see p. 161). Tel: 51 9080. Sophisticated 1920s atmosphere and good food.

Inexpensive

Pancake Kitchen, 13 Gilbert Place, City. Tel: 211 7912. Snacks and chess, 24 hours a day, 7 days a week.

Pier Hotel, 2 Jetty Rd., Glenelg. Tel: 295 4116. Counter meals on the beach.

Stag Hotel, corner of Rundle St. and East Terrace, City. Tel: 223 2934. Excellent steaks, good service, in a pub located close to the markets.

Italian

Sorrento, 135 Hindley St., City. Tel: 51 6740. Good quality, inexpensive restaurant in Adelaide's busiest street. Hindley St. is also Adelaide's fast food quarter.

Seafood

HMS Buffalo, Glenelg. Tel: 294 7000. On the harbour, a restaurant in a reproduction of the first ship to reach Adelaide.

Paul's, 79 Gouger St., City. Tel: 51 9778. Superb food.

The Contented Sole, 354 Shepherds Hill Rd., Blackwood. Tel: 278 7099. Superb food.

Steaks and grill

Leon's Wine Tavern, 194 The Parade, Norwood. Tel: 332 1702. Local steak and wines at reasonable prices. Popular with the under-30s.

Pink Pig, 52 O'Connell St., North Adelaide. Tel: 267 2139. Another popular eating and meeting place.

Special atmosphere

Old Mill, 98 Main St., Hahndorf. Tel: 388 788. A half-hour from Adelaide along the south-eastern freeway, in the heart of the famous Adelaide Hills. A little bit of Germany, including a Bavarian band. Reservations necessary.

Festival Centre Bistro and its big brother, the **Riverside Restaurant.** King William Rd., City. Tel: 51 6430. For food and entertainment before or after the show in the Festival Centre. Superb surroundings.

Shopping

All the big department stores are located around the Rundle St. Mall, said to be the busiest in Australia.

Aboriginal arts

There is a wide selection of Aboriginal arts and crafts at **Primitive Arts and Crafts,** North Terrace, City. Tel: 223 8449.

Antiques

Adelaide Antique Market, 59 Palteney St., City.

Opals

The many merchants of South Australian opals include:

Olympic Opals, 142 Melbourne St., North Adelaide. Tel: 267 5525.

Opal Field Gems, 29 King William St., City. Tel: 212 5300.

The Opal Mine, 30 Gawler Place, City. Tel: 223 4023.

Entertainment and cultural life

Festivals and performances

The **Adelaide Festival,** held over three weeks in March of every even-numbered year, is the most visible manifestation of Adelaide's efforts in the area of culture. The success of the Festival Centre outside Adelaide Festival times fully justifies the construction of this imposing multicultural complex which regularly sells out for performances of ballet, theatre, rock, etc.

Programs and tickets: **Adelaide Festival Centre,** King William Rd., City. Tel: 216 8796.

Cinemas

Adelaide's cinema programs, on the other hand, fall short of the city's reputation as the film capital of Australia. This reputation stems from the fact that most of the successful films of the Australian 'New Wave' were produced in Adelaide and sent from there to Hollywood.

Pubs and nightlife

Adelaide shares Sydney's sympathy for 'liberal' drinking laws. Pubs are open until midnight on Fridays and Saturdays, and for two hours around dinner time on Sunday. Among those pubs which dare to display the neon sign 'Beer is Best' in the wine capital of Australia are the **Botanic Hotel** (North Terrace), **The Earl of Zetland** (Flinders St.) and the **Tattersalls Hotel** (Hindley St.).

All three are in the 1900s style, with mirrors, brass, red wallpaper and wooden bars, and are frequented by real or aspiring businessmen.

Other pubs include:

Largs Pier (The Esplanade, Largs Pier). Typical, popular beachside pub.

The Leg Trap Hotel (Bartley Terrace, West Lakes). Launched by one of Australia's most famous cricketers, Ian Chappell.

The Adelaide Casino (North Terrace). Two gaming levels open noon to 4 am, plus restaurants and bars.

Music and dancing

The Old Lion (Melbourne St., North Adelaide). Disco complex for the under-35s.

Tivoli Hotel, 261 Pirie St., City. Rock music Tues. to Thurs.

Most of the city's clubs and discos are to be found in Melbourne and Hindley Sts. but many rock groups also perform in suburban pubs. A complete entertainment guide is published in the *Advertiser* or the *News*, the dailies behind press magnate Rupert Murdoch's success.

▬▬ GETTING TO KNOW ADELAIDE

Montefiore Hill, North Adelaide, the City

Any walk around the city must start at the statue commemorating Colonel Light's 'vision'. It is located at **Montefiore Hill,** about 20 minutes on foot north of the city. From there, your own vision is more likely to be that of a modest provincial city, in the positive sense of the phrase. In the foreground, the green lawn and red roofs of the grandstands at Adelaide Oval, Adelaide's famous cricket ground, contrast with the igloo design of the Festival Centre. Farther away is the city itself—a few tower blocks and some monumental Victorian buildings—the blue horizon, the purple sky and the bush, all within arm's reach.

Continue northwards from Montefiore Hill, then eastwards, through the 1900s residential area of **North Adelaide,** where quiet streets lined with elegant stone cottages will bring you to Melbourne Street, South Australia's Fifth Avenue. Follow King William Rd., cross the Torrens and its lake, have a look at the Festival Centre (see p. 165) on your right; then you're in the city. Once beyond North Terrace, where **Parliament House,** the **Museum,** the **Art Gallery** and the railway station are, you will come upon Adelaide's two busiest streets. On the left (as you look south) is the pedestrian zone of Rundle Mall, and on the right, cosmopolitan Hindley St. South of this intersection, all along King William Rd., is everyday Adelaide, with its marble-fronted banks, rococo pubs and the concrete office blocks running its affairs.

Adelaide Hills**

The most fortunate (in all senses of the word) of Adelaide's citizens live 19 mi/30 km from the city, in a series of villages in the hills and valleys of the Mount Lofty Ranges. Because of its location close to the city, this area is known as the **Adelaide Hills.** The highest point, Mount Lofty Summit, is no higher than 2329 ft/710 m but the hills enjoy a pleasant climate all year round, slightly cooler than the plain below. Rainfall is good and the hills are covered in eucalypt forests, meadows, and groves of almond and cherry trees. Artists and retired school heads tend their gardens there in the tranquillity of cool summer evenings. The Adelaide Hills represent to perfection the way of life dear to Australians.

The hills are reached via the south-eastern highway (the road from Melbourne). Enjoy spectacular views of the city below before leaving the highway at **Hahndorf** (18 mi/28 km from Adelaide), a village in the German style and renowned for its annual festival (second Saturday in January). The route continues northwards to **Woodside** (20 mi/32 km), then turns west towards **Ashton,** before returning to Adelaide and its suburbs via Magill Road and North Terrace.

Adelaide Beaches

From **Outer Harbour** in the north to **Marino** in the south, Adelaide has 20 mi/32 km of beaches, the closest of which, **West Beach,** is less than 6 mi/10 km from the centre of the city. Washed by the quiet waters of Gulf St. Vincent, these beaches are among the safest in Australia. The most popular are **Semaphore** in the north and **Glenelg*** in the south. The latter is connected to the city by the only remaining tram line.

▬▬ WHAT TO SEE

South Australian Museum**

North Terrace, City. Tel: 223 8911. *Open daily 10am to 5pm, Wed. 1pm to 5pm and Sun. 2pm to 5pm.*

his museum houses one of the most important collections of Aboriginal
rts and crafts in the world.

ext to it is the **Art Gallery of South Australia** which contains a fine
ollection of works by European and Australian artists.

he Constitutional Museum**

orth Terrace, City. Tel: 212 6066. *Open daily 10am to 5pm, weekends
.30pm to 5pm.*
his includes a well-made audiovisual program which traces the political
story of the state. At Speaker's Corner, the 'live' part of the museum,
eople can express their opinions on a given political subject.

delaide Festival Centre

ng William Rd., City. Tel: 216 8796. *Guided tours Mon. to Sat. 10am to
pm, except for lunch on Sat.*
pened by Queen Elizabeth II in 1977, the Centre has a beautiful location
eside the Torrens. The multicultural complex is even more famous for the
gh standard of its entertainment than for its architecture.

Marineland

ilitary Rd., West Beach. Tel: 356 7555. *Open daily from 10am to 4pm,
xcept Tues.*
quatic shows starring dolphins, seals and various fish. West Beach is the
osest beach to the city, directly to the east.

▬ OUTSIDE ADELAIDE

angaroo Island*

ocated 35 minutes by plane from Adelaide, Kangaroo Island is one of
outh Australia's favourite tourist destinations. The 94 mi/150 km long
land has everything to offer: enticing beaches, picturesque villages,
npressive cliffs, and numerous moderately priced hotels and motels (book
advance in summer). However, the one feature which makes Kangaroo
land unique is its **animal reserves.** There are, of course, the kangaroos
hich gave the island its name, but also emus, koalas, many species of
rds, and, in the south, hundreds of seals which have their own beach at
eal Bay where you can walk up and touch them.

angaroo Island can be reached by plane (**Commodore Airlines** and **Air
ransit**) or boat (*Troubridge, Philanderer III* and *Valerie Jane*). Information
nd reservations at the **South Australian Government Travel Centre** (see
161).

he Barossa Valley*

outh Australia produces 70 percent of Australia's wine and 90 percent of
s brandy in vineyards which cover half of the country's wine-growing
eas. For many Australians, the word 'wine' is synonymous with Barossa
alley. In 1840, a group of German Lutheran refugees, fleeing religious
ersecution in their native Silesia, set about turning this low valley into the
ndisputed wine capital of Australia. The valley is 19 mi/30 km long and is
cated 31 mi/50 km north-east of Adelaide. It receives no more than
) inches/510 mm of rain per year but has charms to please any visitor: the
ght of its Bordeaux-green vineyards against the red earth, the golden hills
nd purple sky; wine-tastings (be careful of the combination of wine and
un) at Château Yaldara or Seppeltsfield, two of the 37 vineyards in the
alley; a quiet lunch in the shade of the pointed tower of a village church.
he valley is well worth a full day's car trip.

eave Adelaide by Highway No 21, heading towards **Gawler,** then turn east
wards **Lyndoch,** the entrance to the valley, 34 mi/55 km from Adelaide.
he road beyond Gawler is known as the Barossa Valley Highway.
anunda, the cultural centre of the valley, is 8 mi/12 km further on, and
uriootpa, its commercial centre, 12 mi/19 km. Especially recommended
nong the many vineyards open to the public is **Seppeltsfield,** on the left

f the road between Tanunda and Nuriootpa, with its enormous expanse
f vines, eucalypts and date palms.

fter lunching at Tanunda (at **La galerie,** 66 Murray St. Tel: 63 2788, for
xample), continue on to **Angaston,** 3 mi/5 km east of Nuriootpa, and take
e scenic drive to the top of **Menglers Hill,** from where you can see all
f the Barossa Valley. Return via **Williamstown, Chain of Ponds** and the
)ectacular **Gorge Road** beside the Torrens River. Every two years (the
?ar without an Adelaide Arts Festival), the valley stages its famous
intage Festival, a four-day long festival held in March or April after the
'ine harvest. Warning: it is best to avoid drinking in the sun if the
?mperature is above 104 °F/40 °C.

URAL SOUTH AUSTRALIA

■ *MURRAY RIVER VALLEY***

ie south-east corner of South Australia is watered by the last
)0 mi/800 km of the Murray River, Australia's Mississippi. In 1830, the
xplorer Charles Sturt rowed down the river and back. Today, the flow of
e river is entirely controlled, from its source in the Snowy Mountains to
s mouth in the Southern Ocean, by a series of locks and barriers. Huge
igation projects have turned its banks into the orchard of Australia.
'aikerie, Berri and **Renmark** on the Sturt Highway are the major towns
this South Australian riverland which continues eastward as far as
lbury on the Victorian/New South Wales border (see map pp. 158-159).
: **Morgan,** 103 mi/165 km north-east of Adelaide, the river makes a
idden turn and heads due south to the sea. This is undoubtedly the most
)ectacular and wildest section of the river, lined with majestic cliffs and
ant eucalypts which house a multitude of wild-bird species.

ie ideal way to discover the river at its own pace is by boat. In South
istralia, you have the choice of three operators (5-day cruises) and three
)ats, all modern and fully equipped: the *Murray River Queen,* leaving from
oolwa (56 mi/90 km south of Adelaide); the *Proud Mary,* leaving from
urray Bridge (50 mi/80 km); and the *Murray Explorer,* leaving from
:nmark (156 mi/250 km).

nother way to discover the river is to rent your own houseboat at Murray
idge, Mannum, Loxton, Berri or Renmark (your driver's license will qualify
iu as a captain).

formation and reservations can be obtained from:
)uth **Australian Government Travel Centre** in Adelaide (see p. 161).
urray **Bridge Information Services,** 17 Bridge St., Murray Bridge.
?l: (085) 32 2900.
:nmark **Tourist Office,** Murray Ave., Renmark. Tel: (085) 86 6704.
you're coming from the eastern states, contact South Australian
)vernment Travel Centres in Melbourne, Sydney or Brisbane.
:her river cruises leave from Echuca, Swan Hill and Mildura on the
:torian portion of the river. Contact the **Victorian Tourist Commission**
Melbourne (see p. 125).

■ *FLINDERS RANGES***

ie Flinders Ranges have the advantage of being the most accessible of
istralia's large rock formations. **Wilpena Pound,** the tourist centre of the
nge, is some 219 mi/350 km long and is connected to Adelaide
31 mi/450 km to the south) by an asphalt highway (Highway No 47 from
)rt Augusta). The scenery is that of a fossilized world, a countryside which

elaide, the Aborigines were there first!

is virile and harsh, unchanged for almost 2 billion years. You will see steep red-granite cliffs, blocks of black basalt, cracked granite boulders, hills as old and bare as in the Aboriginal dreamtime. The entire range holds special mythological significance for the Aborigines, and their wall paintings from 12,000 years ago bear witness to the many legends inspired by its wild beauty. Especially worth visiting are the caves at **Kanyaka** and **Yourambulla,** near Hawker on the road from Wilpena, those around **Wilpena Pound,** at **Chambers Gorge,** between Wilpena and Arkaroola and at **Orroroo,** between Adelaide and Port Augusta. The sites are clearly signposted.

Access

There is a regular Greyhound bus service from Adelaide to Wilpena and Arkaroola.

Accommodation

Arkaroola

▲ Mawson Lodge. Tel: (08) 212 1366. 20 rooms.

Wilpena

▲▲ Wilpena Motel. Tel: (08) 212 6386. 34 rooms.

There are also numerous hotels in the bush towns along the road.

Attractions

Excursions by Land Rover or plane can be organized at the motel. Information on the park: **Flinders Ranges National Park,** PMB 10, Hawker, SA 5434. Tel: (086) 48 0017.

PERTH AND WESTERN AUSTRALIA

On September 27, 1983 at 5.21am (local time) the city of Perth, capital of Western Australia, entered the sporting history books. *Australia II*, the 12–metre racing yacht from the Royal Perth Yacht Club, beat the American defender *Intrepid* by 41 seconds. For the first time since the inception of the America's Cup in 1851, the Cup left the Atlantic, New York and the United States. Its destination was the Indian Ocean, Perth and Western Australia.

Perth captured the attention of sailors, sponsors, sports historians and sailing enthusiasts. Australia may have been obliged to return the Cup to the United States in 1987 but at last the city of Perth was on the map.

Western Australia, which occupies one-third of the country, is so immense, so diverse and so unspoiled that it is almost worth visiting it alone, especially if the tourist with limited time takes into account the distances separating it from the rest of the country. In Western Australia, everything is bigger, starker and more intense than in the east and visitors would be well advised not to miss places like Broome, the Kimberley, Kalgoorlie and the Goldfields. The state has something to offer even the most demanding of visitors.

PERTH

Located more than 2500 mi/4000 km from Sydney, Perth claims to be the most isolated metropolis on earth. For a long time, the city was content to grow quietly, far from the gaze of the country and the world. Founded in 1829 by Captain James Stirling with the sole purpose of preventing the French from settling in that part of the world, Perth had to wait until the 1950s before its development really took off. Successive discoveries of fabulous mineral deposits (iron ore, bauxite, nickel, etc.) in the north of the state spawned a renewed rush to the west and Perth mushroomed. The previously sleepy town sprouted skyscrapers (headquarters for the mining companies) and built highways until it overtook its rival, Adelaide, as the biggest 'small' state capital. The population, too, has grown to the million mark, with three out of every four Western Australians living in Perth.

Wealth, however, did not bring fame until Alan Bond, took matters in hand. A local self-made millionaire, Bond launched his first challenge to the New York Yacht Club in 1974 with the firm

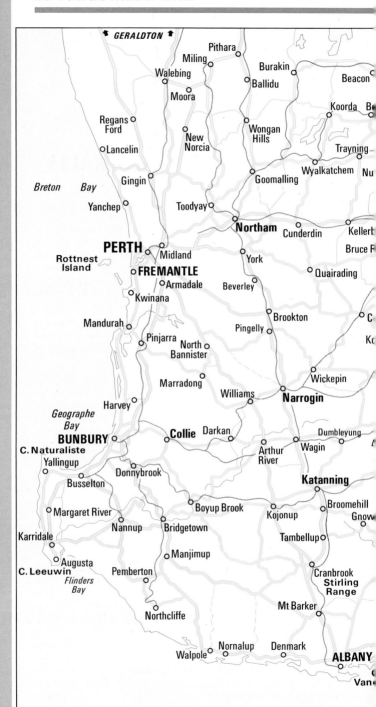

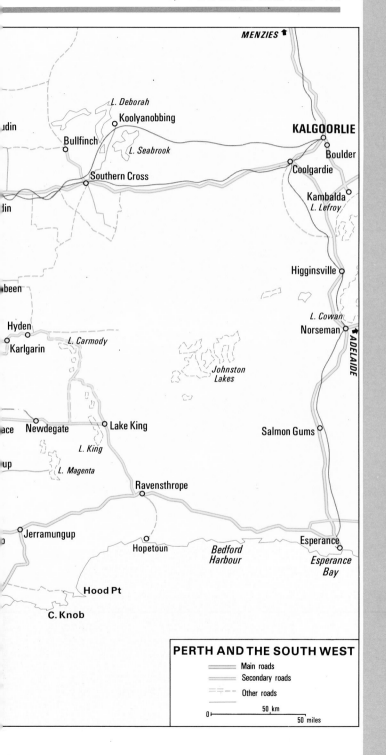

MENZIES ↑

L. Deborah

Koolyanobbing

KALGOORLIE

din

Bullfinch

L. Seabrook

Boulder

Coolgardie

Southern Cross

Kambalda

din

L. Lefroy

been

Higginsville

Hyden

L. Cowan

Karlgarin

L. Carmody

Norseman

Johnston
Lakes

ace

Newdegate

Lake King

Salmon Gums

up

L. King

L. Magenta

Ravensthrope

Jerramungup

Hopetoun

Bedford
Harbour

Esperance

Hood Pt

Esperance
Bay

C. Knob

ADELAIDE ↓

PERTH AND THE SOUTH WEST

Main roads
Secondary roads
Other roads

0   50 km

0   50 miles

intention of bringing the prestigious trophy to the banks of the Swan River and thereby increasing the value of his many properties. Nine years later he succeeded, but after all the rejoicing Perth is not quite sure that it did in fact emerge a winner. There are some who suggest that the price paid for this moment of glory and the foreign investment that followed might have been too high. Hundreds of thousands of people descended on Perth in the southern summer of 1986-87 to watch the defense of the trophy. They all had to be housed, fed and transported, which means that there is no dearth of tourist facilities. However, American-style tourism has left its mark and has endangered the very characteristic which made life on the edge of the Indian Ocean pleasant: tranquillity.

For all its boundless riches, perfect climate (7 hours of sun per day), beaches, and lush natural environment Perth still has a major problem: fresh water. As the summer progresses, the city's reserves are depleted. This consideration probably means that the city is as large as it's ever going to get.

■■■ PRACTICAL INFORMATION

Telephone area code: 09.

Access

Plane

Many of the airlines flying from Europe (**Qantas, British Airways, Air India,** etc.) make Perth their first port of call in Australia. Some give the visitor the choice of arriving in the west and leaving from the east, or vice versa. There are direct flights to Sydney (3 hours 55 min), Melbourne (3 hours 15 min) and Adelaide (3 hours 5 min). Flights to Darwin go through Port Hedland (4.5 hours).

International airlines

Air New Zealand, 50 St. George's Terrace, City. Tel: 325 1099.
British Airways, 140 St. George's Terrace, City. Tel: 322 5011.
Qantas, 93 William St., City. Tel: 322 0222.
Singapore Airlines, 179 St. George's Terrace, City. Tel: 322 2422.
United Airlines, 178 St. George's Terrace, City. Tel: 321 2719.

Domestic airlines

Ansett and Ansett Western Australia, 26 St. George's Terrace, City. Tel: 323 1122.
Australian Airlines, 55 St. George's Terrace, City. Tel: 323 3333.

Regular bus service to and from the airport. **Skybus.** Tel: 328 9777.

Train

If you have enough time, crossing the continent by train is a wonderful experience and much less tiring than bus or car. The *Indian-Pacific,* which as its name suggests, links the two oceans, is one of the most beautiful trains in the world, a sort of air-conditioned luxury hotel on wheels. First class compartments have a private lavatory while in second class, showers and lavatories are located at the end of each carriage. There are three departures per week in each direction. The journey takes 65 hrs from Sydney (2625 mi/4200 km) and 40 hrs from Adelaide (1688 mi/2700 km). Information and reservations in Perth:

East Perth Rail Terminal, Summer St., East Perth. Tel: 326 2811.

Westrail, Perth Rail Station, Wellington St., City. Tel: 326 2690.

Bus

The bus is faster, less expensive and considerably less comfortable than the train. You can count on a minimum 60-hour journey from Sydney and

37 hours from Adelaide. Although the fare itself is not as high, you have to pay for your own food and drink en route. The bus, however, is the only means of public ground transportation between Darwin and Perth. The journey (via Port Hedland) covers 2775 mi/4440 km and takes 60 hours.

Deluxe, 741 Hay St., City.Tel: 322 7877.

Greyhound, 26 St. George's Terrace, City. Tel: 478 1122.

Car

Driving to Perth on the famous Eyre Highway requires considerable patience. At an average 63 mph/100 kmh, driving 12 hours a day, you will take 3.5 days from Sydney to Perth. Heading west from Port Augusta (199 mi/319 km west of Adelaide and the last town before Norseman which is 1250 mi/2000 km further on), you can eat, sleep and fill the car at the following stops (distances are those from Adelaide): **Iron Knob** (243 mi/388 km); **Kimba** (307 mi/491 km), hospital; **Kyancutta** (354 mi/566 km), service-station only; **Wudinna** (362 mi/579 km), hospital; **Minnipa** (386 mi/617 km); **Poochera** (407 mi/651 km); **Wirrulla** (436 mi/698 km); **Ceduna** (496 mi/793 km), hospital; **Penong** (540 mi/864 km); **Nundroo** (589 mi/942 km); **Yalata** (621 mi/993 km), Aboriginal mission, telephone and emergency medical centre but no accommodation; **Nullarbor** (679 mi/1086 km); **BP Travellers Village Motel** at SA/WA border (794 mi/1271 km); **Eucla** (803 mi/1284 km), Flying Doctor base; **Cocklebiddy** (974 mi/1559 km); **Caiguna** (1014 mi/1623 km), Flying Doctor base; **Balladonia** (1128 mi/1805 km); **Norseman** (1248 mi/1996 km), the door to the west.

The stops are only 63 to 126 mi/100 to 200 km apart but don't be deceived—the Nullarbor Plain is a long, treeless stretch of the bush. Check the condition of your car before you leave, battery and wheels in particular. Take a complete tool kit with you and plenty of water, especially if your engine tends to overheat. Beware of the combined effects of heat, poor visibility due to dust, straight stretches of road for miles on end and beer. At night, watch out for kangaroos and cattle. At Norseman you'll be awarded an 'I crossed the Nullarbor' car sticker. You'll have deserved it. You will then have the choice of two routes for the 435 mi/700 km to Perth: via Kalgoorlie in the north or Albany in the south (see pp. 179-182). Reserve ahead if you intend staying at motels along the route. You won't be the only person on the Eyre Highway.

Getting around Perth

Car rental

Avis, 46 Hill St., City. Tel: 325 7677.

Budget, 960 Hay St., City. Tel: 322 1100.

Hertz, 39 Milligan St., City. Tel: 321 7777.

Thrifty, 126 Adelaide Terrace, City. Tel: 325 4700.

Taxis

Black and White. Tel: 328 8288.

Green and Gold. Tel: 328 3455.

Useful addresses

Tourist information

Holiday Western Australia Centre, 771 Hay St., City. Tel: 322 2999. Brochures and help of all kinds, including reservations.

Post office

General Post Office (GPO), 3 Forrest Place, City. Tel: 326 5211. Open Mon. to Fri. 8am to 5pm. After-hours service (stamps only) Mon. to Fri. 5pm to 7pm, Sat. and Sun 9am to noon.

Automobile club

Royal Automobile Club of Western Australia, 228 Adelaide Terrace, City. Tel: 325 0551.

Accommodation

International-standard hotels

▲▲▲▲ **Ansett International,** 10 Irwin St., City. Tel: 325 0481. International hotel with an Australian character. 229 rooms, 14 suites.

▲▲▲▲ **Burswood Island Resort and Casino,** Great Eastern Highway, Victoria Park. Tel: 362 7777. Huge hotel, casino and convention centre complex. 398 rooms, 18 suites.

▲▲▲▲ **Merlin,** corner of Plain St. and Adelaide Terrace, City. Tel: 323 0121. One of Perth's most recent hotels with striking, modern architecture. 369 rooms, 32 suites.

▲▲▲▲ **Parmelia Hilton International,** Mill St., City. Tel: 322 3622. Perth's great modern hotel. 318 rooms, 69 suites.

▲▲▲▲ **Perth Ambassador,** 196 Adelaide Terrace, City. Tel: 325 1455. Chinese decor. 171 rooms, 59 suites.

▲▲▲▲ **Sheraton Perth,** 207 Adelaide Terrace, City. Tel: 325 0501. Another great hotel for business or tourist guests. 410 rooms.

First-class hotels

▲▲▲ **Chateau Perth,** corner of Victoria Ave. and Hay St., City. Tel: 325 0461. Motel. 133 rooms.

▲▲▲ **Park Royal,** 54 Terrace Rd., City. Tel: 325 3822. Motel. 102 rooms.

▲▲▲ **The New Esplanade,** 18 The Esplanade, City. Tel: 325 2000. 36 rooms, 11 suites.

Moderately priced and inexpensive hotels

▲▲ **The Jewell House,** 180 Goderich St., City. Tel: 325 8488. 200 rooms.

▲▲ **Miss Maud European Hotel,** 97 Murray St., City. Tel: 325 3900. 51 rooms.

▲▲ **Perth Youth Hostel,** 60 Newcastle St., City. Tel: 328 1135. Members only.

▲ **YMCA,** 119 Murray St., City. Tel: 325 2744.

In Fremantle

▲▲▲▲ **The Esplanade,** corner of Marine Terrace and Collie St. Tel: 430 4000. A former pub superbly restored and enlarged. 140 rooms.

▲▲ **Federal Hotel,** 23 William St. Tel: 335 1645. 27 rooms.

In Guildford

▲ **Rose & Crown,** 105 Swan St. Tel: 279 4208. The oldest hotel in Western Australia, 9 mi/14 km from the city. 27 rooms.

On the beach

▲ **West Beach Lagoon,** 251 West Coast Highway, Scarborough. Tel: 341 6122. A little more expensive than the Sands Motor Hotel, and more tourist-oriented with a family atmosphere. 70 rooms.

▲ **Sands Motor Hotel,** 23 Hastings St., Scarborough. Tel: 341 1122. Good but inexpensive motel, 8 mi/12 km from the city. 57 rooms.

Food

Elegant restaurants

Perth's high-society meets at the **River Room** of the Sheraton, the **Garden Restaurant** of the Parmelia-Hilton and **Langley's** at the Merlin. Other elegant restaurants include:

Churchill's, behind the Concert Hall. Tel: 325 4033. Elegant, and expensive.

The famous Tudor-style shopping arcades of Perth's London Court.

The Establishment, 35a Hampton Rd., Nedlands. Tel: 386 5508. Expensive and fashionable. BYO.

Hilite 33, Centre Tower, St. George's Terrace, City. Tel: 325 4844. Perth's revolving restaurant offers views over the city and the Swan River.

Ord Street Café, 27 Ord St., West Perth. Tel: 321 6021. Good and quite expensive.

French

Le Canard, 12 Napoleon St. Tel: 384 4571. *Nouvelle cuisine.*

La French Tavern, 135 Stirling Highway, Nedlands. Tel: 386 5006.

Prideau's, 176 Stirling Highway, Nedlands. Tel: 386 8933.

Italian

L'Alba Café, 100 Lake St. Tel: 328 3750.

Mama Maria, 105 Aberdeen St. Tel: 227 9828.

Papa Luigi's, 33 South Terrace. Fremantle. Tel: 430 4522. Well patronized.

Uncle Vince's Pizza, 73 Lake St. Tel: 328 3525.

Vino Vino, 151 James St. Tel: 328 5403.

Mexican

Pancho's Mexican Villa, 885 Albany Highway, East Victoria Park. Tel: 361 2135.

Oriental

Emperor's Court, 66 Lake St. Tel: 328 8860. Chinese.

Jun and Tommy's, 113 Murray St. Tel: 325 7341. Japanese fast food.

Koto 39 High St., Fremantle. Tel: 336 2455. Japanese.

Seafood

Fishy Affair, 132 James St., City. Tel: 328 3939.

Oyster Bar, 88 James St., City. Tel: 328 7888.

Oyster Beds, 26 Riverside Rd., East Fremantle. Tel: 339 1611. Built on stilts in the harbour.

Shopping

The department stores and the main shopping arcades are located around the Hay St. Mall (pedestrian zone) in the centre of the City.

Aboriginal arts

Aboriginal Traditional Arts, 242 St. George's Terrace, City. Tel: 32 1440. Genuine articles guaranteed by the government.

Crafts

Mount Lawley Craft Centre, 676a Beaufort St., Mount Lawley. Tel: 271 2023. Sheepskins, carved wood, clothes, etc.

Opals and precious stones

Gold & Silver Bullion Sales of Australia, London Court, St. George's Terrace, City. Tel: 325 8766. Ingots, nuggets, gold and silver coins.

The Opal Centre, Shop 1, St. Martin's Arcade, City. Tel: 325 8588.

Opal Exploration Co, 1st floor, 616 Hay St., City. Tel: 325 2907.

Entertainment and cultural life

The **Perth Concert Hall,** 5 St. George's Terrace, City (Tel: 325 3399) and the **Entertainment Centre** in Wellington St., City (Tel: 322 4766) bear witness to Perth's efforts in the direction of international-standard culture. The Concert Hall inclines to the classical and the Centre (8000 seats) to the popular. The attractions presented are often of a surprising quality for such a small and remote city. Programs are listed in the newspapers. The Festival of Perth (last two weeks in February) is not as famous as its Adelaide cousin but it manages to attract numerous international stars.

Pubs and nightlife

In Perth, you drink Swan beer (made famous by the brewery's owner Alan Bond). It is one of the city's greatest claims to fame, along with the fact that many pubs (which unfortunately close at 10pm) present excellent rock groups.

Selected pubs

Two pleasant and well-patronized pubs are the **Freemason's Hotel** in Midland and the **Subiaco Hotel** in Subiaco. On the beach at Cottlesloe is the **Ocean Beach Hotel.**

The fashionable bars in the city are the **Shafto Lane,** the **Blue Note** and the **Golden Rail.** The **Wentworth** and **Savoy Plaza** are typical old-style 'Aussie' bars. Other 'in' spots are **Cagney's** in Claremont, **Steve's** in Nedlands, **The Brewery Alehouse** in Nedlands, where you can drink 'home-made' beer, and **Kim's** in Claremont.

Music and dancing

If you want to dance to local but very good rock bands, the following places are recommended:

Café Bar and Brasserie, 88 Broadway, Nedlands. Tel: 386 5147.

The Equator, 160 Beaufort St., City. Tel: 227 9107. A strictly 'local' meeting-place for Perth 'fringe' groups, artists, etc.

The Herdsman, 33 Herdsman Parade, Wembley.

Meccano's, in the Old Melbourne pub in the city.

Raffles, Kintail Rd., Canning Bridge.

Red Parrot, 89 Milligan St., North Perth. Tel: 328 9870.

ore sophisticated (and expensive):

louds, in the Sheraton Hotel (see p. 174).

annibal's, 69 Lake St., Northbridge. Tel: 328 1065.

uliana's, in the Parmelia Hilton (see p. 174).

rograms can be found in the daily *West Australian*.

GETTING TO KNOW PERTH

he City

erth has the clean, bright, modern look of a suburban shopping centre, but comes as a welcome relief after four days on a dusty road. Between the ermanently blue waters of the Swan River and the railway line, four treets contain the major shops and offices: Wellington, Murray and Hay treets, and St. George's Terrace which are sectioned at right angles by alf a dozen cross-streets. Along the river, Perth sparkles with the lights of s enormous road interchanges.

he size of the City (0.6 mi/1 km long) means that you can see it all on one f the free City Clipper buses which runs every 10 minutes. If you want to xplore the suburbs, ask for a map from the **Metropolitan Passenger ransport Trust (MTT)** information office at 125 St. George's Terrace, City el: 325 8511). If you're walking, go down **Hay St. Mall** to **London Court.** ne Court is the best-known of Perth's shopping arcades and is a narrow edestrian zone built in 1937 in neo-Tudor style, with wrought-iron shop gns, stained-glass windows and exposed beams. The most elegant outiques and restaurants are to be found here. London Court opens onto **t. George's Terrace.** Each year, the mining companies and government inistries add new skyscrapers there, alongside the carefully preserved tone or brick buildings from the 1850s. The remainder of the city retains aces of Perth from the days of the conquest of the west: a 19th-century ub, water tanks with corrugated-iron roofs, a shop sign painted on a wall. owever, it is the limpid, deep and mysterious blue of the sky which puts erth in true perspective, as an outpost of civilization at the end of the vorld, with residents who, perhaps through force of circumstances, are the nost spontaneously friendly in Australia.

or a view over the entire City and a quiet picnic, go to **Kings Park*** at the nd of St. George's Terrace. It covers 988 acres/400 ha of typical Australian ush, with eucalypts and grass-trees.

he suburbs

he suburbs of Perth were designed according to the classic Australian nodel, although they lack the Victorian Baroque areas of other cities. The nost typical suburbs, such as **West Perth, Leederville** and **Subiaco,** ontain simple wooden houses with corrugated-iron roofs and wide erandahs. In summer, the green lawns lie scorched by the sun because f the regular water shortages that hit the city. The smartest residential uburbs extend along the river: **Nedlands, Dalkieth, Peppermint Grove** nd **Crawley,** where you will find the relaxed campus of the University of Vestern Australia.

he beaches

erth's fabulous white-sand beaches are to be found north of the mouth f the Swan River. They can all be reached in 20 minutes or so by bus from ne city centre. From south to north, they are: **Mosman, Cottlesloe** (the east frequented), **Swanbourne** (a nudist beach on Army land and thus elonging to the federal government), **City Beach***, and the surf beaches f **Floreat Beach, Scarborough*** (the most exciting, like something from Beach Boys song), **North Beach,** and **Sorrento.** Scarborough was the cene of the 1987 America's Cup races. Further north, but not far away, the eaches are absolutely empty.

East of Perth are the hills of the **Darling Range** and the towns o
Kelmscott, Kalamunda and **Roleystone***. This bushland area is really th
escarpment of a huge inland plateau and is home to Perth's artists and
craftsmen, far from the city crowds and the extreme heat. Coach tours
follow the Albany, then Brookton highways.

WHAT TO SEE

Western Australian Museum

Frances St., City. Tel: 328 4411. *Open Mon. to Thurs. 10.30am to 5pm., Fr.
to Sun. 1pm to 5pm.*
A comprehensive display of Aboriginal artifacts, vintage cars, the skeleton
of a blue whale, an 11 metric-ton meteorite and the restored Old Perth
Gaol.

Western Australian Art Gallery

47 James St., City. Tel: 328 7233. *Open daily 10am-5pm.*
A fine collection of European and Australian paintings, including contempo
rary works plus some very well-executed Western Australian bar
paintings.

OUTSIDE PERTH

Fremantle**

Located south of the mouth of the Swan, 11 mi/18 km from Perth along th
Stirling (northern) or Canning (southern) highways, Fremantle is reminis
cent of the old part of Perth. It probably resembles the city 30 years ag
but with the bustling atmosphere of a large seaport. The town o
Fremantle, which was founded several days before Perth, now boasts
population of about 25,000. It did a fine job of preserving its history an
authentic working-class suburban character until the day it became the lan
base for the America's Cup. Governments, both local and federal, investe
large amounts of money in marinas and slipways for the yachts, pres
centres, hotels, etc. The various competing teams simply took over certai
hotels and restaurants and made them their national headquarters.

In spite of it all, Fremantle has retained its character. Its quiet street
leading to the docks are filled with colonial houses, stone buildings, pub
and ethnic restaurants. Artists display their works in local galleries or at th
Fremantle Markets (corner of South Terrace and Henderson St. Te
335 2515. Open Fri. 9am to 9pm, Sat. 9am to 1pm), next to fresh lobster
and second-hand clothing. The **Western Australian Maritime Museum**
on Cliff St. is also worth a look. It is *open Wed. and Fri. to Sun. 1pm to 5p*
and is located in a convict-built stone building dating from 1851. The ver
interesting collection includes objects associated with maritime exploratio
of the Western Australian coast by the Dutch in the 17th century.

Rottnest Island*

Located some 13 mi/20 km off the coast, this 6 mi/10 km long island is
favourite destination for Perth children. The sea is particularly clear, car
virtually non-existent and the *guokkas,* the tiny marsupials that gav
Rottnest (= rat nest) its name, are as cute as they come. The trip takes tw
hours by boat from Jetty No 4 at the end of Barrack St., City. Tel: 325 6033
There are hotels on the island and an evening boat back to Perth. Th
America's Cup race was held over a course laid out between Rottnes
Island and the coast. A popular hotel on Rottnest is the ▲▲ **Rottnes
Lodge Resort.** Tel: 292 5018. 62 rooms.

Yanchep

Yanchep was another one of Alan Bond's coups: the establishment of
marina and a town on a stretch of deserted beach at the edge of th
Yanchep National Park. It is known as Sun City and was intended as
kind of Surfers Paradise of the west coast, its success supposedl

guaranteed by an expected Australian win in the America's Cup. Bond sold Sun City to Japanese interests before he could put his theory to the test but it remains a surprise in the middle of the bush, with its artificial harbour, stone ramparts, golf course and typically suburban houses in Perth's newest semi-residential district.

The **Yanchep National Park** covers nearly 7410 acres/3000 ha. Its main attractions are its bush, caves and birdlife. For information on the park, contact the **Park Superintendent,** Yanchep National Park, Yanchep. Tel: (095) 61 1661. Access via Waneroo Rd. (31 mi/50 km).

THE GOLDFIELDS
AND THE AUSTRALIAN SOUTH-WEST

The area between Perth, Kalgoorlie, Esperance and Albany (see map pp. 170-171) is one of the most beautiful in Australia. Its size makes it perfect for a week's car trip.

Access

You can get to Kalgoorlie from Perth by plane **(Ansett Western Australia),** bus **(Ansett-Pioneer** or **Greyhound**—8 or 9 hours), train (the *Prospector*—7 to 8 hours), or car (Highway No 94—1 day).

From the east, you can reach Kalgoorlie via Norseman by car or take a direct train from Port Augusta. You can also do the Grand Tour by car: Perth - Kalgoorlie - Norseman - Esperance - Albany - Perth or vice versa (1125 mi/1800 km). Both **Greyhound** and **Deluxe Coaches** offer a regular bus service on the Norseman - Esperance - Albany stretch (8 hours), while a **Westrail** bus (owned and operated by the state railways) covers the Albany - Perth section.

▬ *KALGOORLIE, CAPITAL OF THE GOLDFIELDS****

Located 375 mi/600 km east of Perth, this town remains the centre for 1890s Gold Rush nostalgia.

Kalgoorlie and the Gold Rush

The Great Eastern Highway (No 94) passes through the state wheat-belt—Western Australia produces one-third of Australia's wheat—before plunging into the desert at the town of **Southern Cross,** 230 mi/368 km from Perth. There it traverses the region of minerals and sheep, finally reaching Coolgardie, the most accessible of the Goldfields' 'ghost' towns. There is nothing ghost-like about the twin cities of **Kalgoorlie** and **Boulder,** 25 mi/40 km from Coolgardie. They have a permanent population of 20,000 plus a large number of tourists bitten by the gold-fever bug. In 1902, its heyday, Kalgoorlie boasted 30,000 residents, 93 hotels (pubs), 8 breweries and more than 100 mines, not to mention hundreds more individual shafts, most of them along the Golden Mile, the richest square mile of real-estate in the world. The tunnels of these mines descend as deep as 3900 ft/1200 m, over a network 938 mi/1500 km long. They have yielded more than 100 million tons of quartz containing 1200 tons of fine gold. The high costs of this kind of mineral exploration seriously curtailed mining operations in the area after World War II but Kalgoorlie did not cease gold production completely—the **Mt. Charlotte Mine** is still operational today and the rising gold price has made it economical to reopen others.

At the present time, the Goldfields region of Western Australia alone produces over half of Australia's gold. Geologists are certain that the area has still to yield much more gold than has ever been extracted. Looking for gold has become a favourite Australian pastime and the pretext for long, irresistible forays into the bush from Kalgoorlie, one of the most popular starting-points for amateur prospectors. If you'd like to take part in the Gold

Rush of the 1980s, you must start by obtaining a Miner's Right, a license to prospect. Under English law, the sub-soil of territories governed by the Crown belongs to the Crown. As the representative of the Crown, the state concerned can only lease concessions to prospectors and miners.

Don't worry, a Miner's Right costs only 10 dollars and is valid forever. You can get one in 15 minutes, without even having to prove your identity, from the Department of Mines, Brookman St., Kalgoorlie. With this precious document in your pocket, all the gold that you find on Crown land or on your leased portion of it is yours to keep. The main victory won by the Eureka Stockade miners responsible for such amazingly liberal legislation lies in the fact that you do not have to pay tax on your finds and you even have the right to have 50 tons of minerals per year crushed free of charge in the State Battery.

All you have to do now is find the gold. Your best chances will be either to go 'panning', that is washing supposedly gold-bearing soil in a pan in a river until the gold dust collects in the bottom, or to rent a metal detector from one of the specialist shops in Kalgoorlie. They will tell you how and where to use it. You are more likely to find a nugget after heavy rain; you may even come across a piece of the American *Spacelab* which crashed to earth in the Australian desert...

Discovering Kalgoorlie

Kalgoorlie, along with its sister city Boulder, is an interesting town and one of the most authentic and best preserved in Australia. You will surely like the Baroque architecture of the pubs and former administration buildings in **Hannan St.** (Kalgoorlie) and **Burt St.** (Boulder). The dilapidated wooden houses on the outskirts of Kalgoorlie will conjure up images of the past. Don't forget to stroll along **Hay St.** which runs parallel to Hannan. This wide, dusty street, bordered by fences of corrugated iron was, until recently, the foremost red-light district of the Australian West. Two or three establishments uphold Hay St.'s reputation today. The girls sit in armchairs on the verandas of corrugated-iron cottages, knitting or sipping coffee in the glow of a red light. Empty sites indicate the previous locations of other houses, their residents long gone, no doubt, to service the more profitable markets of the big iron-ore mines in the Pilbara region.

Equally nostalgic are the sights offered by the famous **Golden Mile.** Here nothing has changed since the mines closed: gigantic rusty iron or wooden derricks; buildings with creaking doors; gaping mine-shafts, literally side by-side, in which a thrown rock makes no perceptible sound; reddish moon-like mountains of crushed quartz; barbed-wire enclosures now separating only piles of gravel. In the setting sun, the whole scene becomes a last homage to the incredible determination of the men who worked, sifted and dug up this lifeless red dirt. The town is now experiencing a new Gold Rush and the mines are slowly reopening—until the gold price drops again.

An asphalt road at the end of **Boulder Rd.** will take you to the most interesting part of the Golden Mile, an area theoretically closed to the public, mainly because of the safety problems posed by the hundreds of unfenced, open shafts. However, if you're very careful it's not strictly forbidden to explore the area. At sunset, the view of the Golden Mile from high in the hills is unforgettable. One of the mines, the **Hainault Tourist Gold Mine,** Boulder Block Rd., Golden Mile, Kalgoorlie. Tel: (090) 21 4281 which was in continuous operation from 1897 until 1968, has been restored and converted for tourism. You can visit the mine buildings and descend 200 ft/60 m down one of its shafts.

Useful addresses

Ansett Western Australia, Maritana St. Tel: (090) 21 2277.

Avis, 520 Hannan St. Tel: (090) 21 1472.

Holiday WA Centre, 250 Hannan St. Tel: (090) 21 1413.

Accommodation and food

The 19th-century pubs with their wide verandas are magnificent. They include:

▲ **The Exchange Hotel,** Hannan St. Tel: (090) 21 2833. 16 rooms.

▲ **The Palace Hotel,** Hannan St. Tel: (090) 21 2788. 47 rooms.

▲ **Sandalwood,** Hannan St. Tel: (090) 21 4455. Comfortable motel. 54 rooms.

▲ **Surrey House Private Hotel,** 9 Boulder Rd. Tel: (090) 21 1340. A guest house with atmosphere and good homestyle cooking. 14 rooms.

COOLGARDIE AND THE GHOST TOWNS***

Kalgoorlie is the only Goldfield town to have kept its population. Other towns in the area experienced the same lightning growth and the same orgy of Baroque architecture. However, they did not survive the fever of the 1890s and today all that remain are a few reasonably preserved houses, some pubs with wooden verandas and a few heaps of rusty iron marking the site of an abandoned mine beside a red-dirt road leading into the desert. **Coolgardie** is the most accessible of these ghost towns, 25 mi/40 km from Kalgoorlie on the road to Perth. The town claimed 25,000 inhabitants, 23 hotels, 3 breweries and 7 newspapers in 1900. Today, 700 people live in the few buildings still standing along the main street, exploiting the new code of the Eyre Highway: tourism. The **Goldfields Museum** houses a collection of objects and equipment used during the Gold Rush and attracts 60,000 visitors a year.

North of Kalgoorlie, the asphalt road leading to **Laverton** (225 mi/360 km) extends no further into the desert. With the exception of Laverton, the towns along the way have not yet found their second breath. Laverton saw its population increase beyond 1900 levels following the opening in 1970 of a nickel mine 19 mi/30 km away. Kanowna's population has fallen from 12,000 at the turn of the century to 0; Ora Banda's from 2000 to 50; Broad Arrow's from 2400 to 20; Menzies' from 10,000 to 90; Kookynie's from 1500 to 10; and Leonora's from 1000 to 500. However, **Menzies** (81 mi/130 km north of Kalgoorlie) and **Leonora** (163 mi/260 km) have been able to survive at a reduced level and offer hotels, shops and service-stations. The same facilities are available in Laverton. Further on, another road crosses the 1063 mi/1700 km of desert to reach Alice Springs. Coach tours will take you to the more interesting locations on this route and the driver will teach you how to use a metal-detector. Contact **Gold Rush Tours,** Maritana St., Kalgoorlie. Tel: (090) 21 2954.

ALBANY AND THE SOUTH-WEST

With its temperate climate, varied countryside and relatively dense, well-established population, the south-west of Western Australia is comparable to Victoria or Tasmania. As in areas on the Tasman Sea, the water and the sky are a transparent, pastel colour, quite surprising after the strong contrasts of the Pacific. The towns and villages of the south-west, most of them founded in the early 19th century, have retained the true flavour of rural communities, totally isolated from the rest of the world, or from the faraway, overcrowded metropolis of Perth.

Take at least two days to see this area, either en route between Perth and Adelaide, or as part of a trip to the Goldfields.

Bunbury, the main town on the Indian Ocean coast (116 mi/185 km south of Perth), is the gateway to the twin capes region, with Cape Naturaliste in the north and Cape Leeuwin in the south. The coastline includes 40 mi/64 km of superb surf beaches, said to be the best in Australia and, in the interior, a series of magnificent caves, which have been opened to tourists, are among the most spectacular in the world: **Yallingup Cave**

(20 mi/32 km west of Busselton), **Mammoth Cave** (16 mi/26 km south c Margaret River), **Lake Cave** (1.25 mi/2 km from Mammoth) and **Jewe Cave** (further south, 5 mi/8 km north of Augusta). For information on visit to the caves:

Tourist Office, corner of Bussell Highway and Wallcliffe Rd., Margare River. Tel: (097) 57 2147.

The Southern Ocean coast between Augusta and Albany contains one o Australia's most beautiful forests, the **Pemberton Forest.** Its giant *karri* (local eucalypts) sometimes reach heights of 295 ft/90 m, shelterin exquisite unspoilt beaches (in the **William Bay National Park** betwee Walpole and Denmark) and quiet, picturesque villages such as **Denmarl** (31 mi/50 km west of Albany).

Albany was founded in 1826, three years before Perth, and is the economic capital of the region. This is evidenced by the huge wheat silo that disfigure the otherwise splendid landscape of King George Sound, the natural harbour on which Albany is located. The town itself (pop approx. 20,000) has hardly changed since the end of the 19th century an was forgotten by the rest of the world until the relatively recent arrival o tourists attracted by its provincial charm, its quiet, its deserted beaches an its temperate climate (cold and humid in winter). Albany is also famous fo its whaling station which ceased operations in 1978 following a spirited legal battle with ecologists. You can now visit the buildings and the rust machinery of Cheynes Beach Whaling Station, at Frenchmans Bay 16 mi/25 km west of the town, on Princess Royal Harbour. Information

Albany Travel Centre, 171 York St. Tel: (098) 41 1613.

Returning to Perth (240 mi/400 km by the direct Albany Highway route you pass through a slightly hilly sheep-farming area interspersed wit eucalypt forests and pastures, and a sprinkling of quiet villages and isolate wooden farm buildings. You can also return via **Esperance** (313 mi/500 kn from Albany) before turning north to **Norseman** (138 mi/220 km from Esperance), a sleepy, former gold-mining town located at the foot of a giar heap of crushed quartz. There you rejoin the Eyre Highway leading t Adelaide or the Goldfields. Another famous attraction of the area is **Wave Rock** * (219 mi/350 km west of Perth). As its name suggests, the rock i in the form of a petrified stone wave, 49 ft/15 m high. It is locate 2.5 mi/4 km from the small town of **Hyden** and involves a complicated an very long detour (438 mi/700 km from Albany to Perth), across the state' wheat-belt, via the towns of Lake Grace, Corrigin and Brookton in th direction of Albany-Perth.

Accommodation

Albany

▲ **Albany Hotel,** York St. Tel: (098) 41 1031. 9 rooms.

▲ **Royal George Hotel,** 34 Stirling Terrace. Tel: (098) 41 1466 18 rooms.

▲ **London Hotel,** Stirling Terrace. Tel: (098) 41 1048.

Bunbury

▲ **The Rose Hotel,** Victoria St. Tel: (097) 21 4533. 24 rooms.

Margaret River

▲ **Margaret River Hotel,** Bussell Highway. Tel: (097) 57 2655 31 rooms.

PERTH TO DARWIN:
BROOME AND THE KIMBERLEY

This description has been included here because the hug distances and endless landscape involved seem to offer a fittin conclusion to any tour of Western Australia.

wallaby, one of the numerous Australian marsupials.

Darwin is 2629 mi/4206 km and a minimum four or five days rive from Perth. It goes without saying that this journey is suited genuine lovers of wide open spaces. Other people, especially ose without the time for such a journey, may care to cover the istance by plane (see p. 186). However, visitors should try, if ossible, to visit Broome, arguably the most interesting town in ustralia.

BROOME★★★

cated more than 1250 mi/2000 km from Perth, in the heart of the imberley mountains, Broome (pop. 2000) seems to spring straight out of Joseph Conrad novel. The town made its fortune from pearl fishing in the arly days of this century. A handful of English and Irish boat owners, some

Japanese divers and a few Chinese merchants set up business there
marrying the local Aboriginal women and leaving their descendants to form
one of the most unusual races in the region. Today, there are only four
luggers (pearling boats) left out of a fleet of 400 in 1910, and the modern
Japanese divers bring only mother-of-pearl and cultured pearls to the
surface. The town also serves as one of the largest regional centres for the
export of cattle raised on the huge cattle stations in the Kimberley. The
weird mixture of Australian cowboys, Japanese fishermen and indefinable
mixed-race oyster shell sorters coexists without much trouble in the
corrugated-iron houses or elegant colonial mansions raised on stilts and
sheltered by clumps of bougainvilleas and mango trees. In the evening
everyone gathers at the **Roebuck Bay Hotel** (see below), the most famous
pub in Western Australia, its atmosphere supercharged by a local rock band
which would put AC/DC to shame. The locals call Broome 'gutsy'. Discover
it for yourself before some promoter turns it into the 'Pearl of the Indian
Ocean'. The wide-open, largely unexplored spaces and the considerable
hidden riches of this part of the Kimberley make it Australia's last frontier
and very hard to reach.

Accommodation

▲▲ **Continental Motel,** Weld St. Tel: (091) 92 1002. 53 rooms.

▲▲ **Tropicana Motel,** Robinson St. Tel: (091) 92 1204. 78 rooms.

▲ **Mangrove Motel,** Dampier Terrace. Tel: (091) 92 1303. 24 rooms.
2 suites.

▲ **Roebuck Bay Hotel,** Dampier Terrace. Tel: (091) 92 1221. Sometimes boisterous front bar. Recently renovated. 32 rooms.

Attractions

For the experience of a lifetime in the Western Australian desert, try a
camel train leaving from Broome. Information and bookings:

Abdul Casserley (tour organizer), PO Box 685, Broome, WA 6725, or ring
the **Vali Hai Take Away** restaurant. Tel: 92 1473.

▬▬ THE KIMBERLEY

The Kimberley is among the most inaccessible areas on the continent. The
only roads are dirt tracks and the only towns the big mining camps. The
harsh, lush beauty of the region, with its gigantic cattle stations, and rich
mixture of cowboys, prospectors, miners and Aborigines is well worth a
detour.

Attractions

Safaris

Tour organizers offer safaris (or more precisely, expeditions) into the area.
These trips take 5 to 15 days or more.

Broome Tourist Bureau, PO Box 352, Broome, WA 6725. Tel: (091)
92 1176. Leaves from Broome.

Amesz Adventure Tours, 223 Collier Rd., Bayswater, WA 6053. Tel: (09)
27 6725. Leaves from Perth.

Kimberley Safaris, PO Box 63, Derby, WA 6728. Tel: (091) 91 1084. Leaves
from Derby.

North-West Camping Safaris, PO Box 375, Broome, WA 6725. Tel: (09)
92 1118. Leaves from Broome.

THE NORTHERN TERRITORY: DARWIN AND ALICE SPRINGS

The Northern Territory is big, even by Australian standards. It covers 540,400 sq mi/1.4 million sq km and supports a population of around 130,000, half of whom live in the capital, Darwin. The inhabitants, like all other Australians living north of the 26th parallel, readily admit to being a race apart. They embody to extremes the more outrageous traits of the national character. To live in the territory, you need more than a little courage, a highly developed sense of 'mateship', a lack of discrimination in cultural matters, a consuming lust for money and, the *sine qua non* of territory life, an extraordinary capacity for beer.

The original inhabitants—35,000 Aborigines and several thousand cattle breeders—have become minority groups among a population distinguished primarily by the fact that it is transient. Darwin is almost exclusively a city of bureaucrats, both civil and military (the air-base in Darwin is the most important in Australia). Alice Springs is given over totally to tourism and the majority of the miners, prospectors and cowboys, attracted by the supposedly easy money in the territory's beef and uranium-mining industries, return to the south once they've made their fortunes.

Founded in 1869 in the hope of attracting a permanent population to the continent's northern coast, and thereby guarding (at least symbolically) against the threat of the 'yellow hordes', Darwin has never become anything more than a tropical mini-Canberra.

The territory has no large cities, just bush—hundreds of thousands of square miles of all kinds of bush. It is as if the *dreamtime* spirit that the Aborigines believe created the Northern Territory ran through the gamut of possibilities: desert, steppes, canyons, dunes, rocks, craters, cliffs, marshes, jungles... Enthusiastically, it added a generous selection of wildlife. A traditionalist, it started with kangaroos, emus, giant lizards and parrots. Then it turned to South-East Asia, a boomerang's throw away, for wild buffalo and crocodiles. Finally, in response to the demands of the impatient men who arrived later, it commissioned a battalion of Afghan camel-drivers, complete with camels and donkeys. In its wisdom, the spirit let these beasts multiply. Now, there are at least 20,000 wild camels and an unknown number of donkeys throughout the deserts. With further touches of its magic wand, the spirit created the blood-reds, violets, grey-greens and psychedelic or-

anges of the territory soil, completing its creation and making i
ready for the modern invasion of 300,000 tourists a year.

DARWIN

Darwin's history is that of a western outpost on the doorstep
of Asia. Incongruous it may be, but it's there to stay. First surveyer
in 1869 by George Goyder, Darwin was partly destroyed by
Japanese bombers in 1942, saved by the construction of an asphalt
road linking it with Alice Springs and the transcontinental railway
network, and then devastated by Cyclone Tracy on Christmas Day
1974. Sixty-eight people were killed and the city was practically
wiped off the map. After a mammoth nationally backed reconstruction program, Darwin now has some 63,000 inhabitants
Aborigines are more numerous and more in evidence in Darwin
than elsewhere but the racial tension which might have resulted ha
been replaced by a mutual indifference. Darwin itself is not overly
interesting. The weather is warm and humid all year round
especially during the 'wet', the season of rain and cyclones from
November to March. For the visitor, the area's real interest begins
about 125 mi/200 km away, in Kakadu National Park.

▬▬ PRACTICAL INFORMATION

Telephone area code: 089.

Access

Plane

Because of its military air-base, Darwin has Australia's largest airport an
is connected with Europe and Asia by direct **Garuda** and **Qantas** flights

Ansett, Ansett-Airlines of Western Australia, and **Australia Airlnes** fl
from Darwin to Perth (via Broome and Port Hedland), Adelaide, Melbourne
Sydney (via Alice Springs) and Brisbane (via Mt. Isa). Flights take 6.5 hour
to/from Sydney and 3.5 hours to/from Adelaide. **Ansett Northern Territor**
handles flights within the territory and Arnhem Land.

International airlines

Garuda, 16 Bennett St. Tel: 82 3344.
Qantas, 19 The Mall. Tel: 82 3355.

Domestic airlines

Ansett, Ansett Northern Territory and **Ansett Western Australia,** 4
Smith St. Tel: 80 3333.
Australian Airlines, 16 Bennett St. Tel: 82 3311.

Bus

To/from Adelaide via Alice Springs: 2019 mi/3230 km, 49 hours plu
connection at Alice Springs (2 hours).

To/from Brisbane via Three Ways, Mt. Isa and Townsville: Darwin-Three
Ways (on the road to Alice Springs) 625 mi/1000 km, 13 hours; Three
Ways-Townsville (via Mt. Isa) 956 mi/1530 km, 20 hours; Townsville
Brisbane 888 mi/1420 km, 25 hours. Total: 2469 mi/3950 km, 58 hours plu
connections.

To/from Brisbane via Three Ways, Mt. Isa and Longreach: Darwin-Three
Ways 625 mi/1000 km, 13 hours; Three Ways-Mt. Isa 394 mi/630 km
8 hours; Mt. Isa-Brisbane 1188 mi/1900 km, 28 hours. Total
2206 mi/3530 km, 49 hours plus connections.

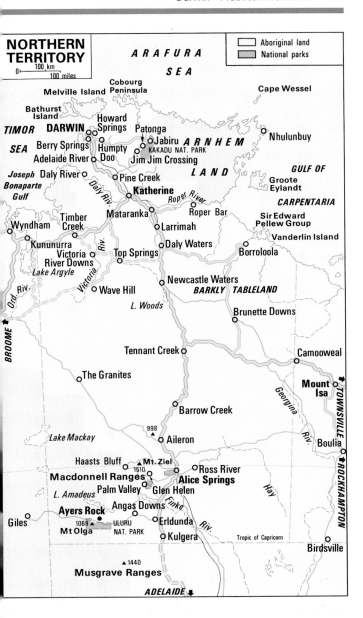

NORTHERN TERRITORY

0 ├─── 100 km
├─── 100 miles

Aboriginal land
National parks

ARAFURA SEA

Cobourg Peninsula

Melville Island

Cape Wessel

Bathurst Island

TIMOR **DARWIN**
Howard Springs
Patonga

Nhulunbuy

SEA Berry Springs
Humpty Doo
Jabiru *ARNHEM*
KAKADU NAT. PARK

Adelaide River
Jim Jim Crossing

Joseph Daly River
Pine Creek
LAND

Bonaparte Gulf
Katherine
Groote Eylandt

Roper River

GULF OF CARPENTARIA

Mataranka
Roper Bar

Wyndham
Timber Creek
Larrimah
Sir Edward Pellew Group

Kununurra
Daly Waters
Vanderlin Island

Victoria River Downs
Top Springs
Borroloola

Lake Argyle

Ord. Riv.
Victoria Riv.
Wave Hill
Newcastle Waters
BARKLY TABLELAND

BROOME
L. Woods
Brunette Downs

Tennant Creek
Camooweal

The Granites
Mount Isa

Georgina Riv.

TOWNSVILLE

Barrow Creek

Lake Mackay
998 ▲ Aileron
Boulia

Haasts Bluff
▲Mt. Ziel
Ross River

1510
Macdonnell Ranges
Alice Springs

ROCKHAMPTON

L. Amadeus
Palm Valley
Glen Helen

Angas Downs
Finke Riv.
Hay

Ayers Rock
Giles
1069 ▲ ●
Mt Olga
ULURU NAT. PARK
Erldunda

Kulgera
Tropic of Capricorn
Birdsville

▲1440
Musgrave Ranges

ADELAIDE ↓

To/from Sydney and Melbourne: via Adelaide, 73 hours to Sydney, 60 hours to Melbourne; via Brisbane, 66 hours to Sydney (via Longreach), 77 hours to Melbourne. Plus connections.

Note that the normal (non-discounted) bus fare is about half the normal economy air fare.

Ansett-Pioneer, 63 Smith St. Tel: 81 6433.

Greyhound, 67-69 Mitchell St. Tel: 81 8510.

Car

Three main routes connect Darwin with the rest of Australia.

Alice Springs to Darwin: 960 mi/1536 km
The Stuart Highway is fully asphalted between Darwin and Alice Springs. In the territory, it is known as 'The Track'. If you don't have any problems, you can cover this stretch in a day. There is not much to see along the way except desert.

You can buy food and fuel at the following points (mi/km figures are the distances from Alice Springs): **Aileron** (89 mi/143 km); **Ti Tree Well** (121 mi/194 km); **Barrow Creek** (178 mi/284 km); **Wauchope** (247 mi/395 km); **Tennant Creek** (319 mi/510 km, the first town on the way north, hospital, police station); **Three Ways** (335 mi/536 km, at the junction of the Barkly Highway to Mt. Isa); **Renner Springs** (439 mi/703 km, small town); **Elliott** (479 mi/766 km, small town); **Dunmarra** (542 mi/867 km); **Daly Waters** (573 mi/916 km, small town, 2 mi/3 km from the highway); **Katherine** (740 mi/1184 km, most important town between Alice Springs and Darwin, hospital, police station); **Pine Creek** (803 mi/1284 km, small town); **Emerald Springs** (825 mi/1320 km); **Hayes Creek** (834 mi/1335 km); **Adelaide River** (887 mi/1419 km, small town); **Noonamah** (933 mi/1493 km from Alice Springs and 27 mi/43 km from Darwin).

Brisbane to Darwin via Mt. Isa: 2469 mi/3950 km
The Brisbane-Mt. Isa stretch (1438 mi/2300 km from Brisbane) is covered on p. 93.

The Barkly Highway is paved all the way from Darwin to Three Ways (625 mi/1000 km). You can buy food and fuel along the 406 mi/650 km route between Mt. Isa and Three Ways at the following points (mi/km from Mt. Isa—add 1438 mi/2300 km for the Mt. Isa to Brisbane stretch): **Camooweal** (118 mi/188 km, the only town until Katherine), **Barry Caves** (226 mi/361 km), **Frewena** (324 mi/518 km). In an emergency, contact the Avon Downs (161 mi/257 km from Mt. Isa) or Soudan (199 mi/318 km) cattle stations. All the above routes require careful driving and a well-prepared car, plus reserves of water, fuel and food.

Perth to Darwin: 2629 mi/4206 km
The road is asphalted all the way. The Western Australian part of the route is detailed in the Perth section on p. 183.

Getting around Darwin

Car rental

Avis, 145 Stuart Highway. Tel: 81 9922.

Hertz, 29 Daly St. Tel: 33 1333.

Territory, 149 Stuart Highway. Tel: 81 8400. Off-road vehicles available.

Thrifty, 131 Stuart Highway. Te: 81 8555.

Useful addresses

Tourist information 31 Smith Street Mall. Tel: 81 6611.

Before leaving for the north, contact one of the following **Northern Territory Government Tourist Offices:**

Adelaide: 9 Hindley St. Tel: (08) 212 1133.
Alice Springs: 51 Todd St. Tel: (089) 52 1299.
Brisbane: 48 Queen St. Tel: (07) 229 5799.
Canberra: 35 Ainslie Ave. Tel: (062) 57 1177.
Hobart: 93 Liverpool St. Tel: (002) 34 4199.
Melbourne: 415 Bourke St. Tel: (03) 67 6948.
Perth: 62 St. George's Terrace. Tel: (09) 322 4255.
Sydney: 89 Kind St. Tel: (02) 235 2822.

Post office

General Post Office (GPO), 21 Knuckey St. Tel: 80 8200.

Automobile club

Automobile Association, 81 Smith St. Tel: 81 3837.

Accommodation

International-standard hotels

▲▲▲▲ **Diamond Beach Hotel Casino,** Gilruth Ave, Mindil Beach. Tel: 81 7755. All-new hotel-casino complex. 92 rooms, 14 suites.

▲▲▲▲ **Four Seasons,** Dashwood Crescent, City. Tel: 81 5333. 75 rooms, 15 suites.

▲▲▲▲ **Sheraton Darwin Hotel,** 32 Mitchell St., City. Tel: 82 0000. 233 rooms, 12 suites.

▲▲▲▲ **Travelodge,** 122 The Esplanade, City. Tel: 81 5388. 181 rooms, 2 suites.

Moderately priced and inexpensive hotels

▲▲ **Cherry Blossom Motel,** 108 The Esplanade, City. Tel: 81 6734. 19 rooms.

▲▲ **Darwin Motor Inn,** 97 Mitchell St., City. Tel: 81 1122. 34 rooms.

▲ **Darwin Youth Hostel,** Beaton Rd., Berrimah. Tel: 84 3107. Members only. 7.5 mi/12 km from the city. 48 beds.

▲ **Larrakeyah Lodge,** 50 Mitchell St., City. Tel: 81 7550. 56 rooms.

Food

The hotels serve the most elaborate meals but there are also numerous restaurants of all nationalities, among them:

The Beagle, Museum Complex, Conacher St., Fannie Bay. Tel: 81 7791. Elegant, international cuisine.

Capri, 37 Knuckey St., City. Tel: 81 2931. Italian.

Le Bénitier, 13 Shepherd Rd., City. Tel: 81 1041. French.

Lee Dynasty, 21 Cavenagh St., City. Tel: 81 7808. Chinese, expensive.

The Rock Oyster, 17 Cavenagh St., City. Tel: 81 7877. Seafood.

The Sheik's Tent, Aralia St., Nightcliff. Tel: 85 4952. Lebanese, inexpensive, atmospheric.

Shopping

You will find a very wide selection of Aboriginal arts and crafts at the **Aboriginal Heritage Gallery,** 44 Smith St., City. Tel: 81 1394.

Entertainment and cultural life

Cultural performances (ballet, theatre, music) at the **Darwin Performing Arts Centre,** Beaufort Hotel complex, The Esplanade, City. Tel: 81 9022.

Festivals and celebrations in the Northern Territory

First week in April: horse racing at Renner Springs.
First week in May: Bang Tail Muster (rodeo) at Alice Springs; horse racing at Aileron.
Second week in May: Camel Cup (camel racing) in Alice Springs.
June: Beer Can Regatta in Darwin (boats made from empty beer cans).
August: Alice Springs Rodeo; Tennant Creek Rodeo; Henley-on-Todd Regatta, Alice Springs (bottomless 'boats' carried in a race along a dry river bed).
Second week in September: Aboriginal Week in Tennant Creek (dedicated to Aborigines and their culture).

Nightlife

Gambling, live entertainment, disco at the **Diamond Beach Casino** (see above). Incredible atmosphere with cowboys and miners in their Sunday best.

Dancing

Le Club, 70 McMinn St., City. Tel: 81 5530.

Sunnies, 3 Edmond St., City. Tel: 81 9761.

WHAT TO SEE

Aquascene
Doctor's Gully, City. Tel: 81 7837.
Watch fish feeding at high tide. Many are tame enough to be hand-fed. As tides vary, so do feeding times.

Artillery Museum
Eastpoint Reserve (6 mi/10 km from Darwin past Fannie Bay). Tel: 81 9702. *Open daily 9.30am to 5pm (May to Oct.), 11am to 4pm (Nov. to Apr.), weekends 9.30am to 5pm.*
Collection of war items, photos and newspaper clippings. Blockhouses, command posts and observation tower.

Botanical Gardens
Gilruth Ave, City. Tel: 81 9155.
The 84 acre/34 ha gardens contain more than 400 species of tropical shrubs, trees and orchids.

Darwin Crocodile Farm
Stuart Highway (25 mi/40 km south of the city). Tel: 88 1450. *Open daily 9am to 5pm.*
Australia's first crocodile farm houses more than 1000 saltwater and freshwater crocodiles, some up to 13 ft/4 m long.

Northern Territory Museum of Arts and Natural Sciences
Bullocky Point, Fannie Bay. Tel: 82 4211. *Open Mon. to Fri. 9am to 6pm, weekends 10am to 6pm.*
Variety of historical displays, paintings and artifacts of Australian and South-East Asian origin.

OUTSIDE DARWIN

Darwin makes a good base from which to set out on safaris to the more remote areas. The Kakadu National Park, the part of the Arnhem Land Plateau open to the public, is the main tourist attraction in the 'Top End'.

Kakadu National Park***
Located 125 mi/200 km east of Darwin, Kakadu National Park must be the only national park in the world to owe its existence to a uranium mine. The area, which is not part of the Arnhem Land Reserve, contains one of the world's richest deposits of uranium. As elsewhere in Australia, subterranean deposits belong to the Crown—that is, to the federal government. It supervises the allocation of mining rights to private companies. However, when private companies began excavating this particular deposit, they ran into strong opposition from the local Aborigines, for whom the area has had a deep religious significance for 50,000 years. A protracted environmental battle ensued, resulting in the establishment of a national park designed to protect the region from the harmful effects of uranium mining. On April 5, 1979, a first section of 2509 sq mi/6500 sq km was opened to the public. Today, the park covers more than 5018 sq mi/13,000 sq km and has been included on the UNESCO World Heritage List. Kakadu's natural and historical pedigree is exceptional: its jungles and marshlands, dominated by the weathered sandstone of the **Arnhem Land Plateau,** are home to an enormous variety of plants and animals (crocodiles and buffalo are the biggest stars). You can see an extraordinary variety of birds, many unique to Australia, at the **Yellow Billabong.** The **Jim Jim Falls** and the **Twin Falls** are spectacular and the paintings which decorate numerous caves and cliff-faces are extremely beautiful, especially those at **Ubirr** and **Nourlangie Rock.** Flat-bottom boat expeditions can be taken along the park's rivers. The best way to explore the park is in a cross-country vehicle. The park rangers' camp is at the end of the Arnhem Highway, just before Jabiru. For information, write or call the **Northern Territory Conservation Commission** (see p. 192).

Aboriginal bark painting.

Other parks and reserves in the Northern Territory

Note: before entering the territory's Aboriginal reserves, it is essential to have obtained permission from the Aboriginal Council of the reserve concerned (see below). Decisions to grant permission are totally at the discretion of the councils. Generally speaking, you will need to write at least eight weeks before your visit for permission to enter an Aboriginal reserve. You must carry your permit with you at all times.

Some national parks in the Top End are also strictly controlled and are open only to visitors holding a permit from the **Conservation Commission of the Northern Territory** (see p. 192).

These regulations operate in the interests of the tourist as much as of the Commission. Reports of tourists becoming stranded in remote areas or attacked by crocodiles, wild buffalo and the like are not uncommon.

It is difficult to get about the Northern Territory without a cross-country vehicle and an experienced guide. Visitors are advised to contact one of the specialist safari operators in Darwin in order to make the most of the nature, history and ethnography of the Top End. Contact the Northern Territory Government Tourist Office for information and reservations (see p. 188).

Useful addresses

Tourist information

Land Councils—for Aboriginal reserves
Northern Land Council, 47 Stuart Highway, Stuart Park, Darwin. Tel: 81 7011. For the northern area.

Tiwi Land Council, Nhuiu, Bathurst Island, NT 5791. Tel: 78 3963. For Bathurst Island.

Central Land Council, 44 Stuart Highway, Alice Springs, NT 5750. Tel: 52 3800. For the remainder.

For Kakadu National Park
Northern Territory Conservation Commission, Park and Wildlife Unit,
Jabiru. Tel: 79 2437.

For national parks in the Top End
Conservation Commission of the Northern Territory, Gap Rd., Alice
Springs, NT 5750. Tel: 50 8211.

Tour operators

The following companies offer safaris to Kakadu:
Australian Kakadu Tours, The Mall, Darwin. Tel: 81 5144.

Terra Safari Tours, PO Box 1634, Darwin. Tel: 84 3470.

Wimray Safari Tours and **Arura Safari Tours** (contact the tourist office for
information).

Accommodation in Kakadu National Park

▲▲ **Kakadu Holiday Village,** Arnhem Hwy. Tel: 79 0166. Motel
(74 rooms) and caravan park.

▲ **Cooinda Motel and Caravan Park,** off Jabiru Pine Creek Rd.
Tel: 79 2545. 48 rooms in motel.

Ban Ban Springs Station

Finally, for those who want a fabulous stay at one of the territory's large
ranches: **Ban Ban Springs Station,** 125 mi/200 km south of Darwin
(2 hours by road). 740,000 acres/300,000 ha of raw nature, with buffalo,
wild horses, crocodiles, birds, gold mines; excursions on horseback or off-
road vehicle, cattle mustering, camping, helicopter flights (contact the
tourist office or your tour organizer for information).

ALICE SPRINGS AND THE RED CENTRE

Like the kangaroo or the Sydney Opera House, Alice Springs,
that oasis in the wilderness, is always associated with the real
Australia. After two days of driving through sand and bush, the
traveler almost expects to lose all trace of civilization. Instead, there
are supermarkets and eucalypts. The gum trees, mothers in shorts
with their blond, near-naked children and the air-conditioned bar
of the Old Riverside Hotel are more than welcome after the heat,
dust and immense emptiness of the Simpson Desert.

Alice Springs (pop. 20,000) is memorable for its fine galleries
of Aboriginal art, the Flying Doctor Base and the School of the Air
(all of which are well worth a visit). The town's fame as a tourist
spot derives from its geographical position at the centre of
Australia's 'Red Heart', and its relative proximity to the monolithic
Ayers Rock. Visitors be warned, however: flies are the scourge of
the Red Centre. Protect your face by wearing a hat equipped with
veiling and arm yourself with a fly swatter or fan.

■■■ *PRACTICAL INFORMATION*

Telephone area code: 089.

Access

Plane

There are direct flights to Alice Springs from Darwin, Mt. Isa, Perth,
Brisbane, Sydney and Adelaide. Flights with stopovers in the above cities
can be taken from other main centres in Australia. If you're going to

Brisbane, you can take the **Australian Airlines** Sunday flight which stops in the Queensland outback towns of Birdsville, Windorah, Quilpie and Charleville. It is a 'milkrun' flight and covers 1250 mi/2000 km in 8 hours.

Domestic airlines

Ansett, corner of Todd and Parsons Sts. Tel: 50 4100.

Australian Airlines, corner of Todd and Parsons Sts. Tel: 50 5211.

Regional airlines

Ansett Northern Territory, same address as Ansett. Tel: 52 4455.

Train

To Adelaide: the *Ghan,* 24 hours, once a week, twice a week from May to Oct.

To Sydney: the *Alice,* 47 hours, twice a week.

Alice Springs Railway Station. Tel: 52 1011.

Bus

There is a regular bus service between Alice Springs and Adelaide (24 hours), Darwin (21 hours) and other parts of Australia.

Ansett-Pioneer, Todd St. Tel: 52 2422.

Greyhound, Todd St. Tel: 52 7888.

Car

To/from Darwin: 930 mi/1500 km
See 'Alice Springs to Darwin' p. 188.

To/from Adelaide: 1063 mi/1700 km
The road from **Port Augusta,** 200 mi/320 km north of Adelaide, passes through the wilderness but it is asphalted and the distances between filling stations are well indicated. Nevertheless, because it is a long drive, don't forget the usual precautions: car in good condition (especially wheels and battery), complete tool kit, and spare water and fuel. Watch out for cattle and kangaroos (especially at night), 'grids' (horizontal metal bars across the road, designed to prevent cattle from wandering) and 'road trains' (semis with trailers up to 148 ft/45 m long). Count on spending two days on the road, with an overnight stop somewhere like Coober Pedy.

First stop after Port Augusta: **Pimba,** 310 mi/496 km from Adelaide (fuel and meals, camping ground). The road to **Andamooka,** South Australia's other opal town, starts from Pimba. The Woomera Rocket Range on the road to Andamooka is closed to the public.

Kingoonya (412 mi/659 km) has a hotel-restaurant and a service station.

Coober Pedy (586 mi/937 km) is without a doubt the world capital of opal mining and in addition to restaurants and service stations, has three motels:

▲▲ **Coober Pedy Budget Motel.** Tel: (086) 72 5163. 12 rooms.

▲▲ **Opal Inn.** Tel: (086) 72 5054. 72 rooms.

▲▲ **Underground Motel.** Tel: (086) 72 5324. 6 rooms.

Note: if you want to try your hand at opal mining in an unstaked area, you will need a Precious Stones Prospecting Permit from the **Department of Mines,** 191 Greenhill Rd., Parkside, S.A. 5063. Tel: 274 7500. The permit costs A$15, is valid for one year and is issued on the spot. Good luck!

You can also get to Coober Pedy and Andamooka on the daily **Opal Air** (represented by **Ansett**) flight from Adelaide, or by taking an all-inclusive six-day air tour starting from Adelaide with **Skytour** (see p. 157).

Willoughby Homestead (688 mi/1100 km): shop, sandwiches, fuel.

Marla Hotel/Motel (738 mi/1180 km): hotel, restaurant, shops, sandwiches, fuel. Here, the desert takes on the red colour which has given it the nickname of the 'Red Heart'.

Kulgera (883 mi/1413 km): shop, restaurant, police, hotel. You will now be in the Northern Territory. Alice Springs is 173 mi/277 km away, and the turn-off for Ayers Rock 44 mi/70 km. This area and the remainder of the road to Darwin is covered on p. 188.

Getting around Alice Springs

Car rental

Avis, 78 Todd St. Tel: 52 4366.

Budget, 64 Hartley St. Tel: 52 4133.

Hertz, Gap Rd. Tel: 52 2644.

Thrifty, 113 Todd St. Tel: 52 6555.

Useful addresses

Tourist information

Northern Territory Government Tourist Office, 51 Todd St. Tel: 52 1299

Information and permits for Aboriginal reserves
Central Land Council for the Northern Territory, 75 Hartley St Tel: 52 3800.

National parks information
Conservation Commission of the Northern Territory, Gap Rd Tel: 50 8211.

Post office

General Post Office (GPO), 33 Hartley St. Tel: 52 1020.

Accommodation

First-class hotels

▲▲▲ **Alice Springs Gap,** 115 Gap Rd. Tel: 52 6611. Motel 52 rooms.

▲▲▲ **Alice Motor Inn,** 27 Undoolya Rd. Tel: 52 2322. Motel 20 rooms.

▲▲▲ **Diamond Springs Casino and Country Club,** Barnett Drive Tel: 52 5066. Very pleasant hotel and casino opened in 1982 70 rooms, 5 suites.

▲▲▲ **Oasis,** Gap Rd. Tel: 52 1444. Motel. 122 rooms.

▲▲▲ **Telford Territory,** Leichhardt St. Tel: 52 2066. Motel 73 rooms.

Moderately priced and inexpensive hotels

▲▲ **Alice Springs Youth Hostel,** corner of Todd St. and Stott Terrace. Tel: 52 5016. 60 beds.

▲▲ **Arura Safari Lodge,** 18 Warburton St. Tel: 52 4722.

▲▲ **Melanka Lodge,** Todd St. Tel: 52 2233. Motel. 237 rooms.

Food

Along with tourists, exotic restaurants have invaded Alice Springs. The choice is surprisingly good for a town of this size, as is the fact that the most consistently good food is offered by hotel restaurants.

Elegant

The Stuart Auto Museum Restaurant, Old South Rd. Tel: 52 4844

Chinese

Chopsticks, Ermond Arcade, Hartley St. Tel: 52 3873.

Golden Inn, 9 Undoolya Rd. Tel: 52 6910.

Italian

Il Sorrentino Tavern, Todd Mall. Tel: 52 2000.

Tavern at Alice Springs: an oasis in the desert.

La Casalinga, 105 Gregory Terrace. Tel: 52 4508.

Mia Pizza Bar, Ermond Arcade, Hartley St. Tel: 52 2964.

Music and food

The Stuart Arms Hotel, Todd Mall. A good pub. Lunchtime meals, rock groups in the evening.

Outside Alice Springs

Chateau Hornsby, Patrick Rd. Tel: 52 5711. Winery, 6 mi/15 km from Alice Springs.

Shopping

Alice Springs is the undisputed capital of Aboriginal art in Australia. The town contains numerous galleries and the choice of items is very wide, from a genuine Arnhem Land bark painting to a plastic boomerang. Prices can be quite high, in accordance with the quality of the work (several hundred dollars for a very fine 'x-ray' painting).

Arunta Art Gallery, Todd St. Tel: 52 1544.

Centre for Aboriginal Arts and Crafts, 88 Todd St. Tel: 52 3408. Government-operated.

Mbantua Store (Finke River Mission), 55 Gap Rd. Tel: 52 1732.

Attractions

Safaris

As in the area around Darwin, it is advisable at Alice Springs to explore the bush on a guided safari tour. The most original and authentic tours are offered by Ian Conway. Conway, a half-caste Aborigine, knows the Alice Springs area better than most and has access to numerous tribal encampments. He goes out of his way to acquaint visitors with the traditions he considers his own. His camping safaris in off-road vehicles will also enable you to witness and help in the capture of wild camels.

Information:
Ian Conway, **Breakaway Safaris,** PO Box 3594, Alice Springs, NT 5750. Tel: 52 1299.

Other specialists include: **Bill King's/AAT, The Camping Connection, Spinifex Tours, Nomad Holidays, Sandrifter Safaris, Centralian Stat** and **Twenty's Travel.**

Tourist offices throughout the country can also book trips starting from the capital cities through **Australian Pacific, Ansett Trailways,** etc. Information and bookings can be obtained at any Northern Territory Government Tourist Office (see p. 188).

Airline and bus companies offer a number of plane/hotel, bus/hotel packages for visitors to Ayers Rock and the Olgas. Because these packages are popular, visitors are advised to select and book as far ahead as possible through a travel agent or a tourist office.

Festivals and celebrations

See 'Entertainment' in Darwin section, p. 189.

WHAT TO SEE

Telegraph Station

1.2 mi/2 km north of town. Tel: 52 1013. *Open daily 8am to 7pm (Apr. to Sept.), 8am to 4pm (Oct. to March).*
Alice Springs grew up as the result of implanting a telegraph station in the middle of the desert in the 1870s. The telegraph line was linked to an undersea line connecting Darwin with Java, permitting Australia to communicate directly with Europe for the first time. The old station has been restored as a telegraph museum, including the bedroom of Alice. She was the wife of the Telegraph Superintendent Charles Todd who was responsible for the construction of the station, and Alice Springs was named after her.

Flying Doctor Network

Stuart Terrace. Tel: 52 1129. *Open Mon. to Sat. 9am to 3.30pm.*
The Royal Flying Doctor Service is quite rightly one of the most famous institutions in Australia. Founded in 1928 by Presbyterian minister John Flynn, the service covers more than 1,930,000 sq mi/5 million sq km of the outback, from some 16 bases located in such centres as Charleville and Mt. Isa in Queensland, Broken Hill in New South Wales, Port Augusta in South Australia, Derby and Wyndham in Western Australia and, of course, Alice Springs. About 2200 communities (stations, prospectors, mining camps, road repair gangs, Aboriginal missions, bush hospitals) are in radio contact twice a day (more often in emergencies) with operators at the bases. Simple medical treatment is given over the radio using coded prescriptions for items in the very full medical kits maintained by people in the bush. In an emergency, a doctor will fly to the patient and, depending on the problem, deal with it on the spot (a birth, for example) or fly the patient back to hospital. This service, which is theoretically free, is funded to a large extent by donations, 60 percent being provided by the people of the outback and the remainder by the government. Everybody, including the Aborigines, benefits from the service. You can visit the radio base at Alice Springs, but it is not possible to accompany a doctor 'on his rounds'.

School of the Air

Head St. Tel: 52 2122. *Open Mon. to Fri. 1.30pm to 3.30pm.*
The School of the Air uses the radio network of the Flying Doctor Service to bring primary education to the isolated children of the outback. The

chool was founded in 1951 and was the first of its kind in the world. There re now 12 such schools in Australia. Most use the Flying Doctor network but two, at Alice Springs and Katherine in the Northern Territory, use their wn equipment, renting two-way radios to families for A\$20 a year. The chool of the Air in Alice Springs transmits over a 313 mi/500 km range to round 100 children aged from four to twelve. You can visit and observe a esson. The teacher asks questions using a microphone and a tiny, far-off oice tries to answer them. The silences are full of desert dust.

AYERS ROCK AND THE OLGAS***
(ULURU NATIONAL PARK)

Ayers Rock is probably as well known abroad as the Sydney Opera House. t deserves its reputation and the 625 mi/1000 km round trip from Alice springs to see it is well worth the trouble. Viewed from a plane, Ayers Rock esembles a kind of seed planted there and forgotten by some deity who oped to see a trunk sprout from its red shell and rise towards the sun, tretching out its branches to the heavens and bringing shade with its oliage to the endless scorched earth below. As you get closer, Ayers Rock ssumes its real dimensions: 1148 ft/350 m high, 2.2 mi/3.5 km long, .6 mi/2.5 km wide and nearly 5.7 mi/9 km in circumference. At its base, t is just a wall of red-brown stone, alternately smooth and furrowed, like he face of an aging Hollywood actress, a stone skin 600 million years old. From its summit it resembles Noah's Ark 40 days after the flood, sitting igh and dry in an expanse of sky, sun and sand. At sunset the rock stages ts main attraction at it changes from brown to red, to orange, to violet, to lue, to green. Then it is evening. Night falls, the rock leaves the stage clad n shadow, the tourists pack their cameras, climb into their buses and open bottle of beer.

Signs warn you that climbing the rock is dangerous (some tourists have lied there from heart attacks), but if you have done some mountaineering, ou can make the climb in 2 1/2 hours (there and back), with the aid of chains fixed to the rock on the steep sections. The Olgas (Katatjuta in Aboriginal mythology), 20 mi/32 km from Ayers Rock, will give you an idea of what the rock will look like in several hundred million years: collapsed, broken, violet, ready to return to the earth, but mysterious. The Aboriginal ribes who 'owned' the Uluru area had their property officially and rrevocably returned to them in October 1985. They, in turn, agreed to lease Ayers Rock and the Olgas to the government which sublets them to the hotel chains and private tour operators.

Access

Plane

Ansett Northern Territory has flights to Connellan Airport near Ayers Rock from Alice Springs (see p. 193). You can also fly to Connellan Airport from Sydney, Perth and Adelaide.

Car

Set aside a whole day for the drive from Alice Springs. 128 mi/205 km south of Alice Springs turn right in the direction of Adelaide. From there you have only 151 mi/242 km of rough, unpaved road ahead of you. You can fill up the car and eat at **Mt. Ebenezer** and **Curtin Springs,** respectively one-third and two-thirds of the way to the rock. If you're coming from Adelaide, turn left after 875 mi/1400 km and continue via **Victory Downs, Mulga Park** and **Curtin Springs** (203 mi/324 km from the Stuart Highway unction). Both routes are closed when it rains.

Bus

Ansette Pioneer and **Greyhound** offer daily bus trips to Ayers Rock 6 hours). For addresses see p. 193.

Accommodation and food

Yulara Tourist Resort, a hotel complex, has been established close to Ayers Rock. It includes shops, restaurants, an information centre and camping/caravan ground, as well as the following hotels.

Ayers Rock showing off its fiery colours.

▲▲▲▲ Sheraton Ayers Rock, Lasseter Highway, Yulara. Tel: 56 2200. 230 rooms, restaurants, swimming pool, tennis courts, etc.

▲▲▲ Four Seasons Ayers Rock Motel, 15 Yulara Drive, Yulara. Tel: 56 2100. 100 rooms, restaurants, swimming pool, etc.

▲▲ Ayers Rock Lodge, Yulara. Tel: 56 2170. 52 rooms, restaurant, barbecue area.

The camping ground (reservations 56 2055) has the advantage of being considerably less expensive than the big hotels. You will find permanent caravans and tents there, fully equipped sites for personal campervans, caravans and tents, plus a swimming pool and shops.

▀ *BIBLIOGRAPHY*

General

APA Productions. *Insight Guide to Australia* (Prentice Hall Press, 1987).

Braddon, Russell. *Thomas Baines and the North Australian Expedition* (Antler Books, London, 1986).

Courtis, Brian, and Douboudin, Tony. *American Express Pocket Guide to Australia* (Prentice Hall Press, 1987).

Hall, George and Brash, Nicholas. *Above Sydney* (Kevin Weldon and Associates Pty McMahon's Point, New South Wales, 1984).

Godwin, John. *Australia on $30 a Day* (Prentice Hall Press, 1988).

Kerr, John and Falkus, Hugh. *From Sydney Cove to Duntroon* (Victor Gollancz Ltd., London, 1982).

Raymond, Robert and Morrison, Reg. *Australia: the Greatest Island* (Landsdowne, Dee Why West, New South Wales, 1979).

Ride, WDL. *Guide to the Native Mammals of Australia* (Oxford University Press Australia, Melbourne, 1970).

On Aborigines

Elkin, A.P. *Aboriginal History* (Angus & Robertson).

Isaacs, Jennifer. *Australian Dreaming* (Landsdowne).

Keneally, Thomas; Adam-Smith, Patsy and Davidson, Robyn. *Australia Beyond the Dreamtime* (BBC Books, London, 1987).

World Travel Map: Australia (John Bartholomew & Son Ltd., Edinburgh, 1987).

▰▰▰ A GUIDE TO AUSTRALIAN ENGLISH

Arvo	Afternoon
Bell (give someone a)	Phone someone
Billabong	Pond in an otherwise dry stream
Billy tea	Tea brewed over an open fire, with gum- leave for extra flavour
Blue (to have a)	To have a fight or argument
Bonnet (car)	Hood of a car (Am.)
Boot	Trunk of a car (Am.)
Brolly	Umbrella
BYO (restaurant)	Bring Your Own (alcohol)
Clobber	Clothing
Corroboree	Aboriginal ceremonial dance
Cozzie	Bathing suit
Drongo	Worthless person
Entrée	Appetizer (not the main course)
Fair dinkum	The real thing; absolutely true, genuine
Footpath	Sidewalk (Am.), pavement (Brit.)
Fossicking	Rock collecting
G'day	Hello, hi
Humpy	Aboriginal's shack
Ice block	Popsicle (Am.), ice lolly (Brit.)
Jackeroo	Young male ranch hand
Jilleroo	Young female ranch hand
Jumbuck	Sheep
Lolly	Candy, sweets
Middy	Medium beer glass
Ocker	Genuinely Australian
Oz	Australia
Ozzie	Australian
Pom(mie)	English person
Pot	Large mug of beer
Rubbish	To make fun of, to put someone down
Sandshoes	Sneakers
School	A group of drinkers
Schooner	Large beer glass
Septic	American (rhyming slang—Septic tank = Yank
Shout	Turn (to buy a round of drinks)
Sickie	Leave of absence due to illness
Singlet	Vest (Brit.), undershirt (Am.)
Smoke-o	Tea break
Sport	Mate
Station	Large ranch
Sweets	Dessert (Am.)
Ta	Thank you
Ta-Ta	Goodbye
Tall poppies	High achievers (to be cut down)
Tea	Dinner (not universal)
Thong	Flip-flop (Brit.)
Tinny	Can of beer
Tube	Can of beer

Tucker	Food
Two pot screamer	Someone unable to hold his liquor
Uni	University
Ute	Pick-up truck
Wowser	Puritan, spoilsport
Yakka	Work

▬▬ INDEX

Abbreviations:
ACT – Australia Capital Territory
NSW – New South Wales
NT – Northern Territory
Qld – Queensland
SA – South Australia
Tas – Tasmania
Vic – Victoria
WA – Western Australia

Page references for regional or municipal maps appear in *italic*.